Adobe
Dreamweaver CC
2015 release

Bē
Tejal Patni

CLASSROOM IN A BOOK®
The official training workbook from Adobe

Jim Maivald

Adobe Press books are published by Peachpit, a division of Pearson Education located in San Francisco, California. For the latest on Adobe Press books, go to www.adobepress.com. To report errors, please send a note to errata@peachpit.com. For information on getting permission for reprints and excerpts, contact permissions@peachpit.com.

Writer: **James J. Maivald**

Acquisitions Editor: **Victor Gavenda**

Development Editor: **Robyn G. Thomas**

Technical Reviewers: **Candyce Mairs and Megan Ahearn**

Production Editor: **Tracey Croom**

Copyeditor: **Scout Festa**

Proofreader: **Patricia Pane**

Indexer: James **Minkin**

Cover Illustration: **Tejal Patni (UAE), behance.net/tejalpatni**

Cover Designer: **Eddie Yuen**

Interior Designer: **Mimi Heft**

Printed and bound in the United States of America

ISBN-13:   978-0-13-430999-6

ISBN-10:   0-13-430999-5

9 8 7 6 5 4 3 2 1

WHERE ARE THE LESSON FILES?

Purchasing this Classroom in a Book gives you access to the lesson files you'll need to complete the exercises in the book.

You'll find the files you need on your **Account** page at peachpit.com on the **Lesson & Update Files** tab.

For complete instructions, see "Accessing the Classroom in a Book files" in the Getting Started section of this book.

The example below shows how the files appear on your **Account** page. The files are packaged as ZIP archives, which you will need to expand after downloading. You can download the lessons individually or as a single large ZIP file if your network connection is fast enough.

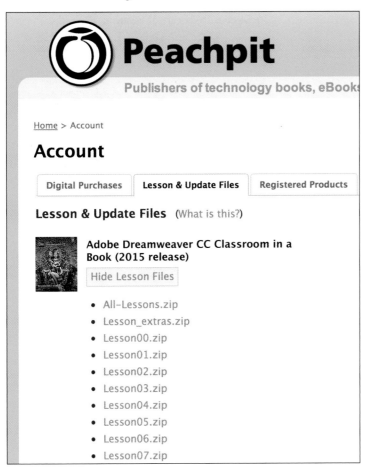

CONTENTS

11 WORKING WITH NAVIGATION 342

12 ADDING INTERACTIVITY 372

13 WORKING WITH WEB ANIMATION AND VIDEO 400

14 PUBLISHING TO THE WEB 418

APPENDIX: Tiny URLs 440

INDEX 441

GETTING STARTED

Adobe® Dreamweaver® CC is the industry-leading web-authoring program. Whether you create websites for others for a living or plan to create one for your own business, Dreamweaver offers all the tools you need to get professional-quality results.

About Classroom in a Book

Adobe Dreamweaver CC Classroom in a Book® (2015 release) is part of the official training series for graphics and publishing software developed with the support of Adobe product experts.

The lessons are designed so you can learn at your own pace. If you're new to Dreamweaver, you'll learn the fundamentals of putting the program to work. If you are an experienced user, you'll find that Classroom in a Book teaches many advanced features, including tips and techniques for using the latest version of Dreamweaver.

Although each lesson includes step-by-step instructions for creating a specific project, you'll have room for exploration and experimentation. You can follow the book from start to finish, or complete only those lessons that correspond to your interests and needs. Each lesson concludes with a review section containing questions and answers on the subjects you've covered.

TinyURLs

At several points in the book, we reference external information available on the Internet. The uniform resource locators (URLs) for this information are often long and unwieldy, so we have provided custom TinyURLs in many places for your convenience. Unfortunately, the TinyURLs sometimes expire over time and no longer function. If you find that a TinyURL doesn't work, look up the actual URL provided in the appendix.

Prerequisites

Before using *Adobe Dreamweaver CC Classroom in a Book (2015 release)*, you should have a working knowledge of your computer and its operating system. Be sure you know how to use the mouse, standard menus, and commands, and also how to open, save, and close files. If you need to review these techniques, see the printed or online documentation included with your Windows or Mac operating system.

Conventions used in this book

Working in Dreamweaver means you'll be working with code. We have used several conventions in the following lessons and exercises to make working with the code in this book easier to follow and understand.

Code font

In many instructions, you will be required to enter HTML code, CSS rules, and properties and other code-based markup. To distinguish the markup from the instructional text, the entries will be styled with a code font, like this:

Examine the following code `<h1>Heading goes here</h1>`

In instances where you must enter the markup yourself, the entry will be formatted in color, like this:

Insert the following code `<h1>Heading goes here</h1>`

Strikethrough

In several exercises, you will be instructed to delete markup that already exists within the webpage or style sheet. In those instances, the targeted references will be identified with strikethrough formatting, like this:

Delete the following values:

```
margin: 10px 20px 10px 20px;
background-image: url(images/fern.png), url(images/stripe.png);
```

Be careful to delete only the identified markup so that you achieve the following result:

```
margin: 10px 10px;
background-image: url(images/fern.png);
```

Missing punctuation

HTML code, CSS markup, and JavaScript often require the use of various punctuation, such as periods (.), commas (,) and semicolons (;), among others, and can be damaged by their incorrect usage or placement. Consequently, periods and other punctuation expected in a sentence or paragraph may be omitted from an instruction or hyperlink whenever it may cause confusion or a possible error, as in the following two instructions:

Enter the following code: `<h1>Heading goes here</h1>`

Type the following link: `http://adobe.com`

Element references

Within the body of descriptions and exercise instructions, elements may be referenced by name or by class or id attributes. When an element is identified by its tag name, it will appear as `<h1>` or `h1`. When referenced by its class attribute, the name will appear with a leading period (`.`) in a code-like font, like this: `.content` or `.sidebar1`. References to elements by their id attribute will appear with a leading hash (#) and in a code font, like this: `#top`. This practice matches the way these elements appear in Dreamweaver's tag selector interface.

Windows vs. OS X instructions

In most cases, Dreamweaver performs identically in both Windows and OS X. Minor differences exist between the two versions, mostly due to platform-specific issues out of the control of the program. Most of these are simply differences in keyboard shortcuts, how dialogs are displayed, and how buttons are named. In most cases, screen shots were made in the OS X version of Dreamweaver and may appear differently from your own screen.

Where specific commands differ, they are noted within the text. Windows commands are listed first, followed by the OS X equivalent, such as Ctrl+C/Cmd+C. Common abbreviations are used for all commands whenever possible, as follows:

WINDOWS	OS X
Control = Ctrl	Command = Cmd
Alternate = Alt	Option = Opt

As lessons proceed, instructions may be truncated or shortened to save space, with the assumption that you picked up the essential concepts earlier in the lesson. For example, at the beginning of a lesson you may be instructed to "press Ctrl+C/Cmd+C." Later, you may be told to "copy" text or a code element. These should be considered identical instructions.

If you find you have difficulties in any particular task, review earlier steps or exercises in that lesson. In some cases if an exercise is based on concepts covered earlier, you will be referred back to the specific lesson.

Installing the program

Before you perform any exercises in this book, verify that your computer system meets the hardware requirements for Dreamweaver, that it's correctly configured, and that all required software is installed.

If you do not have Dreamweaver, you will first have to install it from Creative Cloud. Adobe Dreamweaver must be purchased separately; it is not included with the lesson files that accompany this book. Go to www.adobe.com/products/dreamweaver/tech-specs.html to obtain the system requirements.

Go to https://creative.adobe.com/plans to sign up for Adobe Creative Cloud. Dreamweaver may be purchased with the entire Creative Cloud family or as a standalone app. Adobe also allows you to try Creative Cloud and the individual applications for 30 days for free.

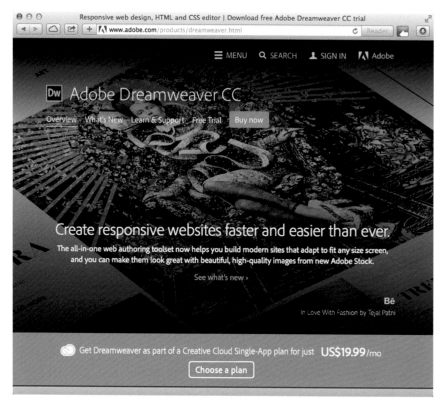

Check out www.adobe.com/products/dreamweaver.html to learn more about the different options for obtaining Dreamweaver.

Updating Dreamweaver to the latest version

Although Dreamweaver is downloaded and installed on your computer hard drive, periodic updates are provided via Creative Cloud. Some updates provide bug fixes and security patches, while others supply amazing new features and capabilities.

The lessons in this book are based on Dreamweaver CC (2015.1 release) and may not work properly in any earlier version of the program. To check which version is installed on your computer, choose Help > About Dreamweaver in Windows or Dreamweaver > About Dreamweaver on the Macintosh. A window will display the version number of the application and other pertinent information.

If you have an earlier version of the program installed, you will have to update Dreamweaver to the latest version. You can check the status of your installation by opening the Creative Cloud manager and logging in to your account.

Windows   OS X

Check out https://helpx.adobe.com/creative-cloud/help/download-install-trials.html to learn how to download and install a limited-period trial of Creative Cloud to your computer or laptop.

Accessing the Classroom in a Book files

In order to work through the projects in this book, you will need to download the lesson files from your Account page at peachpit.com.

If you purchased an eBook from peachpit.com or adobepress.com, the files will automatically appear on your Account page, under the Lesson & Update Files tab.

If you purchased an eBook from a different vendor or a print book, use the unique code in this book to gain access to the lesson files.

To download the Lesson files

1   On a Mac or PC, go to **www.peachpit.com/redeem** and enter the code that you'll find on the card bound into the back of your book.

This code is not the same as the book's ISBN.

2   Click Redeem Code and sign in or create an account. You will be taken to your Account page.

You need to enter the code only once. After you redeem the code, you'll be able to access your lesson files on peachpit.com anytime you want without entering the code again.

3   Click the Lesson & Update Files tab of your Account page to see a list of downloadable files.

4 Click the lesson file links to download them to your computer. You can download the files for individual lessons, or download them all at once in one large file.

The files are compressed into ZIP archives to speed up download time and to protect the contents from damage during transfer. You must uncompress (or "unzip") the files to restore them to their original size and format before you use them with the book. Modern Mac and Windows systems are set up to open ZIP archives by simply double-clicking.

> Hide Lesson Files
>
> - Lesson Files.zip (317 MB) – Last updated Oct 17, 2015
> - Lesson01.zip (197 KB) – Last updated Oct 17, 2015
> - Lesson02.zip (831 B) – Last updated Oct 17, 2015

5 Do one of the following:

- If you downloaded **DWCC2015_lesson_files.zip**, unzipping the archive will produce a folder named **DWCC2015_Lesson_Files** containing all the lesson files used by the book.

- If you downloaded the lessons individually, create a new folder on your hard drive and name it **DWCC2015**. Unzip the individual lesson files to this folder. That way, all the lesson files will be stored in one location. Do not share or copy files between lessons.

Recommended lesson order

The training in this book is designed to take you from A to Z in basic to intermediate website design, development, and production. Each new lesson builds on previous exercises, using supplied files and assets to create an entire website. We recommend that you download all lesson files at once and then perform each lesson in sequential order to achieve a successful result and the most complete understanding of all aspects of web design.

The ideal training scenario will start in Lesson 1 and proceed through the entire book to Lesson 14. Each lesson builds the skills and understanding necessary to complete subsequent tasks. We recommend that you do not skip any lessons, or even individual exercises. Although ideal, this method may not be a practicable scenario for every user. So, each lesson folder contains all the files needed to complete every exercise within it using partially completed or staged assets, allowing you to complete individual lessons out of order, if desired.

However, don't assume that the staged files and customized templates in each lesson represent a complete set of assets. It may seem that these folders contain duplicative materials. But these "duplicate" files and assets, in most cases, cannot be used interchangeably in other lessons and exercises. Doing so will probably cause you to fail to achieve the goal of the exercise.

For that reason, you should treat each folder as a standalone website. Copy the lesson folder to your hard drive, and create a new site for that lesson using the Site Setup dialog. Do not define sites using subfolders of existing sites. Keep your sites and assets in their original folders to avoid conflicts.

One suggestion is to organize the lesson folders in a single *web* or *sites* master folder near the root of your hard drive. But avoid using the Dreamweaver application folder or any folders that contain a web server, such as Apache, ColdFusion, or Internet Information Services (IIS). In most cases, you'd want to use such a local web server as your testing server, which is described in Lesson 14, "Publishing to the Web."

Web Edition

This book comes with a free Web Edition that provides many benefits and can be accessed from any device with a connection to the Internet.

Your Web Edition contains the complete text of the book, plus hours of instructional video keyed to the text and interactive quizzes. In addition, the Web Edition will be updated when Adobe adds significant feature updates between major Creative Cloud releases.

Accessing the free Web Edition

You must register your book purchase on peachpit.com in order to access the free Web Edition:

1 Go to www.peachpit.com/register, and then sign in or create a new account.

2 Enter the book's ISBN: 9780134309996.

3 Answer the questions as proof of purchase.

The Web Edition will appear under the Digital Purchases tab on your Account page.

4 Click the Launch link to access the product.

Bonus material

We've provided additional material for both Lessons 2 and 3 on the Peachpit website. You'll find "HTML Basics Bonus" for Lesson 2 and "CSS Basics Bonus" for Lesson 3 on your account page (Lessons & Update Files tab) once you register your book as described earlier in "Accessing the Classroom in a Book files."

Defining a Dreamweaver site

In the course of completing the following lessons, you will create webpages from scratch and use existing files and resources that are stored on your hard drive. The resulting webpages and assets make up what's called your *local* site. When you are ready to upload your site to the Internet (see Lesson 14, "Publishing to the Web"), you publish your completed files to a web-host server, which then becomes your *remote* site. The folder structures and files of the local and remote sites are usually mirror images of one another.

◆ **Warning:** You must unzip the lesson files before you create your site definition.

The first step is to define your local site:

1 Launch Adobe Dreamweaver CC (2015.1 release) or later.

2 Open the Site menu.

The Site menu provides options for creating and managing standard Dreamweaver sites.

3 Choose New Site.

To create a standard website in Dreamweaver, you need only name it and select the local site folder. Site names typically relate to a specific project or client and appear in the Files panel. This name is intended for your own purposes, so there are no limitations to the name you can create. Use a name that clearly describes the purpose of the website. For the purposes of this book, use the name of the lesson you intend to complete, such as lesson01, lesson02, lesson03, and so on.

4   Type **lesson01** or another name, as appropriate, in the Site Name field.

5   Next to the Local Site Folder field, click the Browse for Folder icon 📁.

The Choose Root Folder dialog appears.

6   Navigate to the appropriate folder containing the lesson files you downloaded from Peachpit.com (as described earlier), and click Select/Choose.

● **Note:** The main folder that contains the site will be referred to throughout the book as the site root folder.

● **Note:** The folder that contains the image assets will be referred to throughout the book as the site default images folder or the default images folder.

You could click Save at this time and begin working on your new website, but we'll add one more piece of handy information.

7   Click the arrow ▶ next to the Advanced Settings category to reveal the categories listed there. Select Local Info.

Although it's not required, a good policy for site management is to store different file types in separate folders. For example, many websites provide individual folders for images, PDFs, videos, and so on. Dreamweaver assists in this endeavor by including an option for a Default Images folder. Later, as you insert images from other places on your computer, Dreamweaver will use this setting to automatically move the images into the site structure.

8 Next to the Default Images Folder field, click the Browse for Folder icon 📁. When the dialog opens, navigate to the appropriate images folder for that lesson or site and click Select/Choose.

● **Note:** The Web URL is not needed for most static HTML sites, but it's required for working with sites using dynamic applications or to connect to databases and a testing server.

Site Setup for lesson01	
Site	Default Images folder: /DWCC2015/Lessons/lesson01/images 📁
Servers	
Version Control	Links relative to: ◉ Document ○ Site Root
▼ Advanced Settings	
Local Info	Web URL: http://
Cloaking	

● **Note:** Resource folders for images and other assets should always be contained within the main site root folder.

The path to the images folder appears in the Default Images Folder field. The next step would be to enter your site domain name in the Web URL field.

9 Enter **http://green-start.org** for the lessons in this book, or enter your own website URL, in the Web URL field.

Site Setup for lesson01	
Site	Default Images folder: /DWCC2015/Lessons/lesson01/images 📁
Servers	
Version Control	Links relative to: ◉ Document ○ Site Root
▼ Advanced Settings	
Local Info	Web URL: http://green-start.org/
Cloaking	

You've entered all the information required to begin your new site. In subsequent lessons, you'll add more information to enable you to upload files to your remote and testing servers.

10 In the Site Setup dialog, click Save.

Site Setup for lesson01	
Site	Default Images folder: /DWCC2015/Lessons/lesson01 📁
Servers	
Version Control	Links relative to: ◉ Document ○ Site Root
▼ Advanced Settings	
Local Info	Web URL: http://green-start.org/
Cloaking	
Design Notes	Enter the Web URL if you don't h...
File View Column...	
	Help Cancel Save

The Site Setup dialog closes.

In the Files panel, the new site name appears in the site list drop-down menu. As you add more site definitions, you can switch between the sites by selecting the appropriate name from this menu.

Whenever a site is selected or modified, Dreamweaver will build, or rebuild, a cache of every file in the folder. The cache identifies relationships between the web pages and the assets within sites, and will assist you whenever a file is moved, renamed, or deleted to update links or other referenced information.

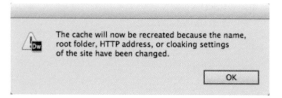

The cache will now be recreated because the name, root folder, HTTP address, or cloaking settings of the site have been changed.

OK

11 Click OK.

Setting up a site is a crucial first step in beginning any project in Dreamweaver. Knowing where the site root folder is located helps Dreamweaver determine link pathways and enables many sitewide options, such as orphaned-file checking and Find and Replace.

Setting up the workspace

Dreamweaver CC (2015.1 release) includes five main workspaces to accommodate various computer configurations and individual workflows. For this book, the Design workspace is recommended.

1 If the Design workspace is not displayed by default, you can select it from the Workspace drop-down menu on the upper-right side of the screen.

2 If the default Design workspace has been modified—where certain toolbars and panels are not visible (as they appear in the figures in the book)—you can restore the factory setting by choosing Reset 'Design' from the Workspace drop-down menu.

Workspace Layout options can also be accessed from the Window menu.

Most of the figures in this book show the Design workspace. When you finish the lessons in this book, experiment with each workspace to find the one that you prefer, or build your own configuration and save the layout under a custom name.

For a more complete description of the Dreamweaver workspaces, see Lesson 1, "Customizing Your Workspace."

Checking for updates

Adobe periodically provides software updates. To check for updates in the program, choose Help > Updates in Dreamweaver. An update notice may also appear in the Creative Cloud update desktop manager.

For book updates and bonus material, visit your Account page on Peachpit.com and select the Lesson & Update Files tab.

Additional resources

Adobe Dreamweaver CC Classroom in a Book (2015 release) is not meant to replace documentation that comes with the program or to be a comprehensive reference for every feature. Only the commands and options used in the lessons are explained in this book. For comprehensive information about program features and tutorials, refer to these resources:

Adobe Dreamweaver Learn & Support: helpx.adobe.com/dreamweaver (accessible in Dreamweaver by choosing Help > Help And Support > Dreamweaver Support Center) is where you can find and browse tutorials, help, and support on Adobe.com.

Dreamweaver Help: helpx.adobe.com/dreamweaver/topics.html is a reference for application features, commands, and tools (press F1 or choose Help > Help And Support > Dreamweaver Online Help). You can also download Help as a PDF document optimized for printing at helpx.adobe.com/pdf/dreamweaver_reference.pdf.

Adobe Forums: forums.adobe.com lets you tap into peer-to-peer discussions and questions and answers on Adobe products.

Resources for educators: www.adobe.com/education and edex.adobe.com offer a treasure trove of information for instructors who teach classes on Adobe software. You'll find solutions for education at all levels, including free curricula that use an integrated approach to teaching Adobe software and that can be used to prepare for the Adobe Certified Associate exams.

Also check out these useful links:

Adobe Add-ons: creative.adobe.com/addons is a central resource for finding tools, services, extensions, code samples, and more to supplement and extend your Adobe products.

Adobe Dreamweaver CC product home page: www.adobe.com/products/ dreamweaver has more information about the product.

Adobe Authorized Training Centers

Adobe Authorized Training Centers offer instructor-led courses and training on Adobe products. A directory of AATCs is available at training.adobe.com/ trainingpartners.

1 CUSTOMIZING YOUR WORKSPACE

Lesson overview

In this lesson, you'll familiarize yourself with the Dreamweaver CC (2015.1 release) program interface and learn how to do the following:

- Use the program Welcome screen
- Switch document views
- Work with panels
- Select a workspace layout
- Adjust toolbars
- Personalize preferences
- Create custom keyboard shortcuts
- Use the Property inspector
- Use the Extract workflow

 This lesson will take about 40 minutes to complete. Download the project files for this lesson from the Lesson & Update Files tab on your Account page at www.peachpit.com, store them on your computer in a convenient location, and define a site based on the lesson01 folder, as described in the "Getting Started" section of this book. Your Account page is also where you'll find any updates to the lessons or to the lesson files. Look on the Lesson & Update Files tab to access the most current content.

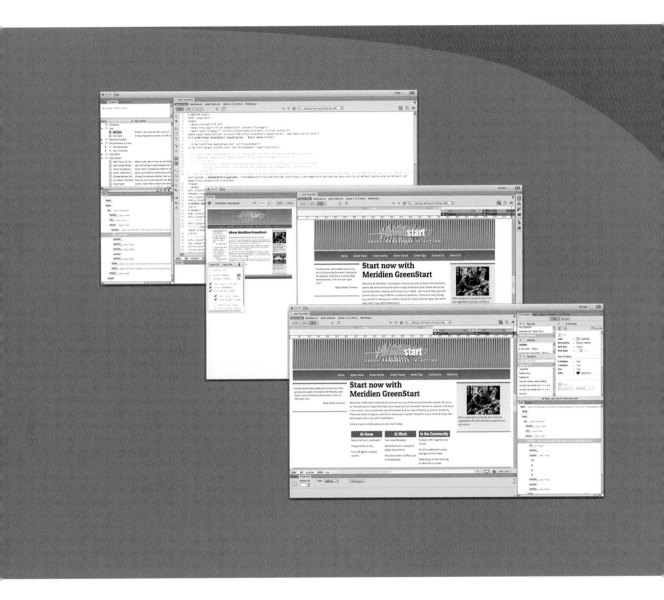

Dreamweaver offers a customizable and easy-to-use WYSIWYG HTML editor that doesn't compromise on power and flexibility. You'd probably need a dozen programs to perform all the tasks that Dreamweaver can do—and none of them would be as fun to use.

Touring the workspace

Dreamweaver is the industry-leading Hypertext Markup Language (HTML) editor, with good reasons for its popularity. The program offers an incredible array of design and code-editing tools. Dreamweaver offers something for everyone.

Coders love the range of enhancements built into the Code view environment, and developers enjoy the program's support for a variety of programming languages and code hinting. Designers marvel at seeing their text and graphics appear in an accurate What You See Is What You Get (WYSIWYG) depiction as they work, saving hours of time previewing pages in browsers. Novices certainly appreciate the program's simple-to-use and power-packed interface. No matter what type of user you are, if you use Dreamweaver you don't have to compromise.

A	Menu bar	**F**	Workspace menu	**K**	Assets panel	**P**	Code view
B	Document tab	**G**	Files panel	**L**	Behaviors panel	**Q**	Tag selectors
C	Referenced files interface	**H**	CC Libraries panel	**M**	Design/Live views	**R**	Property inspector
D	Document toolbar	**I**	CSS Designer	**N**	Scrubber		
E	New Features	**J**	Insert panel	**O**	Coding toolbar		

The Dreamweaver interface features a vast array of user-configurable panels and toolbars. Take a moment to familiarize yourself with the names of these components.

You'd think a program with this much to offer would be dense, slow, and unwieldy, but you'd be wrong. Dreamweaver provides much of its power via dockable panels and toolbars that you can display or hide and arrange in innumerable combinations to create your ideal workspace. In most cases, if you don't see a desired tool or panel, you'll find it in the Window menu.

This lesson introduces you to the Dreamweaver interface and gets you in touch with some of the power hiding under the hood.

Using the Welcome Screen

The Dreamweaver Welcome screen provides quick access to recent pages, easy creation of a range of page types, and a direct connection to several key Help topics. The Welcome screen appears when you first start the program or when no other documents are open. The Welcome screen has gotten a facelift in the last few versions and deserves a quick review to check out what it offers. For example, it now has four main tabs: Create, New Features, Getting Started, and Tips & Techniques. Click the name of the tab to access these features.

Create

If the Create tab looks familiar it's because it has been around in one form or another for many versions of Dreamweaver. As it has always done, it provides instant access to a list of up to your last ten files. At this moment, your screen may not display any filenames at all if you have not used Dreamweaver previously. Choosing a file from this list is a quick alternative to choosing File > Open when you want to edit an existing page.

In addition to recent documents, the Create tab enables you to create up to eight different web file types with a single click, including HTML, CSS, JavaScript, and PHP, as well as predefined starter templates and site setup interfaces.

New Features

When you select New Features in the Welcome screen, you see a list of the most recent features that have been added to the program. Click one of the topics and get a video- or text-based overview of these new tools and workflows. This tab is updated dynamically as new features are added to Dreamweaver.

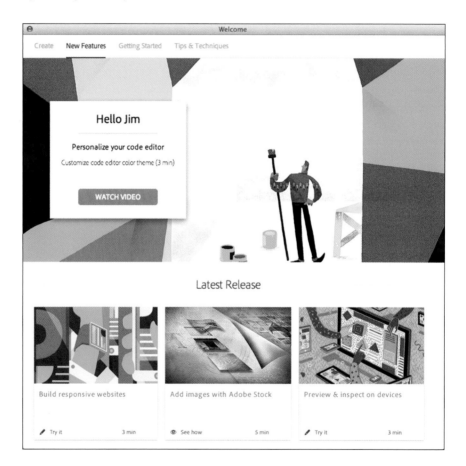

Getting Started

Select Getting Started to access quick tutorials that can get you up and running in various basic techniques and workflows in Dreamweaver. Learn how to create a new layout or style it with CSS. Sample files and assets can be downloaded within each tutorial as needed.

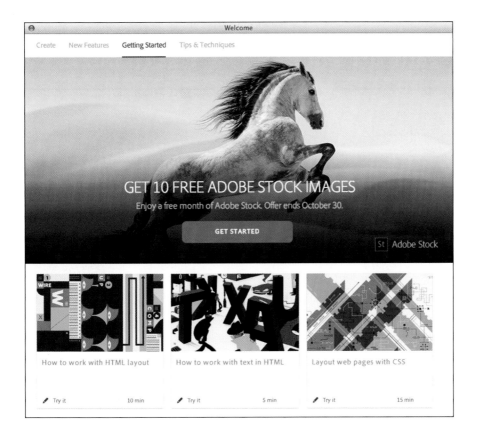

Tips & Techniques

For more advanced tutorials, check out Tips & Techniques. Learn how to create a responsive website, preview your new designs on your favorite mobile devices, or access web fonts.

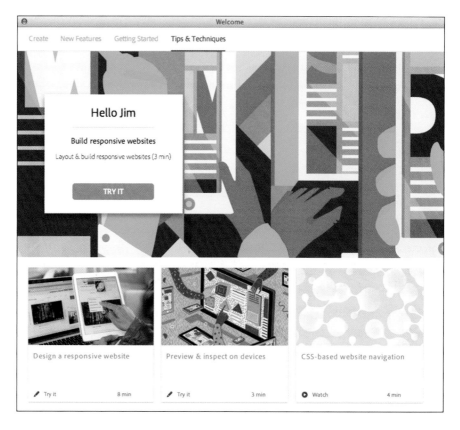

You may use the Welcome screen at any time while working in this book. When you've completed the lessons, you may prefer not to use the Welcome screen or even to see it. If so, you can close it by clicking the Close icon at the top of the screen. To bring back the Welcome screen, select Help > Welcome.

Exploring New Feature Guides

Another new enhancement to Dreamweaver CC (2015.1 release) is the New Feature guides, which will pop up from time to time as you access various features. The pop-ups will call your attention to new features or workflows that have been added to the program and provide handy tips to help you get the most out of them.

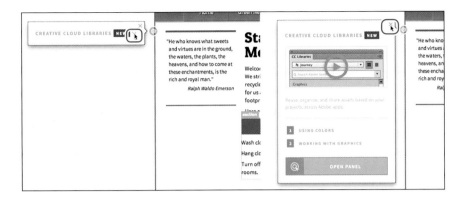

When a tip appears, you can reveal the entire content by clicking the pop-up. You can then close the pop-up by clicking the Close icon ✕ in the upper-right corner of each tip. When you close the tip, it will not appear again. If desired, you can display the tips again by resetting the option in Preferences.

Switching and splitting views

Dreamweaver offers dedicated environments for coders and designers as well as a new option that allows you to work with Photoshop mockups.

Code view

Code view focuses the Dreamweaver workspace exclusively on the HTML code and a variety of code-editing productivity tools. To access Code view, click the Code view button in the Document toolbar.

Code view

Design view

Design view shares the workspace with Live view and focuses the Dreamweaver workspace on its WYSIWYG editor, which provides a reasonable depiction of the webpage as it would appear in a browser. With the advancements in CSS and HTML, Design view is no longer as WYSIWYG as it once was. But it does offer an interface that speeds up the creation and editing of your content. And at the moment, it's also the only way to access certain Dreamweaver tools or workflows, as you will see in the upcoming lessons.

To activate Design view, choose it from the Design/Live views drop-down menu in the Document toolbar. Most HTML elements and basic cascading style sheets (CSS) formatting will be rendered properly within Design view, with the major exceptions of CSS3 properties, dynamic content, interactivity, such as link behaviors, video, audio, jQuery widgets, and some form elements. This may be the first version of Dreamweaver in which you spend more time in Live view than in Design view.

Design view

Live view

Live view is the new default workspace of Dreamweaver CC. It speeds up the process of developing modern websites by allowing you to *visually* create and edit webpages and web content in a browser-like environment, and it supports and previews most dynamic effects and interactivity.

To use Live view, choose it from the Design/Live views drop-down menu in the Document toolbar. When Live view is activated, most HTML content will function as it would in an actual browser, allowing you to preview and test most dynamic applications and behaviors.

In previous versions of Dreamweaver, the content in Live view was not editable. This has all changed. You can now edit text, add and delete elements, create classes and ids, and even style elements, all in the same window. It's like working on a live webpage right inside Dreamweaver.

Live view is integrally connected to the CSS Designer, allowing you to create and edit advanced CSS styling and build fully responsive webpages without having to switch views or waste time previewing the page in a browser.

Live view

Split view

Split view provides a composite workspace that gives you access to both the design and the code simultaneously. Changes made in either window update in the other in real time.

To access Split view, click the Split view button in the Document toolbar. Dreamweaver splits the workspace horizontally by default. When using Split view, you can display the Code view with either Live or Design view.

Split view (horizontal)

● **Note:** Split view can pair Code view with either Design or Live view.

If desired, you can also split the screen vertically by selecting the Split Vertically option on the View menu. When the window is split, Dreamweaver also gives you options for how the two windows display. You can put the code window on the top, bottom, left, or right. You can find all these options in the View menu. Most screen shots in the book that show Split view show Design or Live view at top or left.

Split view (vertical)

Live Source Code

Live Source Code is an HTML code-troubleshooting display mode available whenever Live view is activated. To access Live Source Code, activate Live view and then click the Live Source Code icon <> at the top of the document window. While active, Live Source Code displays the HTML code as it would appear in a live browser on the Internet.

The code window will interactively render changes to the elements, attributes, and styling as you interact with the content in the page. You can see this interaction by changing the width of the screen using the Scrubber until the horizontal navigation menu collapses to an icon. When you click the icon to open the menu, in Code view you will see that a class attribute of open is added to the menu interactively. The class is then removed when you close the menu. Without the live source code, you would not be able to see this interaction and behavior.

Be aware that while Live Source Code is active, you will not be able to edit the HTML code, although you can still modify external files, such as linked style sheets.

Inspect mode

Inspect mode is a CSS troubleshooting display mode available whenever Live view is activated. It is integrated with the CSS Designer and allows you to identify CSS styles applied to content within the page by moving the mouse cursor over elements within the webpage. Clicking an element freezes the focus on that item.

The Live view window highlights the targeted element and displays the pertinent CSS rules applied or inherited by that element. You can access Inspect mode at any time by clicking the Live view button whenever an HTML file is open and then clicking the Inspect icon ◯ at the top of the document window.

Working with panels

Although you can access most commands from the menus, Dreamweaver scatters much of its power in user-selectable panels and toolbars. You can display, hide, arrange, and dock panels at will around the screen. You can even move them to a second or third video display if you desire.

Standard panel grouping

The Window menu lists all the panels available in the program. If you do not see a desired panel on the screen, choose it from the Window menu. A checkmark appears next to its name in the menu to indicate that the panel is open. Occasionally, one panel may lie behind another on the screen and be difficult to locate. In such situations, simply choose the desired panel from the Window menu and the panel will rise to the top of the stack.

Minimizing panels

To create room for other panels or to access obscured areas of the workspace, you can minimize or expand individual panels in place. To minimize a standalone panel, double-click the tab containing the panel name. To expand the panel, click the tab once.

Minimizing a panel by double-clicking its tab

You can also minimize one panel within a stack of panels individually by double-clicking its tab. To open the panel, click once on its tab.

Minimizing one panel in a stack using its tab

To recover more screen real estate, you can minimize panel groups or stacks down to icons by double-clicking the title bar. You can also minimize the panels to icons by clicking the double arrow icon ▶▶ in the panel title bar. When panels are minimized to icons, you access any of the individual panels by clicking its icon or button. The selected panel will appear on the left or right of the icon, wherever room permits.

Collapsing a panel to icons or buttons

Closing panels and panel groups

Each panel or panel group may be closed at any time. You can close a panel or panel group in several ways; the method often depends on whether the panel is floating, docked, or grouped with another panel.

To close an individual panel that is docked, right-click in the panel tab and choose Close from the context menu. To close an entire group of panels, right-click any tab in the group and choose Close Tab Group.

To close a floating panel or panel group, click the Close icon ✖ that appears in the left corner of the title bar of the panel or panel group. To reopen a panel, choose the panel name from the Window menu. Reopened panels will sometimes appear undocked. Feel free to dock them as desired.

Dragging

You can reorder a panel tab by dragging it to the desired position within the group.

Dragging a tab to change its position

Floating

A panel that is grouped with other panels can be floated separately. To float a panel, drag it from the group by its tab.

Pulling a panel out by its tab

To reposition panels, groups, and stacks in the workspace, simply drag them by the title bar. To pull out a single panel group when it's docked, grab it by the tab bar.

Dragging a whole
docked panel group to
a new position

Grouping, stacking, and docking

You can create custom groups by dragging one panel into another. When you've moved the panel to the correct position, Dreamweaver highlights the area, called the *drop zone*, in blue. Release the mouse button to create the new group.

Creating new groups

In some cases, you may want to keep both panels visible simultaneously. To stack panels, drag the desired tab to the top or bottom of another panel. When you see the blue drop zone appear, release the mouse button.

Creating panel stacks

Floating panels can be docked to the right, left, or bottom of the Dreamweaver workspace. To dock a panel, group, or stack, drag its title bar to the edge of the window on which you wish to dock. When you see the blue drop zone appear, release the mouse button.

Docking panels

Selecting a workspace layout

A quick way to customize the program environment is to use one of the prebuilt workspaces in Dreamweaver. These workspaces have been optimized by experts to put the tools you need at your fingertips.

Dreamweaver CC (2015.1 release) includes five prebuilt workspaces: Beginner, Code, Default, Design, and Extract. To access these workspaces, choose them from the Workspace menu located at the upper-right side of the program window.

Beginner workspace

The Beginner workspace simplifies the program interface by focusing on the bare essentials. It provides the new user a good balance between design and code, with a minimum number of panels displayed.

Beginner workspace

Code workspace

Users who work mostly with code will want to use the Code workspace, because it optimizes the panels and windows to provide an effective workspace for coding.

Code workspace

Default workspace

The Default workspace maximizes the document window and emphasizes the power provided by various panels, such as CC Libraries, Snippets, Insert, and CSS Designer.

Default workspace

Design workspace

The Design workspace focuses the available screen real estate on the Design and Live view window. Design is the default workspace for screen shots in this book.

Design workspace

Extract workspace

The Extract workspace provides a direct connection to the online interface for extracting CSS styles and image assets from Photoshop mockups uploaded to Creative Cloud. You can upload PSD files directly from Dreamweaver or post them in the Creative Cloud app or website once you are logged in to your account.

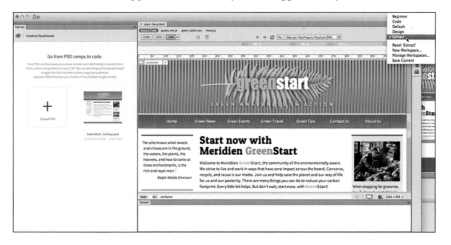

Extract workspace

Working with Extract

Extract is a new workflow that has been added to Dreamweaver CC (2015.1 release). It allows you to create CSS styles and image assets from a

Photoshop-based mockup. You can create your webpage design using text and linked or embedded image layers and post the file to Creative Cloud, where Dreamweaver can access the styles, colors, and images to help you build your basic site design.

Build your design in Photoshop using text, images, and effects stored in layers.

Post your file to your Creative Cloud online folder right inside Dreamweaver.

Access the various layers from the Extract panel inside Dreamweaver, copy styles and text, and even download image assets.

Try these features yourself by uploading **GreenStart_mockup.psd**, in the lesson01 resources folder, to your Creative Cloud account online folder. Go to helpx.adobe. com/creative-cloud/help/sync-files.html to learn how to upload files to your Creative Cloud account.

Adjusting toolbars

Some program features are so handy you may want them available all the time in toolbar form. Two of the toolbars—Document and Standard—appear horizontally at the top of the document window. The Coding toolbar, however, appears vertically, but only in the Code view window. You can display the desired toolbar by choosing it from the View menu. You can also display the toolbar by simply right-clicking the top of the document window and choosing the desired toolbar from the context menu.

Document (Live view)

Document (Design view)

Standard   Coding

Personalizing Dreamweaver

As you continue to work with Dreamweaver, you'll devise your own optimal workspace of panels and toolbars for each activity. You can store these configurations in a custom workspace of your own naming.

Saving a custom workspace

To save a custom workspace, first create your desired configuration of panels, choose New Workspace from the Workspace menu, and then give it a custom name.

Saving a custom workspace

Editing preferences

In addition to the ability to order and arrange the program's panels and toolbars, Dreamweaver's Preferences dialog provides advanced customizations for many functions and workflows. There are way too many options to cover in this lesson, but let's make one adjustment to give you a taste of the types of things you can do.

1 Click the Code view button at the top of the document window.

Dreamweaver is sporting a new dark color scheme in Code view. Some designers love it; some hate it. You can change it completely, or merely tweak it, right in Preferences.

2 In Windows, select Edit > Preferences.
   In the Mac OS, select Dreamweaver CC > Preferences.

	Preferences	
Category	**General**	
General	Document options: ☑ Open documents in tabs	
Accessibility	☑ Show Welcome Screen	
Code Coloring	☐ Reopen documents on startup	
Code Format	☑ Warn when opening read-only files	
Code Hints	☑ Enable Related Files	
Code Rewriting	Discover Dynamically-Related Files: Manually ▼	
Copy/Paste		
CSS Styles	Update links when moving files: Prompt ▼	
Extract	Editing options: ☑ Show dialog when inserting objects	
File Compare	☑ Enable double-byte inline input	
File Types / Editors	☑ Switch to plain paragraph after heading	
Fonts	☐ Allow multiple consecutive spaces	
Highlighting	☑ Use <strong> and <em> in place of <b> and <i>	
In-App Updates	☑ Use CSS instead of HTML tags	
Invisible Elements	☑ Warn when placing editable regions within <p> or <h1>–<h6> tags	
Linting	☐ Limit undo actions to the active document	
New Document		
New Feature Guides	Maximum number of history steps: 50	
Preview in Browser	Spelling dictionary: English (United States) ▼	
Site		
Sync Settings		
Technology Previews		
W3C Validator		
Window Sizes		
Help	Close	Apply

The Preferences dialog appears.

3 Select the Code Coloring category.

As you see from the dialog, Dreamweaver gives you fine control over various aspects of the code-editing interface. For example, you can change the colors one by one or select a theme and change them all at once.

4 Select Classic from the Theme drop-down menu.

The colors assigned to each item change. This scheme is the traditional color scheme of previous versions of Dreamweaver. At the moment, the changes have happened only in the dialog.

5 Click Apply in the lower-right corner of the dialog.

The Code window behind the dialog has changed to match the Classic color scheme. You can use this scheme as you work through the upcoming lessons. It is the default scheme used for all the code-based screen shots in the book. But feel free to use any of the predefined schemes or make your own.

6 Click Close.

Saved preferences persist from session to session and through each workspace.

Creating custom keyboard shortcuts

Another powerful feature of Dreamweaver is the ability to create your own keyboard shortcuts as well as edit existing ones. Keyboard shortcuts are loaded and preserved independently of workspaces.

Is there a command you can't live without that doesn't have a keyboard shortcut or that uses one that's inconvenient? Create one of your own. Try this:

Note: The default keyboard shortcuts are locked and cannot be edited. But you can duplicate the set, save it under a new name, and modify any shortcut within that custom set.

1 Choose Edit > Keyboard Shortcuts (Windows) or Dreamweaver CC > Keyboard Shortcuts (Mac OS).

2 Click the Duplicate Set icon ⊞ to create a new set of shortcuts.

3 Enter a name in the Name Of Duplicate Set field. Click OK.

4 Choose Menu Commands from the Commands pop-up menu.

5 In the Commands window, choose File > Save All.

Note that the Save All command does not have an existing shortcut, although you'll use this command frequently in Dreamweaver.

6 Insert the cursor in the Press Key field. Press Ctrl+Alt+S/Cmd+Opt-S.

Note the error message indicating that the keyboard combination you chose is already assigned to a command. Although we could reassign the combination, let's choose a different one.

7   Press Ctrl+Alt+Shift+S/Ctrl+Cmd+S.

This combination is not currently being used, so let's assign it to the Save All command.

8   Click the Change button.

The new shortcut is now assigned to the Save All command.

9   Click OK to save the change.

You have created your own keyboard shortcut—one you can use in upcoming lessons.

Using the Property inspector

One tool vital to your workflow is the Property inspector. In the built-in Dreamweaver workspaces, the Property inspector typically appears at the bottom of the workspace. If it is not visible in your program interface, you can display it by selecting Window > Properties and then dock it to the bottom of the document window as described earlier. The Property inspector is context-driven and adapts to the type of element you select.

Using the HTML tab

Insert the cursor into any text content on your page and the Property inspector provides a means to quickly assign some basic HTML codes and formatting. When the HTML button is selected, you can apply heading or paragraph tags as well as bold, italics, bullets, numbers, and indenting, among other formatting and attributes. The Document Title metadata field is also available in the Property inspector when Design view is active. Enter your desired Document Title in this field, and Dreamweaver adds it automatically to the document <head> section.

HTML Property
inspector

Using the CSS tab

Click the CSS button to quickly access commands to assign or edit CSS formatting.

CSS Property inspector

Image properties

Select an image in a webpage to access the image-based attributes and formatting controls of the Property inspector.

Image Property
inspector

Table properties

To access table properties, insert your cursor in a table and then click the table tag selector at the bottom of the document window.

Table Property inspector

Using the Related Files interface

Webpages are often built with multiple external files providing styling and programming assistance. Dreamweaver enables you to see all the files linked to, or referenced by, the current document by displaying the filenames in the Related Files interface at the top of the document window. This interface displays the name of any external file and will actually display the contents of each file—if it's available—when you simply select the filename in the display.

The Related Files
interface lists all
external files linked
to a document.

To view the contents of the referenced file, click the name. If you are in Live or Design view, Dreamweaver splits the document window and shows the contents of the selected file in the Code view window. If the file is stored locally, you'll even be able to edit the contents of the file when it's selected.

Use the Related Files interface to edit locally stored files.

To view the HTML code contained within the main document, click the Source Code option in the interface.

Choose the Source Code option to see the contents of the main document.

Using tag selectors

One of the most important features of Dreamweaver is the tag selector interface that appears at the bottom of the document window. This interface displays the tags and element structure in any HTML file pertinent to the insertion point of, or selection by, the cursor. The display of tags is hierarchical, starting at the document root at the left of the display and listing each tag or element in order based on the structure of the page and the selected element.

The display in the tag selector interface mimics the structure of the HTML code based on your selection.

The tag selectors also enable you to select any of the elements displayed by simply clicking a tag. When a tag is selected, all the content and child elements contained within that tag are also selected.

Use the tag selectors to
select elements.

The tag selector interface is closely integrated with the CSS Designer panel. You may use the tag selectors to help you style content or to cut, copy, paste, and delete elements.

The tag selector is closely integrated with the styling and editing of elements.

Using the CSS Designer

The CSS Designer has been greatly improved in Dreamweaver CC (2015.1 release). Along with its visual method of creating, editing, and troubleshooting CSS styling, CSS Designer has gained new productivity enhancements for copying and pasting CSS styles from one rule to another. You can also decrease or increase the specificity of new selector names by pressing the up or down arrow keys, respectively.

Copy and paste styles from one rule to another.

Make selectors more or less specific by using the arrow keys.

The CSS Designer panel consists of four windows: Sources, @Media, Selectors, and Properties.

Sources

The Sources window allows you to create, attach, define, and remove internal embedded and external linked style sheets.

@Media

The @Media window is used to define media queries to support various types of media and devices.

Selectors

The Selectors window is used to create and edit the CSS rules that format the components and content of your page. Once a selector, or rule, is created you define the formatting you wish to apply in the Properties window.

In addition to allowing you to create and edit CSS styling, the CSS Designer can also be used to identify styles already defined and applied, and to troubleshoot issues or conflicts with these styles.

Properties

The Properties window features two basic modes. By default, the Properties window displays all available CSS properties in a list, organized in five categories: Layout , Text , Borders , Background , and More . You can scroll down the list and apply styling as desired.

The second mode can be accessed by selecting Show Set at the upper-right edge of the window. In this mode, the Properties pane will then filter the list down to only the properties actually applied to the rule chosen in the Selectors window. In either mode, you can add, edit, or remove style sheets, media queries, rules, and properties.

Selecting the Show Set option limits the property display to only the properties that are styled.

The Properties pane also features a COMPUTED option that displays the aggregated list of styles applied to the selected element. The COMPUTED option will appear anytime you select an element or component on the page. When you're creating any type of styling the code created by Dreamweaver complies with industry standards and best practices.

The COMPUTED option collects in one place all styles applied to the selection.

All and Current modes

In Dreamweaver CC (2015.1 release), the CSS Designer got two new buttons, All and Current, that enable specific functions and workflows within the panel.

When the All button is selected, the panel allows you to create and edit CSS style sheets, media queries, rules, and properties. When the Current button is selected, the CSS troubleshooting functions are enabled, allowing you to inspect individual elements and assess existing styling properties applied to a selected element. In this mode, you are able to edit existing properties, but you're not allowed to add new style sheets, media queries, or rules. This interaction works the same way in all document views modes.

When the Current button is selected, the CSS Designer displays all styling associated with a selected element.

In addition to using the CSS Designer, you may also create and edit CSS styling manually within Code view while taking advantage of many productivity enhancements, such as code hinting and auto completion.

Using the Visual Media Query interface (VMQ)

A new addition to Dreamweaver CC (2015.1 release) is the Visual Media Query (VMQ) interface. Appearing above the document window, the VMQ interface allows you to visually inspect and interact with existing media queries, as well as create new ones on the fly using a simple point-and-click interface.

Open any webpage that is formatted by a style sheet with one or more media queries, and the VMQ interface will appear above the document window, displaying color-coded bars that specify the type of media query that has been defined. Media queries using only a max-width specification will be displayed in green. Media queries using only a min-width specification will be displayed in purple. Ones that use both will be displayed in blue.

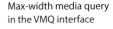

Max-width media query in the VMQ interface

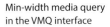

Min-width media query in the VMQ interface

Media using both max-width and min-width specifications

Using the DOM Viewer

The DOM Viewer is another new tool introduced recently that has already been improved in Dreamweaver CC (2015.1 release). It allows you to view the Document Object Model (DOM) to quickly examine the structure of your layout as well as interact with it to select and move existing elements and to insert new ones by drag and drop.

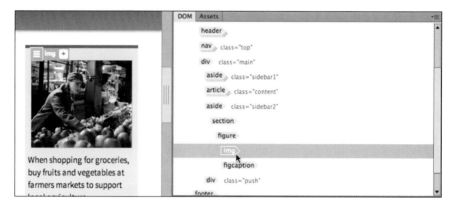

Using the heads-up displays

The movement toward Live view as the default Dreamweaver workspace has driven the development of new methods for editing and managing HTML elements. In Dreamweaver CC (2015.1 release), you will see a handful of new heads-up displays (HUDs) whenever you are working in Live view. All of them, except the Text HUD, allow you to add class or id attributes to the selected element and then insert references to the class or id in your CSS style sheets and media queries.

Position Assist HUD

The Position Assist HUD appears whenever new elements are being inserted in Live view, using either the Insert menu or Insert panel. Typically, the Position Assist HUD will offer the options Before, After, Wrap, and Nest. Depending on what type of element is selected and what item is targeted by the cursor, one or more of the options may be grayed out.

The Position Assist HUD allows you to control how elements and components are inserted in Live view.

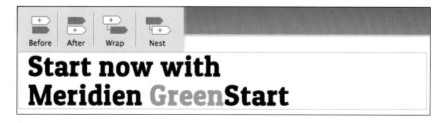

Element HUD

The Element HUD appears whenever you select an element in Live view. When an element is selected in Live view, you can change the selection focus by pressing the up and down arrow keys; the Element HUD will then highlight each element in the page, in turn, based on its position in the HTML structure.

The Element HUD enables you to quickly apply classes, ids, and links, as well as basic formatting.

Image HUD

The Image HUD provides access to the image source, alt text, width and height attributes as well as a field to add a hyperlink.

The Image HUD gives you quick access to the image source and allows you to add hyperlinks.

Text HUD

The Text HUD appears whenever you select a portion of text in Live view. The Text HUD allows you to apply bold <strong>, italic <em>, and hyperlink <a> markup to the text.

The Text HUD lets you apply bold, italics, and hyperlink markup to selected text.

Linting support

Dreamweaver CC (2015.1 release) provides live code error checking. Linting support is enabled by default in Preferences, which means the program monitors your code writing and flags errors in real time. The errors will be displayed in the new Output panel. Double-click the error message and Dreamweaver will jump to the error in the Code view window.

Enabling Linting support in Preferences to check your HTML code for errors.

Linting checks the file for coding errors in real time.

Introducing Emmet

Emmet is a new feature in Dreamweaver CC (2015.1 release) that allows you to supercharge your code-writing tasks. By entering shorthand characters and operators, Emmet enables you to create whole blocks of code with just a few keystrokes. To experience the power of Emmet, try this:

1 Select File > Open. Select **emmet-test.html** in the lesson01 folder and click Open.

2 Click the Code view button at the top of the document window.
   Insert the cursor in the <body> section.

3 Type **div** and press the Tab key.

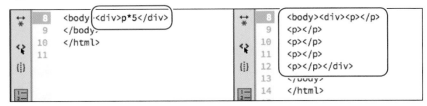

A full `<div></div>` element is created. The cursor should appear within it.

4   Type **p*5** and press Tab.

Five `<p>` elements are created inside the `<div>`. Emmet also allows you to combine these operations to save even more time.

5   Select the `div` tag selector.
Press Delete to remove the content.

The code created in steps 3 and 4 should be deleted.

6   Type **div>p*5** and press Tab.

A `<div>` and five nested `<p>` elements are created all at once. Emmet can also generate placeholder text along with the HTML if desired.

7   Press Ctrl+Z/Cmd+Z to undo step 6.

The shorthand **div>p*5** reappears, replacing the `<div>` and five `<p>` elements.

8   Edit the shorthand phrase as highlighted:
div>p(lorem)*5. Press Tab.

● **Note:** As you work in Code view, you may need to click the Refresh button in the Property inspector to see the tag selectors.

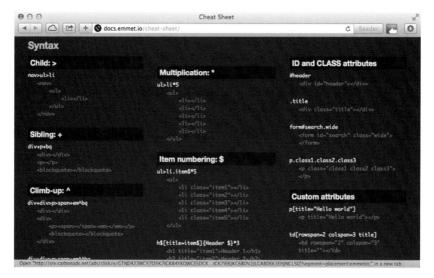

This time, the `<div>` and five nested `<p>` elements appear with lorem ipsum placeholder text. You can see how Emmet can make dreary code-writing tasks much faster and even fun.

Check out http://emmet.io to learn more about Emmet.

Check out http://docs.emmet.io/cheat-sheet/ for a handy Emmet shorthand cheat sheet.

Exploring, experimenting, and learning

The Dreamweaver interface has been carefully crafted over many years to make the job of webpage design and development fast and easy. Feel free to explore and experiment with various menus, panels, and options to create the ideal workspace and keyboard shortcuts to produce the most productive environment for your own purposes. You'll find the program endlessly adaptable, with power to spare for any task. Enjoy.

Review questions

1 Where can you access the command to display or hide any panel?

2 Where can you find the Code, Split, Design, and Live view buttons?

3 What can be saved in a workspace?

4 Do workspaces also load keyboard shortcuts?

5 What happens in the Property inspector when you insert the cursor into various elements on the webpage?

6 What new features have been added to the CSS Designer?

7 What can you do with DOM Viewer?

8 Does the Element HUD appear in Design view?

Review answers

1 All panels are listed in the Window menu.

2 The Code, Split, Design, and Live view buttons are components of the Document toolbar.

3 Workspaces can save the configuration of the document window, the open panels, and the panels' size and position on the screen.

4 No. Keyboard shortcuts are loaded and preserved independently of a workspace.

5 The Property inspector adapts to the selected element, displaying pertinent information and formatting commands.

6 The CSS Designer now allows you to copy and paste styles from one rule to another and to change the specificity of a new selector name by pressing the up and down arrow keys.

7 The DOM Viewer allows you to visually examine the DOM and select and insert new elements.

8 No. HUDs are only visible in Live view.

2 HTML BASICS

Lesson Overview

In this lesson, you'll familiarize yourself with HTML and learn:

- What HTML is and where it came from
- Frequently used HTML tags
- How to insert special characters
- What semantic web design is and why it's important
- New features and capabilities in HTML5

 This lesson will take about 25 minutes to complete. This lesson does not have support files.

HTML is the backbone of the web, the skeleton of your webpage. Like the bones in your body, it is the structure and substance of the Internet, although it is usually unseen except by the web designer. Without it, the web would not exist. Dreamweaver has many features that help you access, create, and edit HTML code quickly and effectively.

What is HTML?

"What other programs can open a Dreamweaver file?"

This question was asked by an actual student in a Dreamweaver class; although it might seem obvious to an experienced developer, it illustrates a basic problem in teaching and learning web design. Most people confuse the program with the technology. They assume that the extension .htm or .html belongs to Dreamweaver or Adobe. Designers are used to working with files ending with extensions, such as .ai, .psd, .indd, and so on; it's just a part of their jobs. They have learned over time that opening these file formats in a different program may produce unacceptable results or even damage the file.

On the other hand, the goal of the web designer is to create a webpage for display in a browser. The power and/or functionality of the originating program has little bearing on the resulting browser display, because the display is all contingent on the HTML code and how the browser interprets it. Although a program may write good or bad code, it's the browser that does all the hard work.

The web is based on HyperText Markup Language (HTML). The language and the file format don't belong to any individual program or company. In fact, it is a *non*-proprietary, plain-text language that can be edited in any text editor, in any operating system, on any computer. Dreamweaver is, in part, an HTML editor, although it is also much more than this. But to maximize the potential of Dreamweaver, you first need to have a good understanding of what HTML is and what it can (and can't) do. This lesson is intended as a concise primer on HTML and its capabilities. It will be a helpful foundation for understanding Dreamweaver.

Where did HTML begin?

HTML and the first browser were invented in 1989 by Tim Berners-Lee, a computer scientist working at the CERN (Conseil Européen pour la Recherche Nucléaire, which is French for European Council for Nuclear Research) particle physics laboratory in Geneva, Switzerland. He intended the technology as a means for sharing technical papers and information via the fledgling Internet that existed at the time. He shared his HTML and browser inventions openly as an attempt to get the scientific community at large and others to adopt them and engage in the development themselves. The fact that he did not copyright or try to sell his work started a trend for openness and camaraderie on the web that continues to this day.

The language that Berners-Lee created over 25 years ago was a much simpler construct of what we use now, but HTML is still surprisingly easy to learn and master. At the time of this writing, HTML is now at version 5, officially adopted as of October 2014. It consists of over 120 *tags*, such as html, head, body, h1, p, and so on.

The tag is inserted between less-than (<) and greater-than (>) angle brackets, as in <p>, <h1>, and <table>. These tags are used to identify, or *mark up*, text and graphics to enable a browser to display them in a particular way. HTML code is considered properly *balanced* when the markup features both an opening (<...>) and a closing (</...>) tag, such as <h1>...</h1>.

When two matching tags appear this way, they are referred to as an *element*; an element entails any contents contained within the two tags, as well. Empty, or void, elements, like the horizontal rule, can be written in an abbreviated fashion using only one tag, such as <hr/>, essentially opening and closing the tag at the same time. In HTML5, empty elements can also be validly expressed without the closing slash, such as <hr>.

Some elements are used to create page structures, others to structure and format text, and yet others to enable interactivity and programmability. Even though Dreamweaver obviates the need for writing most of the code manually, the ability to read and interpret HTML code is still a recommended skill for any burgeoning web designer. Sometimes it's the only way to find an error in your webpage. The ability to understand and read code may also become an essential skill in other fields as more information and content is created and disseminated via mobile devices and Internet-based resources.

Note: If you are dead set against learning how to read and write good HTML, you should check out Adobe Muse. This program allows you to create professional-looking webpages and complete websites using point-and-click techniques in a graphical user interface similar to Adobe InDesign while never exposing you to the code running behind the scenes.

Basic HTML code structure

Here you see the basic structure of a webpage:

Basic HTML Code Structure

Note: Go to the book's online resources at Peachpit.com for bonus hands-on exercises to gain some vital skills and experience writing and editing HTML code. See the "Getting Started" section at the beginning of the book for more details.

You may be surprised to learn that the only text from this code that displays in the web browser is "Welcome to my first webpage." The rest of the code creates the page structure and text formatting. Like an iceberg, most of the content of the actual webpage remains out of sight.

Frequently used HTML elements

HTML code elements serve specific purposes. Tags can create distinct objects, apply formatting, identify logical content, or generate interactivity. Tags that make their own space on the screen and stand alone are known as *block* elements; the ones that perform their duties within the flow of another tag are known as *inline* elements. Some elements can also be used to create *structural* relationships within a page, like stacking content in vertical columns or collecting several elements together in logical groupings. Structural elements can behave like block or inline elements or do their work entirely invisible to the user.

HTML tags

The following table shows some of the most frequently used HTML tags. To get the most out of Dreamweaver and your webpages, it helps to understand the nature of these elements and how they are used. Remember that some tags can serve multiple purposes.

Table 2.1 Frequently used HTML tags

TAG	DESCRIPTION
<!--...-->	Comment. Designates an HTML comment. Allows you to add notes within the HTML code that are not displayed within the browser.
<a>	Anchor. The basic building block for a hyperlink.
<blockquote>	Quotation. Creates a standalone, indented paragraph.
<body>	Designates the document body. Contains the visible portions of the webpage content.
 	Break. Inserts a line break without creating a new paragraph.
<div>	Division. Used to divide webpage content into discernible sections.
<em>	Emphasis. Adds semantic emphasis. Displays as italics by default in most browsers and readers.
<form>	Designates an HTML form. Used for collecting data from users.
<h1> to <h6>	Headings. Creates headings. Implies semantic value. Default formatting is bolded.
<head>	Designates the document head. Contains code that performs background functions, such as meta tags, scripts, styling, links, and other information not overtly visible to site visitors.
<hr>	Horizontal Rule. Empty element that generates a horizontal line.
<html>	Root element of most webpages. Contains the entire webpage, except in certain instances where server-based code must load before the opening <html> tag.
<iframe>	Inline Frame. A structural element that can contain another document.
<img>	Image. Provides the source reference to display an image.
<input>	Input element for a form such as a text field.
<li>	List Item. The content of an HTML list.

TAG	DESCRIPTION
`<link>`	Designates the relationship between a document and an external resource.
`<meta>`	Metadata. Additional information provided for search engines or other applications.
`<ol>`	Ordered List. Defines a numbered list. List items display in a numbered sequence.
`<p>`	Paragraph. Designates a standalone paragraph.
`<script>`	Script. Contains scripting elements or points to an internal or external script.
`<span>`	Designates a document section. Provides a means to apply special formatting or emphasis to a portion of an element.
`<strong>`	Strong. Adds semantic emphasis. Displays as bold by default in most browsers and readers.
`<style>`	Style. Embedded or inline reference for CSS styling.
`<table>`	Designates an HTML table.
`<td>`	Table Data. Designates a table cell.
`<textarea>`	Designates a multi-line text input element for a form.
`<th>`	Table Header. Identifies a cell as containing a header.
`<title>`	Title. Contains the metadata title reference for the current page.
`<tr>`	Table Row. Structural element that delineates one row of a table from another.
`<ul>`	Unordered List. Defines a bulleted list. List items display with bullets by default.

HTML character entities

Entities exist for every letter and character. If a symbol can't be entered directly from the keyboard, it can be inserted by typing the name or numeric value listed in the following table:

Note: Some entities can be created using either a name or a number, as in the copyright symbol, but named entities may not work in all browsers or applications. So either stick to numbered entities or test the specific named entities before you use them.

Table 2.2 HTML character entities

CHARACTER	DESCRIPTION	NAME	NUMBER
©	Copyright	&copy;	&#169;
®	Registered trademark	&reg;	&#174;
™	Trademark		&#153;
•	Bullet		&#149;
–	En dash		&#150;
—	Em dash		&#151;
	Nonbreaking space		

Go to www.w3schools.com/html/html_entities.asp to see a complete list of entities.

What's new in HTML5

Every new version of HTML has made changes to both the number and purpose of the tags that make up the language. HTML 4.01 consisted of approximately 90 tags. HTML5 has removed some of those HTML 4 tags from its specification altogether, and some new ones have been adopted or proposed.

Changes to the list usually revolve around supporting new technologies or different types of content models, as well as removing features that were bad ideas or ones infrequently used. Some changes simply reflect customs or techniques that have been popularized within the developer community over time. Other changes have been made to simplify the way code is created, to make it easier to write and faster to disseminate.

HTML5 tags

The Table 2.3 shows some of the important new tags in HTML5. The specification features nearly 50 new tags in total, while at least 30 old tags were deprecated. As we move through the exercises of this book, you will learn how to use many of these new HTML5 tags as appropriate to help you understand their intended role on the web. Take a few moments to familiarize yourself with these tags and their descriptions.

Go to www.w3schools.com/tags/default.asp to see the complete list of HTML5 elements.

Table 2.3 Important new HTML5 tags

TAG	DESCRIPTION
`<article>`	Designates independent, self-contained content, which can be distributed independently from the rest of the site.
`<aside>`	Designates sidebar content that is related to the surrounding content.
`<audio>`	Designates multimedia content, sounds, music, or other audio streams.
`<canvas>`	Designates graphics content created using a script.
`<figure>`	Designates a section of standalone content containing an image or video.
`<figcaption>`	Designates a caption for a `<figure>` element.
`<footer>`	Designates a footer of a document or section.
`<header>`	Designates the introduction of a document or section.
`<hgroup>`	Designates a set of <h1> to <h6> elements when a heading has multiple levels.
`<nav>`	Designates a section of navigation.

TAG	DESCRIPTION
`<section>`	Designates a section in a document.
`<source>`	Designates media resources for media elements, a child element of video, or audio elements. Multiple sources can be defined for browsers that do not support the default file type.
`<video>`	Designates video content, such as a movie clip or other video streams.

Semantic web design

Many of the changes to HTML were made to support the concept of *semantic web design*. This movement has important ramifications for the future of HTML, its usability, and the interoperability of websites on the Internet. At the moment, each webpage stands alone on the web. The content may link to other pages and sites, but there's really no way to combine or collect the information available on multiple pages or multiple sites in a coherent manner. Search engines do their best to index the content that appears on every site, but much of it is lost due to the nature and structure of old HTML code.

HTML was initially designed as a presentation language. In other words, it was intended to display technical documents in a browser in a readable and predictable manner. If you look carefully at the original specifications of HTML, it looks like a list of items you would put in a college research paper: headings, paragraphs, quoted material, tables, numbered and bulleted lists, and so on.

The element list in the first version of HTML basically identified how the content would be displayed. These tags did not convey any intrinsic meaning or significance. For example, using a heading tag displayed a particular line of text in bold, but it didn't tell you what relationship the heading had to the following text or to the story as a whole. Is it a title or merely a subheading?

The Internet before HTML looked more like MS DOS or the OS X Terminal application. There was no formatting, no graphics, and no user-definable color.

HTML5 has added a significant number of new tags to help us add semantic meaning to our markup. Tags, such as <header>, <footer>, <article>, and <section>, allow you for the first time to identify specific content without having to resort to additional attributes. The result is simpler code and less of it. But most of all, the addition of semantic meaning to your code allows you and other developers to connect the content from one page to another in new and exciting ways—many of which haven't even been invented yet. It's truly a work in progress.

New techniques and technology

HTML5 has also revisited the basic nature of the language to take back some of the functions that over the years have been increasingly handled by third-party plug-in applications and programming.

If you are new to web design, this transition will be painless because you have nothing to relearn, no bad habits to break. If you already have experience building webpages and applications, this book will guide you safely through some of these waters and introduce the new technologies and techniques in a logical and straightforward way. But either way, you don't have to trash all your old sites and rebuild everything from scratch.

Valid HTML 4 code will remain valid for the foreseeable future. HTML5 was intended to make web design easier by allowing you to do more with less work. So let's get started!

See www.w3.org/TR/2014/WD-html5-20140617 to learn more about HTML5.

See www.w3.org to learn more about W3C.

Review questions

1 What programs can open HTML files?

2 What does a markup language do?

3 HTML is composed of how many code elements?

4 What are the three main parts of most webpages?

5 What is the difference between block and inline elements?

6 Is HTML5 the current version of the language?

Review answers

1 HTML is a plain-text language that can be opened and edited in any text editor and viewed in any web browser.

2 A markup language places tags contained within brackets < > around plain-text content to pass information concerning structure and formatting from one application to another.

3 Fewer than 100 tags are defined in the HTML 4 specifications; HTML5 contains over 100.

4 Most webpages are composed of three main sections: root, head, and body.

5 A block element creates a standalone element. An inline element can exist within another element.

6 Yes, HTML5 was formally adopted at the end of 2014. However, full support may take several more years. And, as with HTML 4, some browsers and devices may support the specification in differing ways.

3 CSS BASICS

Lesson overview

In this lesson, you'll familiarize yourself with CSS and learn:

- CSS (cascading style sheets) terms and terminology

- The difference between HTML and CSS formatting

- How the cascade, inheritance, descendant, and specificity theories affect the way browsers apply CSS formatting

- New features and capabilities of CSS3

 This lesson will take about 1 hour and 15 minutes to complete. If you have not already done so, download the project files for this lesson from the Lesson & Update Files tab on your Account page at www.peachpit.com, store them on your computer in a convenient location, and define a new site in Dreamweaver based on this folder, as described in the "Getting Started" section of this book. Your Account page is also where you'll find any updates to the chapters or to the lesson files. Look on the Lesson & Update Files tab to access the most current content.

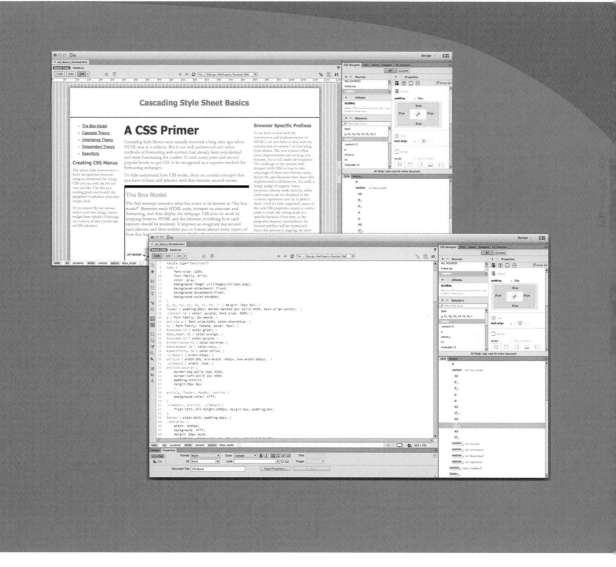

Cascading style sheets control the look and feel of a webpage. The language and syntax of CSS is complex, powerful, and endlessly adaptable. It takes time and dedication to learn and years to master, but a modern web designer can't live without it.

What is CSS?

HTML was never intended to be a design medium. Other than allowing for bold and italic, version 1 lacked a standardized way to load fonts or format text. Formatting commands were added along the way—up to version 3 of HTML—to address these limitations, but these changes still weren't enough. Designers resorted to various tricks to produce the desired results. For example, they used HTML tables to simulate multicolumn and complex layouts for text and graphics, and they used images when they wanted to display typefaces other than Times or Helvetica.

HTML-based formatting was so misguided a concept that it was deprecated from the language less than a year after it was formally adopted in favor of cascading style sheets (CSS). CSS avoids all the problems of HTML formatting, while saving time and money too. Using CSS lets you strip the HTML code down to its essential content and structure and then apply the formatting separately, so you can more easily tailor the webpage to specific applications.

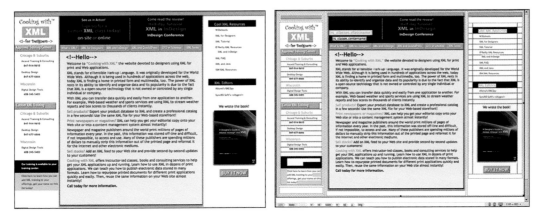

By adding cell padding and margins to the table structure in Dreamweaver (left), you can see how this webpage relies on tables and images to produce the final design (right).

HTML vs. CSS formatting

When comparing HTML-based formatting to CSS-based formatting, it's easy to see how CSS produces vast efficiencies in time and effort. In the following exercise, you'll explore the power and efficacy of CSS by editing two webpages, one formatted by HTML and the other by CSS.

1 Launch Dreamweaver, if it's not currently running.

2 Create a new site based on the lesson03 folder, using instructions in the "Getting Started" section at the beginning of the book. Name the site **lesson03**.

3 Choose File > Open.

4 Navigate to the lesson03 folder, and open **html_formatting.html**.

5 Click the Split view button. If necessary, choose View > Split Vertically to split Code and Live view windows vertically, side by side.

Each element of the content is formatted individually using the deprecated `<font>` tag. Note the attribute `color="blue"` in each `<h1>` and `<p>` element.

6 Replace the word `"blue"` with `"green"` in each line in which it appears. If necessary, click in the Live view window to update the display.

● **Note:** Dreamweaver usually defaults to Live view when you open or create a new page. If not, you may select it from the Document toolbar using the Live/Design drop-down menu.

● **Note:** "Deprecated" means that the tag has been removed from future support in HTML but may still be honored by current browsers and HTML readers.

The text displays in green now in each line where you changed the color value. As you can see, formatting using the obsolete `<font>` tag is not only slow but prone to error too. Make a mistake, like typing **greeen** or **geen**, and the browser will ignore the color formatting entirely.

7 Open **css_formatting.html** from the lesson03 folder.

8 If it's not currently selected, click the Split view button.

The content of the file is identical to the previous document, except that it's formatted using CSS. The code that formats the HTML elements appears in the `<head>` section of this file. Note that the code contains only two `color:blue;` attributes.

9   In the code `h1 { color: blue; }` select the word `blue` and type **green** to replace it. If necessary, click in the Live view window to update the display.

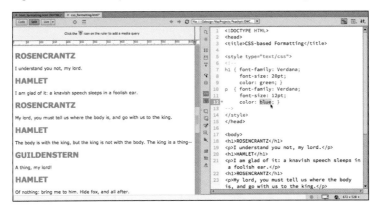

In Live view, all the heading elements display in green. The paragraph elements remain blue.

10 Select the word `blue` in the code `p { color: blue; }` and type **green** to replace it. Click in the Live view window to update the display.

In Live view, all the paragraph elements have changed to green.

In this exercise, CSS accomplished the color change with two simple edits, whereas the HTML `<font>` tag required you to edit every line. Are you beginning to understand why the W3C deprecated the `<font>` tag and developed cascading style sheets? This exercise highlights just a small sampling of the formatting power and productivity enhancements offered by CSS that can't be matched by HTML alone.

HTML defaults

● **Note:** The Code and Live view windows can be swapped top to bottom, left to right by selecting the option under the View menu. See Lesson 1, "Customizing Your Workspace," for more information.

Since the very beginning, HTML tags came right out of the box with one or more default formats, characteristics, or behaviors. So even if you did nothing, much of your text would already be formatted in a certain way in most browsers. One of the essential tasks in mastering CSS is learning and understanding these defaults. Let's take a look.

1   Open **html_defaults.html** from the lesson03 folder. If necessary, select Live view to preview the contents of the file.

The file contains a range of HTML headings and text elements. Each element exhibits basic styling for traits such as size, font, and spacing, among others.

2 Switch to Split view. If necessary, choose View > Split Vertically to split Code and Live view windows side by side. In the Code view window, locate the `<head>` section and try to identify any code that may be formatting the HTML elements.

A quick look will tell you that there is no overt styling information in the file, yet the text still displays different kinds of formatting. So where does the formatting come from? And more importantly, what are the settings being used?

The answer is: It depends. In the past, HTML 4 elements drew characteristics from multiple sources. The W3C, the web standards organization that establishes Internet specifications and protocols, created a default style sheet. You can find this document at www.w3.org/TR/CSS21/sample.html. It defines the standard formatting and behaviors of all HTML elements. This was the style sheet that all browser vendors used to base their default rendering of HTML elements. But that was before HTML5.

HTML5 defaults?

The last decade has seen a consistent movement on the web to separate "content" from its "styling." At the time of this writing, the concept of "default" formatting in HTML seems to be dead. According to specifications adopted by WC3 in 2014, there are no default styling standards for HTML5 elements. If you look for a default style sheet for HTML5 on w3.org, like the one noted for HTML 4, you won't find one. There are no public moves to change this relationship, and for the time being, browser manufacturers are still honoring and applying HTML 4 default styling to HTML5-based webpages. Confused? Join the club.

The ramifications could be dramatic and wide-reaching. Some day, in the not too distant future, HTML elements may not display any formatting at all by default.

Note: If the current trends continue, the lack of an HTML5 default style sheet makes the development of your own site standards even more important.

This doesn't seem to be an imminent danger; HTML5-based webpages continue to display the same default styling we've come to expect from the HTML 4 defaults.

To save time and give you a bit of a head start, I pulled together the following table of some of the most common defaults:

Table 3.1 Common HTML defaults

ITEM	DESCRIPTION
Background	In most browsers, the page background color is white. The background of the elements <div>, <table>, <td>, <th>, and most other tags is transparent.
Headings	Headings <h1> through <h6> are bold and align to the left. The six heading tags apply differing font size attributes, with <h1> the largest and <h6> the smallest. Sizes may vary between browsers.
Body text	Outside of a table cell, paragraphs—<p>, <li>, <dd>, <dt>—align to the left and start at the top of the page.
Table cell text	Text within table cells, <td>, aligns horizontally to the left and vertically to the center.
Table header	Text within header cells, <th>, aligns horizontally and vertically to the center (this is not standard across all browsers).
Fonts	Text color is black. Default typeface and font is specified and supplied by the browser (or by browser defaults specified by the manufacturer, which can be overridden by the user applying preference settings in the browser itself).
Margins	Spacing external to the element border/boundary is handled by margins. Many HTML elements feature some form of margin spacing. Margins are often used to insert additional space between paragraphs and to indent text, as in lists and blockquotes.
Padding	Spacing within the box border is handled by padding. According to the default HTML 4 style sheet, no elements feature default padding.

Browser antics

The next task is to identify the browser (and its version) that is displaying the HTML. That's because browsers frequently differ (sometimes dramatically) in the way they interpret, or render, HTML elements and CSS formatting. Unfortunately, even different versions of the same browser can produce wide variations from identical code.

The best practice is to build and test your webpages to make sure they work properly in the browsers employed by the majority of web users—especially the browsers preferred by your own visitors. The breakdown of browser use of your own visitors can differ quite a bit from the norm. They also change over time, especially now as more and more people abandon desktop computers in favor of tablets and smartphones. In July 2014, the W3C published the following statistics identifying the most popular browsers:

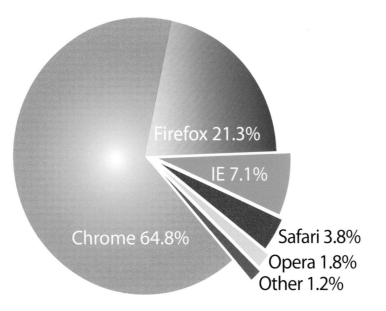

Although it's nice to know which browsers are the most popular among the general public, it's crucial that before you build and test your pages you identify the browsers your target audience uses.

Although this chart shows the basic breakdown in the browser world, it obscures the fact that multiple versions of each browser are still being used. This is important to know because older browser versions are less likely to support the latest HTML and CSS features and effects. To make matters more complicated, these statistics show trends for the Internet overall, but the statistics for your own site may vary wildly.

CSS box model

Browsers normally read the HTML code, interpret its structure and formatting, and then display the webpage. CSS does its work by stepping between HTML and the browser, redefining how each element should be rendered. It imposes an imaginary box around each element and then enables you to format almost every aspect of how that box and its contents are displayed.

The box model is a programmatic construct imposed by HTML and CSS that enables you to format, or redefine, the default settings of any HTML element.

CSS permits you to specify fonts, line spacing, colors, borders, background shading and graphics, margins, and padding, among other things. Most of the time these boxes are invisible, and although CSS gives you the ability to format them it doesn't require you to do so.

1 Launch Dreamweaver, if necessary.
   Open **boxmodel.html** from the lesson03 folder.

2 If necessary, click the Split view button to divide the workspace between the Code view and Live view windows.

The file's sample HTML code contains a heading and two paragraphs with sample text formatted to illustrate some of the properties of the CSS box model. The text displays visible borders, background colors, margins, and padding. To see the real power of CSS, sometimes it's helpful to see what the page would look like without CSS.

● **Note:** The style rendering command is only available in Design view.

3 Switch to Design view.

Choose View > Style Rendering > Display Styles to disable style rendering.

Dreamweaver now displays the page without any applied styling. A basic tenet in web standards today is the separation of the *content* (text, images, lists, and so on) from its *presentation* (formatting). Although the text now is not wholly unformatted, it's easy to see the power of CSS to transform HTML code. Whether formatted or not, this illustrates the importance in the *quality* of your content. Will people still be enthralled by your website if all the wonderful formatting were pulled away?

4 Choose View > Style Rendering > Display Styles to enable the CSS rendering in Dreamweaver again.

The working specifications found at www.w3.org/TR/css3-box describe how the box model is supposed to render documents in various media.

Previewing the completed file

The best way to learn CSS is by creating your own. For the rest of this lesson, you'll learn how CSS works by creating a complete style sheet for a sample HTML file. Let's take a look at the final product of the upcoming exercises.

1 Open the **css_basics_finished.html** file from the site root.

2 If necessary, switch to Split view and observe the content and code in the two windows.

The file contains a complete HTML page with a variety of elements, including headings, paragraphs, lists, and links all fully formatted by CSS. Note the text styling, as well as the colors and borders assigned to other elements. The file should open with Live view active. This is important because some features may not display properly in Design view alone.

3 If necessary, switch to Live view only.

The document window now displays the entire webpage. Live view displays CSS styling more accurately than Design view. For example, in Live view you should see a drop shadow around the main content section. As before, the best way to see the true power of CSS is by shutting it off.

4 Switch to Design view.
Choose View > Style Rendering > Display Styles to toggle off the CSS rendering in Dreamweaver.

The page is no longer formatted by CSS and displays only the default styling you would expect on standard HTML elements. The text content now stacks vertically in a single column with no colors, borders, backgrounds, or shadows.

5 Choose View > Style Rendering > Display Styles to toggle on the CSS rendering in Dreamweaver again.

6 Choose File > Close All.

Close all sample files without saving them.

As you can see, CSS can style all aspects of a webpage with amazing variety and detail. First we'll take a look at how you can use CSS to format text.

Formatting text

You can apply CSS formatting in three ways: *inline*, *embedded* (in an internal style sheet), or *linked* (via an external style sheet). A CSS formatting instruction is known as a rule. A rule consists of two parts—a *selector* and one or more *declarations*. The selector specifies what element, or combination of elements, is to be formatted; declarations contain the styling information. CSS rules can redefine any existing HTML element, as well as define two custom element modifiers, named "class" and "id."

A rule can also combine selectors to target multiple elements at once or to target specific instances within a page where elements appear in unique ways, such as when one element is nested within another.

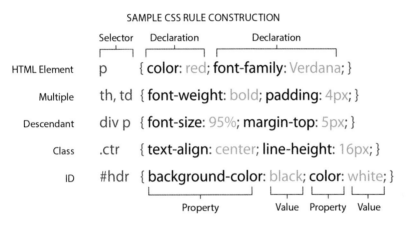

SAMPLE CSS RULE CONSTRUCTION

These sample rules demonstrate some typical constructions used in selectors and declarations. The way the selector is written determines how the styling is applied and how the rules interact with one another.

Applying a CSS rule is not a simple matter of selecting some text and applying a paragraph or character style, as in Adobe InDesign or Adobe Illustrator. CSS rules can affect single words, paragraphs of text, or combinations of text and objects. A single rule can affect an entire webpage, a single paragraph, or just a few words or letters. Basically, anything that has an HTML tag on it can be styled, and there is even an HTML tag specifically intended to style content that has no tag.

Many factors come into play in how a CSS rule performs its job. To help you better understand how it all works, the exercises in the following sections illustrate four main CSS concepts, which I'll refer to as theories: cascade, inheritance, descendant, and specificity.

CSS rule syntax: write or wrong

CSS is a powerful adjunct to HTML. It has the power to style and format any HTML element, but the language is sensitive to even the smallest typo or syntax error. Miss a period, comma, or semicolon and you may as well have left the code out of your page entirely.

For example, take the following simple rule:

```
p { padding: 1px;
    margin: 10px; }
```

It applies both padding and margins to the paragraph <p> element.

This rule can also be written properly without spacing as:

```
p{padding:1px;margin:10px;}
```

The spaces and line breaks used in the first example are unnecessary, merely accommodations for the humans who may write and read the code. The browsers and other devices processing the code do not need them. But the same cannot be said of the various punctuation marks sprinkled throughout the CSS.

Use parentheses ( ) or brackets [ ] instead of braces { }, and the rule (and perhaps your entire style sheet) is useless. The same goes for the use of colons ":" and semicolons ";" in the code.

Can you catch the error in each of the following sample rules?

```
p { padding; 1px: margin; 10px: }
p { padding: 1px; margin: 10px; ]
p { padding 1px, margin 10px, }
```

Similar problems can arise in the construction of compound selectors too. For example, putting a space in the wrong place can change the meaning of a selector entirely.

The rule `article.content { color: #F00 }` formats the <article> element and all its children in this code structure:

```
<article class="content"><p>…</p></article>
```

On the other hand, the rule `article .content { color: #F00 }` would ignore the previous HTML structure altogether, and format only the <p> element in the following code:

```
<article class="content"><p class="content">…</p></article>
```

A tiny error can have dramatic and far-reaching repercussions. To keep their CSS and HTML functioning properly, good web designers keep their eyes peeled for any little error, misplaced space, or punctuation mark. As you work through the following exercises, keep a careful eye on all the code for any similar errors. As mentioned in the "Getting Started" section, some instructions in this book may omit an expected period or other punctuation in a sentence when including it might cause confusion or possible errors.

Cascade theory

The cascade theory describes how the order and placement of rules in the style sheet or on the page affects the application of styling. In other words, if two rules conflict, which one wins out? Let's take a look at how cascade influences CSS formatting.

1 Open **css_basics.html** from the lesson03 folder in Split view.

   The file contains a complete HTML page with various elements, headings, paragraphs, lists, and links that are currently formatted only by default HTML styling.

2 Save the file as **mycss_basics.html** in the site root folder.

   Dreamweaver creates a copy of the file using the new name and displays two tabs at the top of the document window. Since the original file is still open it could cause confusion during the following exercises. Let's close the original file.

3 Select the document tab for the **css_basics.html** file. Choose File > Close.

   The **mycss_basics.html** file should be the only one open.

4 Click the Split view button, if necessary, and observe the <head> section in the Code view window for any CSS rules.

▶ **Tip:** Dreamweaver CC (2015.1 release) will open most files in Live view by default. In the following exercises be aware that certain commands will only function in Design view. Be prepared to switch between Live and Design view as necessary.

Note that the code contains a <style> section but no CSS rules.

5 Insert the cursor between the <style> and </style> tags.

6 Type `h1 { color:gray; }` and, if necessary, click in the Live view window to refresh the display.

● **Note:** As you type the rule markup, Dreamweaver provides code hints as it did with the HTML code in Lesson 2. Feel free to use these hints to speed up your typing, or simply ignore them and continue typing.

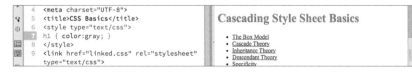

The h1 headings throughout the page now display in gray. The rest of the text still displays the default formatting. Congratulations, you wrote your first CSS rule.

Note: CSS does not require line breaks between rules, but it does make the code easier to read.

7   In Code view, insert the pointer at the end of the rule created in step 6. Press Enter/Return to create a new line.

8   Type `h1 { color:red; }` and click in the Live view window, if necessary, to refresh the display.

```
 4    <meta charset="UTF-8">
 5    <title>CSS Basics</title>
 6    <style type="text/css">
 7    h1 { color:gray; }
 8    h1 { color:red; }
 9    </style>
10    <link href="linked.css" rel="stylesheet"
```

Cascading Style Sheet Basics

- The Box Model
- Cascade Theory
- Inheritance Theory
- Descendant Theory
- Specificity

Tip: Live view should automatically refresh the display when you edit content in the Code window. But if you don't see the display change as described, you may need to refresh the display manually.

The h1 headings now display in red. The styling of the new rule supersedes the formatting applied by the first. It's important to understand that the two rules are identical except that they apply different colors: red or gray. Both rules want to format the same elements, but only one will be honored.

It's clear the second rule won, but why? In this case, the second rule is the last one declared, making it the *closest* one to the actual content. Whether intentional or not, a style applied by one rule may be overridden by declarations in a subsequent rule.

9   Select the rule `h1 { color: gray; }`

10 Choose Edit > Cut.

Tip: In Code view, you can also drag and drop code once it's selected.

11 Insert the pointer at the end of the rule `h1 { color: red; }` and press Enter/Return to insert a new line.

12 Choose Edit > Paste or press Ctrl+V/Cmd+V.

The rule applying the gray color now appears last. You have switched the order of the rules.

13 If necessary, click in the Live view window to refresh the preview display.

```
 4    <meta charset="UTF-8">
 5    <title>CSS Basics</title>
 6    <style type="text/css">
 7    h1 { color:red; }
 8    h1 { color:gray; }
 9    </style>
10    <link href="linked.css" rel=
```

Cascading Style Sheet Basics

- The Box Model
- Cascade Theory
- Inheritance Theory
- Descendant Theory
- Specificity

The h1 headings display in gray again. *Cascade* applies to styles whether the rules are embedded in the webpage or located in a separate external, linked style sheet.

14 Select **linked.css** in the Related Files interface.

When you select the name of referenced file, the contents of that file appear in the Code view window. If the file is stored on a local hard drive, Dreamweaver allows you to edit the contents without actually opening the file itself.

15 Insert the pointer in line 2. Type `h1 { color:orange; }` and press Ctrl+S/ Cmd+S to save the file. Click in the Design view window to refresh the display.

The `h1` headings now display in orange.

16 Select Source Code in the Related Files interface. Locate the `<link>` reference for **linked.css** in the `<head>` section.

The `<link>` element appears after the `<style>` element. Based strictly on cascade, this means that any rule that appears in the linked file will supersede duplicate rules in the embedded sheet.

17 Click the line number for the external CSS `<link>` reference to select the entire reference. Drag the entire `<link>` reference above the `<style>` element. Click in the Live view window to refresh the display.

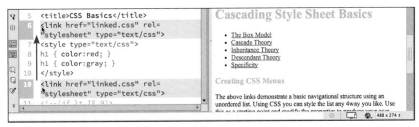

The headings revert to gray.

18 Select File > Save All.

As you can clearly see, the order and *proximity* of the rules within the markup are powerful factors in how CSS is applied. When you try to determine which

Note: !important
is an attribute you
can append to any
CSS value to make it
supersede values set by
other equivalent rules.
It can trump cascade,
inheritance, and
sometimes even more
specific rules.

CSS rule will be honored and which formatting will be applied, browsers typically
honor the following order of hierarchy, with number 4 being the most powerful:

1. Browser defaults.

2. External or embedded style sheets. If both are present, the one declared last
   supersedes the earlier entry in conflicts.

3. Inline styles (within the HTML element itself).

4. Styles with the value attribute !important applied.

Inheritance theory

The inheritance theory describes how an element can be affected by one or more
rules at the same time. Inheritance can affect rules of the same name as well as
rules that format parent elements—ones that contain other elements. Let's take a
look at how inheritance influences CSS formatting.

1 If necessary, open **mycss_basics.html** from the lesson03 folder. In Split view,
   observe the HTML code.

   The webpage contains headings, paragraphs, lists, and HTML5 semantic
   elements formatted by HTML defaults, as well as CSS rules created in the
   previous exercise.

2 Insert the pointer after the rule h1 { color: gray; } in the embedded style
   sheet. Press Enter/Return to insert a new line.

3 Type h1 { font-family:Arial; } and click in the Live view window to refresh
   the display.

```
 6  <link href="linked.css" rel=
    "stylesheet" type="text/css">
 7  <style type="text/css">
 8  h1 { color:red; }
 9  h1 { color:gray; }
10  h1 { font-family:Arial; }
11  </style>
```

Cascading Style Sheet Basics

- The Box Model
- Cascade Theory
- Inheritance Theory
- Descendant Theory
- Specificity

The h1 elements appear in Arial and gray. The other content remains formatted
by default styling.

Now there are four CSS rules that format <h1> elements. Can you tell, by
looking at the Live view window, which of the rules is formatting the <h1> text?
If you said *two* of them, you're the winner.

At first glance, you may think that the rules formatting <h1> elements are
separate from each other. And technically, that's true. But if you look closer,
you'll see that the new rule doesn't contradict the others. It's not resetting
the color attribute as you did in the previous exercise; it's declaring a new,
additional attribute. In other words, since both rules do something different,

both will be honored, or inherited, by the h1 element. All <h1> elements will be formatted as gray *and* Arial.

Far from being a mistake or an unintended consequence, the ability to build rich and elaborate formatting using multiple rules is one of the most powerful and complex aspects of cascading style sheets.

4   Insert the pointer after the last h1 rule. Insert a new line in the code.

5   Type h2 { font-family:Arial; color:gray; } and click in the Live view window to refresh the display.

► **Tip:** Rules typically contain multiple property declarations.

The h2 element appears in Arial and gray; it originally displayed in a serif font in black.

6   After the h2 rule, type the following code:

```
h3 { font-family:Arial; color:gray; }
p { font-family:Arial; color:gray; }
li { font-family:Arial; color:gray; }
```

● **Note:** There is no requirement to create rules in any specific order or hierarchy. You may order them any way you please, as long as you keep in mind how the application of styling is governed by cascade and inheritance.

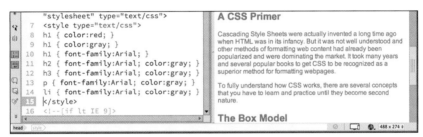

7   If necessary, refresh the Live view window display by clicking in it or clicking the Refresh button in the Properties panel.

All the elements now display the same styling, but it took six rules to format the entire page.

Although CSS styling is far more efficient than the obsolete HTML-based method, inheritance can help you optimize your styling chores even more. For example, all the rules include the statement { font-family:Arial; color:gray; }. Redundant code like this should be avoided whenever possible. It adds to the amount of code in each webpage as well as to the time it takes to download and process it. By using inheritance, sometimes you can create the same effect with a single rule. One way to make your styling more efficient is to apply formatting to a *parent* element instead of to the elements themselves.

8   Create a new line in the <style> section and type the following code:

```
article { font-family: Arial; color: gray; }
```

If you look through the code, you will see that the <article> tag contains much, but not all, of the webpage content. Let's see what happens if we delete some of our CSS rules.

9 Select and delete the rule:

~~h2 { font-family: Arial; color: gray; }~~

Refresh the Live view window display.

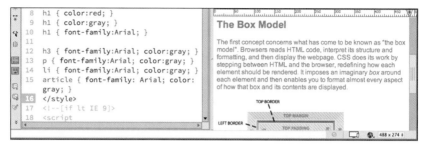

The h2 elements appearing within the <article> element remain formatted as gray Arial. The other h2 element down the page and outside the <article> now appears in HTML default styling.

10 Select and delete all h1 rules. Don't forget the one in the **linked.css** file. Refresh the Live view display.

The h1 elements contained within the <article> element continue to be styled. Those outside the <article> element have also reverted to the HTML defaults. Since the rule targets only the <article> element, only the elements contained within it are styled.

11 Select and delete the rules formatting h3, p, and li. Refresh the Live view display.

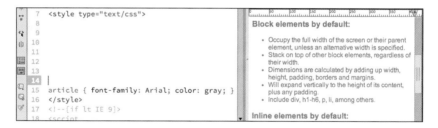

As in step 10, any content contained in the <article> tag remains formatted, while content elsewhere has reverted.

This is the way inheritance works. You could simply recreate the rules to format the other content, but there's a simpler alternative. Instead of adding additional CSS rules, can you figure out a way to use inheritance to format all the content on the page the same way? A hint: Look carefully at the entire structure of the webpage.

Did you think about using the <body> element? If so, you win again. The <body> element contains all the visible content on the webpage and therefore is the parent of all of it.

12 Change the rule selector from `article` to **body** and delete any blank lines. Choose File > Save All. Refresh the Live view display, if necessary.

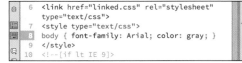

Once again, all the text displays in gray Arial. By using inheritance, only one rule is needed to format all the content instead of six. You'll find that the <body> element is a popular target for setting various default styles.

Descendant theory

Inheritance provides a means to apply styling to multiple elements at once, but CSS also provides the means to target styling to specific elements.

The descendant theory describes how formatting can target particular elements based on their position relative to others. This technique involves the creation of a selector name that identifies a specific element, or elements, by combining multiple tags, as well as id and class attributes. Let's take a look at how descendant selectors influence CSS formatting.

1 If necessary, open **mycss_basics.html** from the lesson03 folder. In Split view, observe the structure of the HTML content.

The page contains headings and paragraphs in various HTML5 structural elements, such as `article`, `section`, and `aside`. The rule `body {font-family:Arial; color: gray; }` applies a default font and color to the entire page. In this exercise, you will learn how to create descendant CSS rules to target styling to specific elements in context.

2 In Code view, insert the pointer at the end of the `body` rule. Press Enter/Return to insert a new line.

3 Type `p { font-family:Garamond; }` and refresh the Live view display.

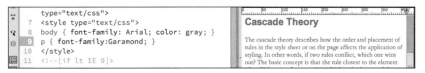

All p elements on the page display in Garamond. The rest of the page continues to be formatted as before.

By creating a selector using the p tag, the font formatting has been overridden for all p elements no matter where they appear. You may be thinking that since the p rule appears *after* the body rule, this type of styling simply relates to the cascade order. Let's try an experiment to see if that's true.

Tip: In this particular page, you could also use the <div> element to achieve the same result. But since <div> is a frequently used element, it might pose unpredictable conflicts in the future. Since webpages have only one <body> element, it is definitely the preferred target.

Note: Dreamweaver frequently edits externally linked files. Use Save All whenever changes on your page may affect multiple files in your site.

Note: Step 3 assumes you have Garamond installed on your computer. If it is not, select another serif style font, like Times.

4 Click the line number for the p rule.

Drag the p rule above the body rule.

Refresh the Live view display.

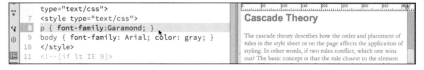

The p rule now appears above the body rule, but the styling did not change.

● **Note:** We will examine the role of specificity later in this lesson.

If the styling of p elements were determined simply by cascade, you would expect the headings to revert to gray Arial. Yet here, the styling is unaffected by changing the order of the rules. Instead, by using a more specific tag name in the selector, the new p rule becomes more powerful than the generic body rule. By properly combining two or more tags in the selector, you can craft the CSS styling on the page in even more sophisticated ways.

5 Create a new line after the p rule.

On the new line, type:

```
article p { font-size:120%; color:darkblue; }
```

By adding a p tag immediately after `article` in the selector, you are telling the browser to format only p elements that are children, or *descendants*, of `article` elements. Remember, a *child* element is one contained or nested within another element.

6 If necessary, refresh the Live view display.

All paragraphs appearing within the `<article>` element now display in dark blue, 120 percent larger than the other paragraph text on the page.

7 Choose File > Save All.

Although it may be hard to understand at this moment, the styling in other rules—both body and p—are still being inherited by the newly formatted paragraphs. But wherever two or more rules conflict, a descendant selector will win over any less specific styling.

Using classes and ids

So far, you've learned that you can create CSS rules that format specific HTML elements and ones that can target specific HTML element structures or relationships. In some instances, you may want to apply unique formatting to an element that is already formatted by an existing rule. In such cases, you can use CSS classes or id attributes to target that element.

In **mycss_basics.html**, all h1 elements are formatted identically regardless of where they appear in the layout. In the following exercise, you'll use classes and ids to differentiate the styling among the headings.

1 Insert a new line after the rule `article p`.

Type `h1 { font-family:Tahoma; color:teal; }` and refresh the display.

All h1 headings now display in the color teal and the font Tahoma.

Although it's tagged identically to the other h1 headings, "A CSS Primer" is the main heading in the `<article>` element. To make it stand out from the other headings, you can use the class attribute assigned to its parent to target it for special formatting.

2 Create the following new rule:

`.content h1 { color:red; font-size:300%; }`

The heading "A CSS Primer" displays in red, 300 percent larger than the body text.

In CSS syntax, the period (.) refers to a *class* attribute, and the hash (#) means *id*. By adding `.content` to the selector, you have targeted the styling only to h1 elements in `<article class="content">`.

In the same way, you can assign custom styling to the subheadings (h2). You can use the id attributes of each `<section>`.

3 Create the following rules:

```
#box_model h2 { color:orange; }
#cascade h2 { color:purple; }
#inheritance h2 { color:darkred; }
#descendant h2 { color:navy; }
#specificity h2 { color:olive; }
```

4 Choose File > Save All.

If necessary, refresh the display.

All the h2 headings now display unique colors.

What's important to understand here is that no formatting or additional attributes have been added to any of the headings themselves. They are being formatted based solely on their position within the structure of the code.

Understanding descendant selectors

CSS formatting can be very confusing for designers coming from the print world. Print designers are accustomed to applying styles directly to text and objects, one at a time. In some cases, styles can be based on one another, but this relationship is intentional. In print-based styling, it's impossible for one paragraph or character style to affect another unintentionally. On the other hand, in CSS, the chance of one element's formatting overlapping or influencing another's happens all the time.

It may be helpful to think of it as if the elements were formatting themselves. When you use CSS properly, the formatting is not intrinsic to the element but to the entire page and to the way the code is structured. The following exercise will help you understand this concept.

1 In Code view, click the line number for the "The Box Model" heading (approximately line 50).

2 Choose Edit > Copy or press Ctrl+C/Cmd+C.

3 Insert the pointer at the end of the h2 element "Cascade Theory" (approximately line 81) and create a new line.

4 Choose Edit > Paste or press Ctrl+V/Cmd+V and then refresh the display.

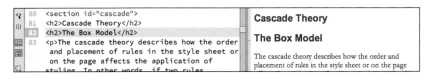

The heading "The Box Model" appears following and formatted identically to the heading "Cascade Theory."

5 Insert the pointer at the end of the "Inheritance Theory" heading and create a new line.

6 Press Ctrl+V/Cmd+V to paste the heading again.

The heading matches the styling of the "Inheritance Theory" heading.

As you can see, the formatting of the heading in the original instance does not travel with the text. That's the point of separating content from presentation—you can insert the content anywhere and it will adopt the formatting native to that position. It even works in reverse.

7 In Code view, select and copy the "Inheritance Theory" heading.

8 Insert the pointer after the original "The Box Model" heading and press Ctrl+V/Cmd+V.

The heading appears and adopts the same styling as "The Box Model."

Once again, the pasted text matches the formatting applied to the other h2 element within the `<article>`, ignoring its original styling altogether. Now that you've seen how descendant theory works there's no need for the extra headings.

9 Choose File > Revert. Click Yes to revert the file to the previously saved version.

The ability to separate the content from its presentation is an important concept in modern web design. It allows you great freedom in moving content from page to page and structure to structure without worrying about the effects of residual or latent formatting. Since the formatting doesn't reside with the element itself, the content is free to adapt instantly to its new surroundings.

Specificity theory

Conflicts between two or more rules are the bane of most web designers' existence and can waste hours of time in troubleshooting CSS formatting errors. In the past, designers would have to spend hours manually scanning style sheets and rules one by one trying to track down the source of styling errors.

Specificity describes how browsers determine what formatting to apply when two or more rules conflict. Some refer to this as *weight*—giving certain rules higher priority based on order (cascade), proximity, inheritance, and descendant relationships. One way to make it easier to see a selector's weight is by giving numeric values to each component of its name. For example, each HTML tag gets 1 point, each class gets 10 points, each id gets 100 points, and inline style attributes get 1000 points. By adding up the component values of one selector, its specificity can be calculated and compared to another. The higher specific weight wins.

● **Note:** Don't confuse CSS weight with code weight, described in Lesson 2, "HTML Basics."

As you have learned in this lesson, CSS rules often don't work alone. They may style more than one HTML element at a time and may overlap or inherit styling from one another. Each of the theories described so far has a role to play in how CSS styling is applied through your webpage and across your site. When the style sheet is loaded, the browser will use the following hierarchy—with number 4 being the most powerful—to determine how the styles are applied, especially when rules conflict:

1. Cascade

2. Inheritance

3. Descendant structure

4. Specificity

Of course, knowing this hierarchy doesn't help much when you are faced with a CSS conflict on a page with dozens or perhaps hundreds of rules and multiple style sheets. Luckily, Dreamweaver has several tools that can help you in this endeavor. The first one we'll look at is named Code Navigator.

Calculating specificity

Can you do the math? Look at the following list of selectors and see how they add up. Now look through the list of rules you created in the previous exercises in **mycss_basics.html.** Can you determine the weight of each of those selectors and figure out which rule is more specific on sight?

```
* (wildcard)  { }   0 + 0 +   0 + 0   =      0 points
h1            { }   0 + 0 +   0 + 1   =      1 point
ul li         { }   0 + 0 +   0 + 2   =      2 points
.class        { }   0 + 0 + 10 + 0    =     10 points
.class h1     { }   0 + 0 + 10 + 1    =     11 points
a:hover       { }   0 + 0 + 10 + 1    =     11 points
#id           { }   0 + 100 +  0 + 0  =    100 points
#id.class     { }   0 + 100 + 10 + 0  =    110 points
#id.classh1   { }   0 + 100 + 10 + 1  =    111 points
style=" "     { }   1000 + 0 + 0 + 0  =   1000 points
```

Code Navigator

Code Navigator is an editing tool within Dreamweaver that allows you to instantly inspect an HTML element and assess its CSS-based formatting. When activated, it displays all the embedded and externally linked CSS rules that have some role in formatting a selected element, and it lists them in the order of their cascade application and specificity. Code Navigator works in all Dreamweaver-based document views.

1 If necessary, open **mycss_basics.html** from the lesson03 folder. In Split view, observe the CSS code and the structure of the HTML content. Then, note the appearance of the text in the Live view window.

The page contains headings, paragraphs, and lists in various HTML5 structural elements, such as `article`, `section`, and `aside`, styled by CSS rules you created in the previous exercises.

2 In Live view, insert the pointer in the "A CSS Primer" heading.

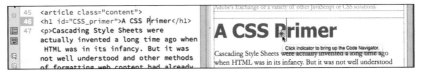

When Code Navigator is enabled, after a moment, an icon that looks like a ship's wheel appears. This icon provides access to Code Navigator.

3 Click the Code Navigator icon. If the Code Navigator does not appear automatically, right-click the heading and choose Code Navigator from the context menu or press Ctrl+Alt+N/Cmd+Opt+N.

A small window appears, displaying a list of three CSS rules that apply to this heading.

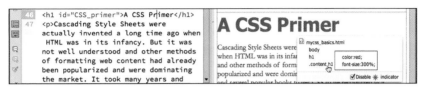

If you position the pointer over each rule in turn, Dreamweaver displays any properties formatted by the rule and their values. The rule with the highest specificity (most powerful) is at the bottom of the list.

Unfortunately, Code Navigator doesn't show styling applied via inline styles, so you'll have to check for these types of properties separately and calculate the effect of inline styles in your head. Otherwise, the sequence of rules in the list indicates both their cascade order and their specificity.

When rules conflict, rules farther down in the list override rules that are higher up. Remember that elements may inherit styling from one or more rules, and default styling—that is not overridden—may still play a role in the final presentation. Unfortunately, Code Navigator doesn't display what, if any, default styling characteristics may still be in effect.

The `.content h1` rule appears at the bottom of the Code Navigator window, indicating that its specifications are the most powerful ones styling this element. But many factors can influence which of the rules may win. Sometimes the specificity of two rules is identical; then, it's simply the order (cascade) in which rules are declared in the style sheet that determines which one is actually applied.

As you saw earlier, changing the order of rules can often affect how the rules work. There's a simple exercise you can perform to determine whether a rule is winning because of cascade or specificity.

4 In the Code view window, click the line number for the `.content h1` rule.

5 Drag the rule to the top of the embedded style sheet.

6 Click in the Live view window to refresh the display.

The styling did not change.

> ▶ **Tip:** Code Navigator may be disabled by default. To have it display automatically, deselect the Disable option in the Code Navigator window when it's visible.

> ● **Note:** Code Navigator doesn't display inline CSS rules. Since most CSS styling is not applied this way, it's not much of a limitation, but you should still be aware of this blind spot as you work with Code Navigator.

7 Insert the pointer into the text of the <h1> element "A CSS Primer" and activate Code Navigator.

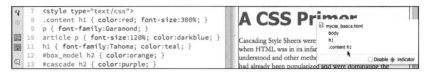

Although the rule was moved to the top of the style sheet, the order of the rules in Code Navigator did not change. The .content h1 selector has a specificity higher than either the body or h1 selectors. In this instance, it would win no matter where it was placed in the code. But specificity can change by simply modifying the selector.

8 Select and delete the ~~.content~~ class notation from the .content h1 selector.

9 Click in the Live view window to refresh the display.

Did you notice how the styling changed? The "A CSS Primer" heading reverted to the color teal, and the other h1 headings scaled to 300 percent. Do you know why this happened?

10 Insert the pointer in the "A CSS Primer" heading and activate Code Navigator.

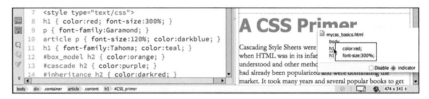

By removing the class notation from its selector, it now has equal value to the other h1 rule, but since it is the first one declared, it loses precedence by virtue of its cascade position.

11 Using Code Navigator, examine and compare the rules applied to the headings "A CSS Primer" and "Creating CSS Menus."

The Code Navigator shows the same rules applied to both.

By removing the .content class from the selector, the rule no longer targets only h1 headings in the <article class="content"> element; it's now styling all h1 elements on the page.

12 Choose Edit > Undo to restore the .content class to the h1 selector. Refresh the Live view display.

All the headings return to their previous styling.

13 Insert the pointer in the heading "Creating CSS Menus" and activate Code Navigator.

The heading is no longer styled by the `.content h1` rule.

14 Choose File > Save All.

Is it starting to make more sense? Don't worry, it will—over time. Until that time, just remember that the rule appearing last in Code Navigator has the most influence on any particular element.

CSS Designer

Code Navigator was introduced in Dreamweaver CS4 and has been an invaluable aid for troubleshooting CSS formatting. Yet the latest tool in Dreamweaver's CSS arsenal is much more than a good troubleshooting tool. CSS Designer not only displays all the rules that pertain to any selected element but also allows you to create and edit CSS rules at the same time.

When you use Code Navigator, it shows you the relative importance of each rule, but you still have to access and assess the effect of all the rules to determine the final effect. Since some elements can be affected by a dozen or more rules, this can be a daunting task for even a veteran web coder. CSS Designer eliminates this pressure altogether by providing a Properties window that computes the final CSS display for you. And best of all, unlike Code Navigator, CSS Designer can even compute the effects of inline styles too.

1 Open **mycss_basics.html** in Split view.

2 If necessary, choose Window > CSS Designer to display the panel.

The CSS Designer panel features four windows: Sources, @Media, Selectors, and Properties. Feel free to adjust the heights and widths of the windows as needed. The panel is also responsive: It will even take advantage of the extra screen space, if you drag out the edge, by splitting into two columns.

3 Insert the pointer in the heading "A CSS Primer."

The CSS Designer has two basic modes: *All* and *Current*. When the All mode is engaged, the panel allows you to review and edit all existing CSS rules and create new rules. In Current mode, the panel allows you to identify and edit the rules and styling already applied to a selected element.

4 If necessary, click the Current button in the CSS Designer panel.

When the Current mode is active the panel displays the CSS rules that are affecting the heading. In the CSS Designer, the most powerful rules appear at the top of the Selectors window, the opposite of Code Navigator.

5 Click the rule `.content h1` in the Selectors panel.

By default, the Properties window of CSS Designer displays a list of properties that you can style for this element. The list is not exhaustive, but it contains most of the properties you will need.

Showing a seemingly endless list of properties can be confusing as well as inefficient. For one thing, it makes it difficult to differentiate the properties assigned from those that aren't. Luckily, CSS Designer allows you to limit the display to only the properties currently applied to the selected element.

6 Click the Show Set option in the CSS Designer panel menu to enable it, if necessary.

When Show Set is enabled, the Properties panel shows only the items that have been set in that rule.

7 Select each rule that appears in the Selectors window and observe the properties of each. To see the expected result of all the rules combined, select the COMPUTED option.

The COMPUTED option analyzes all the CSS rules affecting the element and generates a list of properties that should be displayed by browsers or HTML readers. By displaying a list of pertinent CSS rules and then computing how the CSS should render, the CSS Designer does Code Navigator one step better. But it doesn't stop there. Whereas Code Navigator allows you to select a rule to edit it in Code view, the CSS Designer lets you edit the CSS properties right inside the panel itself. Best of all, CSS Designer can even compute and edit *inline* styles too.

8 Select COMPUTED in the Selectors window. In the Properties window, change the `color` property from `red` to `purple`. Press Enter/Return to complete the change.

> ▶ **Tip:** Click to edit the text-based color name. You can also select colors by using the color picker.

The heading displays in purple. What you may not have noticed is that the change you made was actually entered directly in the rule that contributed the styling.

9 In the Code view window, scroll to the embedded style sheet and examine the `.content h1` rule.

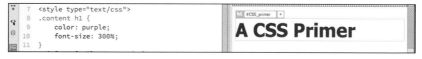

As you can see, the color was changed within the code and added to the proper rule.

10 Save all files.

The CSS Designer is like an amalgam of Code Navigator and Dreamweaver's old CSS Styles panel. In upcoming exercises, you'll get the chance to experience all aspects of the CSS Designer as you learn more about cascading style sheets.

Multiples, classes, and ids, oh my!

By taking advantage of the cascade, inheritance, descendant, and specificity theories, you can target formatting to almost any element anywhere on a webpage. But CSS offers a few more ways to optimize and customize the formatting and increase your productivity even further.

Applying formatting to multiple elements

To speed things up, CSS allows you to apply formatting to multiple elements at once by listing each in the selector, separated by commas. For example, the formatting in these rules:

```
h1 { font-family:Verdana; color:gray; }
h2 { font-family:Verdana; color:gray; }
h3 { font-family:Verdana; color:gray; }
```

can also be expressed like this:

```
h1, h2, h3 { font-family:Verdana; color:gray; }
```

CSS shorthand

Although Dreamweaver will write most of the CSS rules and properties for you, at times you will want, or need, to write your own. All properties can be written out fully, but many can also be written using a shorthand method. Shorthand does more than make the job of the web designer easier; it reduces the total amount of code that has to be downloaded and processed. For example, when all properties of margins or padding are identical, such as:

```
margin-top:10px;
margin-right:10px;
margin-bottom:10px;
margin-left:10px;
```

the rule can be shortened to `margin:10px;`

When the top and bottom and left and right margins or padding are identical, like this:

```
margin-top:0px;
margin-right:10px;
margin-bottom:0px;
margin-left:10px;
```

it can be shortened to `margin:0px 10px;`

But even when all four properties are different, like this:

```
margin-top:20px;
margin-right:15px;
margin-bottom:10px;
margin-left:5px;
```

they can be shortened to `margin:20px 15px 10px 5px;`

In these three examples, you can see clearly how much code can be saved using shorthand. There are way too many references and shorthand techniques to cover here. To get a full description, check out www.w3.org/community/webed/wiki/CSS_shorthand_reference.

In the following exercises, I'll use common shorthand expressions wherever possible; see if you can identify them as we go.

Creating class attributes

Frequently, you will want to create unique formatting to apply to objects, paragraphs, phrases, words, or even individual characters appearing within a webpage. To accomplish this, CSS allows you make your own custom attributes, named class and id.

Class attributes may be applied to any number of elements on a page, whereas id attributes should appear only once per page. If you are a print designer, think of classes as being similar to a combination of Adobe InDesign's paragraph, character, table, and object styles all rolled into one. Class and id names can be a single word, an abbreviation, any combination of letters and numbers, or almost anything, but they may not contain spaces. In HTML 4, ids could not start with a number. There don't seem to be any similar restrictions in HTML5, but for backward compatibility you should probably avoid starting class and id names with numbers.

Although there's no strict rule or guideline on how to create them, classes should be more general in nature, and ids should be more specific. Everyone seems to have an opinion, but at the moment there is no absolutely right or wrong answer. However, most agree that they should be descriptive, such as `"co-address"` or `"author-bio"` as opposed to `"left-column"` or `"big-text"`. This will especially help to improve your site analytics. The more sense Google and other search engines can make of your site's structure and organization, the higher your site will rank in the search results.

To declare a CSS class selector, insert a period before the name within the style sheet, like this:

```
.content
.sidebar1
```

Then, apply the CSS class to an entire HTML element as an attribute, like this:

```
<p class="intro">Type intro text here.</p>
```

Or to individual characters or words using the <span> tag, like this:

```
<p>Here is <span class="copyright">some text</span> formatted
differently.</p>
```

Creating id attributes

HTML designates id as a unique attribute. Therefore, any id should be assigned to no more than one element per page. In the past, many web designers used id attributes to style or identify specific components within the page, such as the header, the footer, or specific articles. With the advent of HTML5 elements—header, footer, aside, article, and so on—the use of id and class attributes for this purpose became less necessary. But ids can still be used to identify specific text elements, images, and tables to assist you in building powerful hypertext navigation within your page and site. You will learn more about using ids this way in Lesson 12, "Working with Navigation."

To declare an id attribute in a CSS style sheet, insert a number sign, or hash mark, before the name, like this:

```
#cascade
#box_model
```

Here's how you apply the CSS id to an entire HTML element as an attribute:

```
<div id="cascade">Content goes here.</div>
<div id="box_model">Content goes here.</div>
```

Or to a portion of an element:

```
<p>Here is <span id="copyright">some text</span> formatted
differently.</p>
```

● **Note:** For the online bonus lesson, go to the book's online resources at Peachpit.com for bonus hands-on exercises to gain some vital skills and experience writing and editing CSS code. See the "Getting Started" section at the beginning of the book for more details.

CSS3 overview and support

In the previous exercise, the last two properties both seemed to apply a drop shadow to the main content container. Did you notice that one used a -webkit- prefix? This notation is a temporary accommodation for certain browsers as they implement new CSS3 properties. The specifications provide some amazing, and long-needed, new features for styling the modern web.

The Internet doesn't stand still for long. Technologies and standards are evolving and changing constantly. The members of the W3C have been working diligently to adapt the web to the latest realities, such as powerful mobile devices, large flat-panel displays, and HD images and video—all of which seem to get better and cheaper every day. This is the urgency that currently drove the development of HTML5 and CSS3.

Many of these new standards have not been officially defined yet and browser vendors are implementing them in varying ways. But don't worry. The latest version of Dreamweaver has been updated to take advantage of the latest changes, and it provides many new features based on these evolving standards. This includes ample support for the current mix of HTML5 elements and CSS3 formatting. As new features and capabilities are developed, you can count on Adobe to add them to the program as quickly as possible using Creative Cloud.

As you work through the lessons that follow, you will be introduced to and actually implement many of these new and exciting techniques in your own sample pages.

CSS3 features and effects

CSS3 has over two dozen new features. Many are ready now and have been implemented in all the modern browsers; others are still experimental and are supported less fully. Among the new features, you will find

- Rounded corners and border effects
- Box and text shadows
- Transparency and translucency
- Gradient fills
- Multicolumn text elements

You can implement all these features and more via Dreamweaver today. The program will even assist you in building vendor-specific markup when necessary. To give you a quick tour of some of the coolest features and effects brewing, I've provided a sample of CSS3 styling in a separate file.

1 Open **css3_demo.html** from the lesson03 folder. Display the file in Split view and observe the CSS and HTML code.

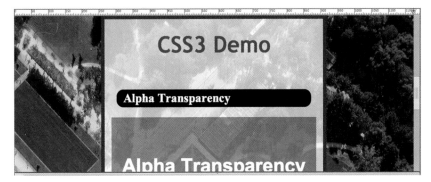

Some of the new effects can't be previewed directly in Design view. You'll need to use Live view or an actual browser to get the full effect.

2 If necessary, activate Live view to preview all the CSS3 effects.

The file contains a hodgepodge of features and effects that may surprise and even delight you—but don't get too excited. Although many of these features are already supported in Dreamweaver and will work fine in modern browsers, there's still a lot of older hardware and software out there that can turn your dream site into a nightmare. And there's at least one additional twist.

Some of the new CSS3 features have not been standardized, and certain browsers may not recognize the default markup generated by Dreamweaver. In these instances, you may have to include specific vendor commands to make them work properly. Like the box shadow in the previous exercise, these commands are preceded by a vendor prefix, such as `-ms-`, `-moz-`, and `-webkit-`. If you look carefully in the code of the demo file, you'll be able to find examples of these within the CSS markup.

Additional CSS support

CSS formatting and application is so complex and powerful that this short lesson can't cover all aspects of the subject. For a full examination of CSS, check out the following books:

• *Bulletproof Web Design: Improving Flexibility and Protecting Against Worst-Case Scenarios with HTML5 and CSS3 (3rd edition)*, Dan Cederholm (New Riders Press, 2012) ISBN: 978-0-321-80835-6

• *CSS3: The Missing Manual (3rd Edition)*, David Sawyer McFarland (O'Reilly Media, 2013) ISBN: 978-1-449-32594-7

• *HTML5 & CSS3 for the Real World*, Alexis Goldstein, Louis Lazaris, and Estelle Weyl (SitePoint Pty. Ltd, 2011) ISBN: 978-0-9808469-0-4

• *Stylin' with CSS: A Designer's Guide (3rd edition)*, Charles Wyke-Smith (New Riders Press, 2012) ISBN: 978-0-321-85847-4

Review questions

1 Should you use HTML-based formatting?

2 What does CSS impose on each HTML element?

3 True or false? If you do nothing, HTML elements will feature no formatting or structure.

4 What four "theories" affect the application of CSS formatting?

5 What is the difference between block and inline elements?

6 True or false? CSS3 features are all experimental, and you shouldn't use them at all.

Review answers

1 No. HTML-based formatting was deprecated in 1997 when HTML 4 was adopted. Industry best practices recommend using CSS-based formatting instead.

2 CSS imposes an imaginary box on each element. This box, and its content, can then be styled with borders, background colors and images, margins, padding, and other types of formatting.

3 False. Even if you do nothing, many HTML elements feature default formatting.

4 The four theories that affect CSS formatting are cascade, inheritance, descendant, and specificity.

5 Block elements create standalone structures; inline elements appear at the insertion point.

6 False. Many CSS3 features are already supported by modern browsers and can be used right now.

4 WEB DESIGN BASICS

Lesson overview

In this lesson, you'll learn the following:

- The basics of webpage design
- How to create page thumbnails and wireframes
- How to use Photoshop to generate site image assets automatically

 This lesson will take about 45 minutes to complete. If you have not already done so, download the project files for this lesson from the Lesson & Update Files tab on your Account page at www.peachpit .com, store them on your computer in a convenient location, and define a new site in Dreamweaver based on this folder, as described in the "Getting Started" section of this book. Your Account page is also where you'll find any updates to the chapters or to the lesson files. Look on the Lesson & Update Files tab to access the most current content.

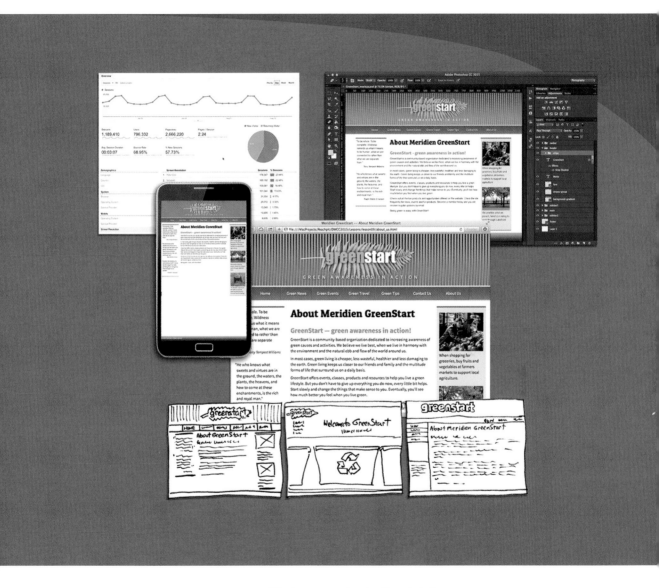

Whether you use thumbnails and wireframes,
Photoshop, or just a vivid imagination, Dreamweaver
can quickly turn your design concepts into complete,
standards-based CSS layouts.

Developing a new website

Before you begin any web design project for yourself or for a client, you need to answer three important questions:

- What is the purpose of the website?
- Who is the audience?
- How do they get here?

What is the purpose of the website?

Will the website sell or support a product or service? Is your site for entertainment or games? Will you provide information or news? Will you need a shopping cart or database? Do you need to accept credit card payments or electronic transfers? Knowing the purpose of the website tells you what type of content you'll be developing and working with and what types of technologies you'll need to incorporate.

Who is the audience?

Is the audience adults, children, seniors, professionals, hobbyists, men, women, everyone? Knowing *who* your audience will be is vital to the overall design and functionality of your site. A site intended for children probably needs more animation, interactivity, and bright, engaging colors. Adults will want serious content and in-depth analysis. Seniors may need larger type and other accessibility enhancements.

A good first step is to check out the competition. Is there an existing website performing the same service or selling the same product? Are they successful? You don't have to mimic others just because they're doing the same thing. Look at Google and Yahoo—they perform the same basic service, but their site designs couldn't be more different from one another.

How do they get here?

This sounds like an odd question when speaking of the Internet. But just as with a brick-and-mortar business, your online customers can come to you in a variety of ways. For example, are they accessing your site on a desktop computer, laptop, tablet, or cellphone? Are they using high-speed Internet, wireless, or dial-up service? What browser are they most likely to use, and what is the size and resolution of the display? These answers will tell you a lot about what kind of experience your customers will expect. Dial-up and cellphone users may not want to see a lot of graphics or video, whereas users with large flat-panel displays and high-speed connections may demand as much bang and sizzle as you can send at them.

So where do you get this information? Some you'll have to get through painstaking research and demographic analysis. Some you'll get from educated guesses based on your own tastes and understanding of your market. But a lot of it is actually available on the Internet itself. W3Schools, for one, keeps track of tons of statistics regarding access and usage, all updated regularly:

- w3schools.com/browsers/browsers_stats.asp provides information about browser statistics.

- w3schools.com/browsers/browsers_os.asp gives the breakdown on operating systems. In 2011, they started to track the usage of mobile devices on the Internet.

- w3schools.com/browsers/browsers_display.asp lets you find out the latest information on the resolution, or size, of screens using the Internet.

If you are redesigning an existing site, your web-hosting service itself may provide valuable statistics on historical traffic patterns and even the visitors themselves. If you host your own site, you can incorporate third-party tools, such as Google Analytics and Adobe Omniture, into your code to do the tracking for you for free or for a small fee.

Analytics provides comprehensive statistics on the visitors to your site. Google Analytics, pictured here, is a popular choice.

As of the fall of 2015, Windows still dominates the Internet (80 to 85 percent), with most users favoring Google Chrome (60 percent), followed by Firefox (21 percent), with various versions of Internet Explorer (7 percent) a distant third. The vast majority of browsers (99 percent) are set to a resolution higher than 1024 pixels by 768 pixels. If it weren't for the rapid growth in usage of tablets and smartphones for accessing the Internet, these statistics would be great news for most web designers and developers. But designing a website that can look good and work effectively for both flat-panel displays and cellphones is a tall order.

Responsive web design

Each day, more people are using cellphones and other mobile devices to access the Internet. Some people may use them to access the Internet more frequently than they use desktop computers. This presents a few nagging challenges to web designers. For one thing, cellphone screens are a fraction of the size of even the smallest flat-panel display. How do you cram a two- or three-column page design into a meager 300 to 400 pixels? Another problem is that mobile device manufacturers have dropped support for Flash-based content on their devices.

Until recently, web design usually required that you target an optimum size (height and width in pixels) for a webpage and then build the entire site on these specifications. Today, that scenario is becoming a rare occurrence. Now, you are presented with the decision to either build a site that can adapt to displays of multiple different dimensions (responsive) or build two or more separate websites to support desktop *and* mobile users at the same time (adaptive).

Your own decision will be based in part on the content you want to provide and on the capabilities of the devices accessing your pages. Building an attractive website that supports video, audio, and other dynamic content is hard enough without throwing in a panoply of different display sizes and device capabilities. The term *responsive web design* was coined, in a book of the same name (2011), by a Boston-based web developer named Ethan Marcotte; he describes the notion of designing pages that can adapt to multiple screen dimensions automatically. As you work through the following lessons, you will learn many techniques for responsive web design and implement them in your site and asset design.

Many of the concepts of print design are not applicable to the web, because you are not in control of the user's experience. A page carefully designed for a typical flat panel is basically useless on a cellphone.

Scenario

For the purposes of this book, you'll be working to develop a website for Meridien GreenStart, a fictitious community-based organization dedicated to green investment and action. This website will offer a variety of products and services and require a broad range of webpage types, including dynamic pages using technologies such as jQuery, which is a form of JavaScript.

Your customers come from a wide demographic that includes all ages and education levels. They are people who are concerned about environmental conditions and who are dedicated to conservation, recycling, and the reuse of natural and human resources.

Your marketing research indicates that most of your customers use desktop computers or laptops, connecting via high-speed Internet services. You can expect to get 20 to 30 percent of your visitors exclusively via cellphone and other mobile devices, and much of the rest will be using mobile from time to time.

To simplify the process of learning Dreamweaver, we'll focus on creating a fixed-width site design first. In Lesson 7, "Designing for Mobile Devices," you'll learn how to adapt your fixed-width design to work with smartphones and tablets.

Working with thumbnails and wireframes

After you have nailed down the answers to the three questions about your website purpose, customer demographic, and access model, the next step is to determine how many pages you'll need, what those pages will do, and finally, what they will look like.

Creating thumbnails

Many web designers start by drawing thumbnails with pencil and paper. Think of thumbnails as a graphical shopping list of the pages you'll need to create for the website. Thumbnails can also help you work out the basic navigation structure for the site. Draw lines between the thumbnails showing how your navigation will connect them.

Most sites are divided into levels. Typically, the first level includes all the pages in your main navigation menu—the ones a visitor can reach directly from the home page. The second level includes pages you can reach only through specific actions or from specific locations, say from a shopping cart or product detail page.

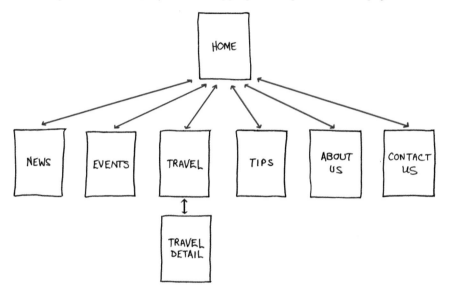

Thumbnails list the pages that need to be built and how they are connected to each other.

Creating a page design

Once you've figured out what your site needs in terms of pages, products, and services, you can then turn to what those pages will look like. Make a list of components you want or need on each page, such as headers and footers, navigation, and areas for the main content and the sidebars (if any). Put aside any items that won't be needed on every page. What other factors do you need to consider? If mobile devices are going to be an important consideration of your design identity, will any of the components be required or optional for these devices? Although many components can be simply resized for mobile screens, some will have to be completely redesigned or reimagined.

1. Header (includes banner and logo)
2. Footer (copyright info)
3. Horizontal navigation (for internal reference, i.e., Home, About Us, Contact Us)
4. Main content (one-column with chance of two or more)

Identifying the essential components for each page helps you create a page design and structure that will meet your needs.

Do you have a company logo, business identity, graphic imagery, or color scheme you want to match or complement? Do you have publications, brochures, or current advertising campaigns you want to emulate? It helps to gather them all in one place so you can see everything all at once on a desk or conference table. If you're lucky, a theme will rise organically from this collection.

Desktop or mobile

Once you've created your checklist of the components that you'll need on each page, sketch out several rough layouts that work for these components. Depending on your target visitor demographics, you may decide to focus on a design that's optimized for desktop computers or one that works best on tablets and smartphones.

Most designers settle on one basic page design that is a compromise between flexibility and sizzle. Some site designs may naturally lean toward using more than one basic layout. But resist the urge to design each page separately. Minimizing the number of page designs may sound like a major limitation, but it's key to producing a professional-looking site that's easy to manage. It's the reason why some professionals, like doctors and airline pilots, wear uniforms. Using a consistent page design, or template, conveys a sense of professionalism and confidence to your visitor. While you're figuring out what your pages will look like, you'll have to address the size and placement of the basic components. Where you put a component can drastically affect its impact and usefulness.

In print, designers know that the upper-left corner of a layout is considered one of the "power positions," a place where you want to locate important aspects of a design, such as a logo or title. This is because in western culture we read from left to right, top to bottom. The second power position is the lower-right corner, because this is the last thing your eyes will see when you're finished reading.

Unfortunately, in web design this theory doesn't hold up for one simple reason: You can never be certain how the user is seeing your design. Are they on a 20-inch flat panel or a 2-inch cellphone?

In most instances, the only thing you can be certain of is that the user can see the upper-left corner of any page. Do you want to waste this position by slapping the company logo here? Or make the site more useful by slipping in a navigation menu? This is one of the key predicaments of the web designer. Do you go for design sizzle, workable utility, or something in between?

Creating wireframes

After you pick the winning design, wireframing is a fast way to work out the structure of each page in the site. A wireframe is like a thumbnail, but bigger, that sketches out each page and fills in more details about the components, such as actual link names and main headings, but with minimal design or styling. This step helps to catch or anticipate problems before you smack into them when working in the code.

Wireframes allow you to experiment with page designs quickly and easily without wasting time with code.

The wireframe for the final design should identify all components and include specific information about content, color, and dimensions.

Once the basic concepts are worked out, many designers take an extra step and create a full-size mockup or "proof of concept" using a program like Adobe Photoshop or even Illustrator. It's a handy thing to do because you'll find that some clients just aren't comfortable giving an approval based only on pencil sketches. The advantage here is that all these programs allow you to export the results to full-size images (JPEG, GIF, or PNG) that can be viewed in a browser as if they were finished webpages. Such mockups are as good as seeing the real thing but may take only a fraction of the time to produce.

In some cases, creating a mockup in Adobe Photoshop, Adobe Fireworks, or Adobe Illustrator can save hours of tedious coding to receive a needed approval.

In addition to creating graphical mockups, Photoshop has tricks geared specifically for web designers, like the Adobe Generator feature.

Creating web assets using Adobe Generator (optional)

Adobe Generator is one of the web-oriented tools that allow you to export web assets from a Photoshop file in a variety of sizes, resolutions, and even file types. Best of all, this feature works in real time, exporting image assets from your file based on user-specified attributes added to the layer name. Let's take a closer look at this great tool.

Working with Adobe Generator

In this exercise, you'll work with an Adobe Photoshop document to prepare assets for your web project.

1 Launch Photoshop CC 2015 or higher.

2 Open **GreenStart_mockup.psd** from the lesson04/resources folder.

The Photoshop file contains a complete mockup of the GreenStart site design, which is composed of various vector-based design components as well as image assets stored in separate layers. Note the use of colors and gradients in the design.

3 Choose File > Save As.
Name the file **resources/myGreenStart_mockup.psd**.

4 If necessary, choose Window > Layers to display the Layers panel. Observe the names and contents of the layers and layer groups.

The layers and layer groups are named for the webpage components.

5 Open the header layer group, and observe the contents.

The header group contains two text elements and four graphical elements. Often, it's difficult to understand how a graphic component is built or for what purpose it is intended by looking at the layer names alone.

Note: This exercise requires the installation of Photoshop CC 2015 or higher and the lesson04 lesson files.

Note: The sample file used in this exercise requires the font Bree Serif, which you can download and install for free from Adobe Typekit. To access this font, and the entire Typekit library, choose Type > Add Fonts from Typekit in Photoshop CC 2015 or higher.

Tip: It's a good idea to save the file under a different name so you can refer back to the original assets should you make an error.

6 In the GreenStart layer, click the eye icon 👁 to toggle the layer visibility off.

The text "greenstart" disappears from the layer.

7 In the fern layer, click the eye icon 👁 to toggle the layer visibility off.

The image of the fern disappears. Using this method, you can identify each element of the header and see what role it plays in the creation of the overall design. The number and type of layers and the level of detail used here aren't necessary for a mockup that you merely want to use for a client approval. This file was set up specifically to create many of the final assets for the page design.

8 Click the eye icon 👁 to toggle the GreenStart and fern layers back on.

Exporting assets from Photoshop

The fern layer will be used to create one component of the header background. Photoshop generates a web asset automatically if you add a file extension to the layer name.

1 Double-click the name of the fern layer, type **fern.png** and press Enter/Return to complete the name.

When activated, Generator works in the background exporting assets in real time.

2 Choose File > Generate > Image Assets.

The next time you look at the Generate menu option, a checkmark will appear beside Image Assets, indicating that Generator is active.

3 Choose File > Open.

Navigate to the lesson04 > resources folder.

A new folder has been created and named **myGreenStart_mockup-assets** by Generator. Whenever you add file extensions to the layer names and enable Generator, it creates a folder and fills it with assets automatically, based on the layer names and settings.

4 Navigate to the **myGreenStart_mockup-assets** folder created by Photoshop.

The folder contains a single image: **fern.png**.

5 Open **fern.png**.

The file contains the fern with a transparent background. Note that the image displays a drop shadow. The shadow is a permanent part of the image, no longer created by a Photoshop effect.

6 Choose Image > Image Size.

Note the dimensions and resolution of the image.

The image is 468 pixels by 157 pixels, at 72 pixels per inch (ppi).

7 Click OK to close the Image Size dialog.

Close **fern.png**.

Creating multiple assets using Generator

Generator can also modify the default export specifications and even create multiple assets at multiple resolutions.

● **Note:** If you do not see the images created as described, check to make sure that the command File > Generate > Image Assets is enabled as described in the previous exercise.

1 Change the layer name fern.png to **200% fern.png+fern.jpg** and press Enter/Return to complete the name.

2 Choose File > Open. If necessary, navigate to the **myGreenStart_mockup-assets** folder.

The folder contains two images: **fern.png** and **fern.jpg**, both created by Generator. Older files with the same names are replaced automatically.

3 Select **fern.png** and open the file.

The file contains the fern, but it appears twice as large as the previous image.

4 Open **fern.jpg**.

The file contains the same fern image, but at the original size. JPEGs do not support transparency, so the background is white. There's no need for the JPEG version of the image. Generator can remove assets automatically too.

5 Change the layer name **200% fern. png+fern.jpg** to **150% fern.png** and press Enter/Return to complete the name.

The specification creates a larger, higher-quality image that will display well in regular browsers and on new higher-resolution devices. By removing "fern.jpg" from the layer name, Generator automatically deletes the JPEG version of the file.

6 Choose File > Open. Navigate to the myGreenStart_mockup-assets folder.

The JPEG version of the file is no longer visible in the folder. As you can see, Photoshop generates assets based on the name of the layer. You can create an entire set of images for your site design from the layers in this file.

7 In the Layers panel, open the header layer group. Change the name of the *stripe* layer group to **stripe.png**.

8 Open the sidebar2 layer group. Change the layer shopping to **shopping.jpg**. Change the layer biking to **biking.jpg**.

Note: In Photoshop, the background is mocked up using two layers: stripe and stripes-group. You are exporting the web background from the smaller stripe layer group, which looks like a folder icon in the Layers panel.

9 Choose File > Open. Navigate to the myGreenStart_mockup-assets folder.

The myGreenStart_mockup-assets folder now contains four image files. These files are identical to the ones you will use to build the site template and populate articles in upcoming lessons. As you can see, Generator offers some handy tools for turning this mockup into real web design assets, but the tricks don't stop there. Photoshop and Dreamweaver have even more collaboration tools to offer, as you will see later.

Check out http://helpx.adobe.com/photoshop/using/generate-assets-layers.html to see a complete explanation of Adobe Generator and how to use it.

Review questions

1 What three questions should you ask before starting any web design project?

2 What is the purpose of using thumbnails and wireframes?

3 Why is it important to create a design that takes into account smartphones and tablets?

4 Why would you use Adobe Photoshop, Illustrator, or Fireworks to design a website?

5 How does Adobe Generator assist in the creation of a website design?

Review answers

1 What is the purpose of the website? Who is the audience? How did they get here? These questions, and their answers, are essential in helping you develop the design, content, and strategy of your site.

2 Thumbnails and wireframes are quick techniques for roughing out the design and structure of your site without having to waste lots of time coding sample pages.

3 Mobile device users are one of the fastest-growing demographics on the web. Many visitors will use a mobile device to access your website on a regular basis or exclusively. Webpages designed for desktop computers often display poorly on mobile devices, making the websites difficult or impossible to use for these mobile visitors.

4 Using Photoshop, Illustrator, or Fireworks, you can produce page designs and mockups much faster than when designing in code with Dreamweaver. Designs can even be exported as web-compatible graphics that can be viewed in a browser to get client approval.

5 Adobe Generator allows you to export site image assets quickly from Photoshop mockups, allowing you to produce multiple sizes and versions of each asset.

5

CREATING A PAGE LAYOUT

Lesson overview

In this lesson, you'll learn how to do the following:

- Examine the chosen page design and evaluate the use of the predefined layouts provided by Dreamweaver.

- Work with the Visual Media Query interface.

- Create a new layout using the BootStrap framework.

- Modify the layout structure to use HTML5 semantic elements.

 This lesson will take about 90 minutes to complete. If you have not already done so, download the project files for this lesson from the Lesson & Update Files tab on your Account page at www.peachpit.com, store them on your computer in a convenient location, and define a new site in Dreamweaver based on this folder, as described in the "Getting Started" section of this book. Your Account page is also where you'll find any updates to the chapters or to the lesson files. Look on the Lesson & Update Files tab to access the most current content.

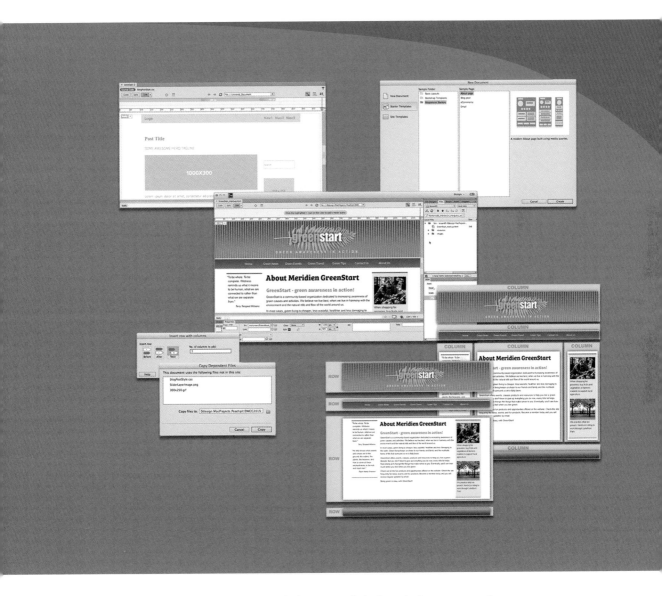

Whether you are designing a single page or an entire website, Dreamweaver provides all the tools you need to complete the project on time and under budget.

Evaluating page design options

In the previous lesson, you went through the process of identifying the pages, components, and structures you would need for a specific website. The selected design balances those needs against a variety of other factors, such as the types of visitors that may come to the site and their means of connecting to it. In this lesson, you will learn how to break down a graphical mockup into actual HTML structures and components and then build that basic layout in code.

Since there are almost unlimited ways to build a particular design, we'll concentrate on building a simple structure that uses the minimum number of HTML5 semantic elements. This will produce a page design that will be the easiest to implement and maintain.

Let's start by taking a look at the mockup created in Lesson 4.

1 Open **GreenStart_mockup.html** from the lesson05 folder.

This file contains an image depicting the final mockup of the GreenStart site design. The design can be broken down into basic components, such as header, footer, navigation, main, and sidebar content elements. If you diagrammed this scheme over the mockup, it might look like the following figure.

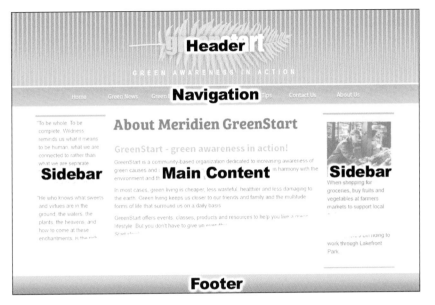

Once you identify the basic page component scheme, you could then break down the diagram into basic HTML elements, like this:

Although the <div> element is perfectly acceptable, and still in wide use as a page component, it is a holdover from HTML 4 and comes with some disadvantages. For example, it makes the underlying code more complex by requiring the use of class attributes to help delineate the various components within the design. Today, web designers are instead using the new HTML5 elements to simplify their designs and to add semantic meaning to their code. If you substitute the <div> elements for HTML5 structures, it's easy to see how much simpler the layout can be.

Now that the page has been diagrammed and broken down into its components, you could start creating the basic structure right away. But before you spend any time creating the new layout by hand, Dreamweaver may offer some better alternatives.

2 Close **GreenStart_mockup.html**.

Working with predefined layouts

Dreamweaver has always tried to offer the latest tools and workflows to all web designers, regardless of their skill level. For example, over the years, the program has provided a selection of predefined templates and various page components to make the task of building and populating webpages fast and easy. Often the first step of building a website was to see if one of these predefined layouts matched your needs, or if your needs could be adapted to one of the available designs.

Dreamweaver CC (2015.1 release) continues this tradition by providing sample CSS layouts and frameworks that you can adapt to many popular types of projects. You can access these samples from the File menu.

1 Choose File > New.

The New Document dialog appears. Dreamweaver allows you to build a wide spectrum of web-compatible documents besides those built using HTML, CSS, and JavaScript. The New Document dialog displays many of these document types, including PHP, XML, and SVG. Predefined layouts, templates, and frameworks can also be accessed from this dialog.

At the time of this writing, Dreamweaver CC (2015.1 release) offers three basic layouts, four responsive starter layouts and six Bootstrap templates. The exact number and features of these layouts may change over time through automatic updates via Creative Cloud. The changes to this list may occur without notice or fanfare, so keep your eyes peeled for new options in this dialog.

All the featured starter layouts are responsive design built using HTML5-compatible structures and will help you gain valuable experience with this evolving standard. Unless you need to support older browsers (such as IE5 and 6), there's little to worry about when using the newer designs. Let's check out these layouts.

2 In the New Document dialog, select Starter Templates > Responsive Starters.

The Starter Templates window of the New Document dialog displays five options: About page, Blog post, eCommerce, Email, and Portfolio.

3 Select **About page**.

Observe the preview image in the dialog.

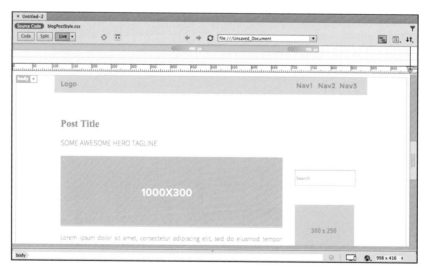

An image appears showing the design of a responsive webpage for desktop, tablet, and smartphone.

4 Select **Blog Post**.

The preview image changes to depict the new design.

5 Select each of the design options in turn.

Observe the preview image in the dialog.

Each template offers a design appropriate for specific applications. None of the templates are identical to our chosen design, but Blog Post is the closest. Let's take a closer look.

6 Select **Blog Post** again.

Click Create.

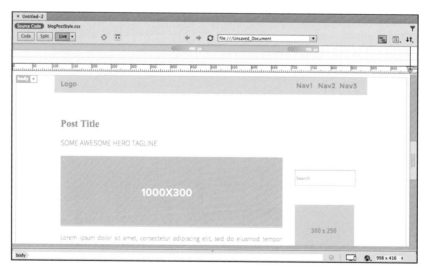

A new, untitled document appears in the workspace based on the starter layout. Before working in any document, it's a good idea to save it.

7 Select File > Save.

The Save As dialog appears.

8 Name the page **page1.html**, and click Save to save the page into the root folder for lesson05.

The file is saved to the site folder. At the same time Dreamweaver creates a BlogPostAssets folder and copies some files to it to support the starter layout.

● **Note:** The support files may not appear immediately in the Files panel.

Dreamweaver designed this page for use as a blog post. The new page is populated with placeholders for text, images, and even menus. To use it, you simply swap out these placeholders with your own words and pictures.

Another attribute of this layout that is not readily apparent at this moment is that it has been built right out of the box to be fully responsive. Fortunately, you can test this functionality right in Dreamweaver.

Live view is the new default workspace for most functions in Dreamweaver CC (2015.1 release). It offers an accurate display of all page components, styling, and even interactivity. You may still switch to Design or Code view for various operations, but you'll find that Live view provides most of the tools you'll ever need in one place.

9 If necessary, switch to Live view.

10 Drag the Scrubber to the left to make the document window narrower.

As the document window narrows, some of the components resize or reformat to adapt to the smaller window. Note that some elements actually change positions within the layout. When the window narrows below 480 pixels, the content displays in a single column.

11 Drag the Scrubber to the right to make the document window wider.

As the window widens, notice that the content continues to adapt to the screen until it resumes its original layout and formatting.

Did you notice that the layout changed abruptly at certain widths? These changes were caused by *media queries* that control the application of the CSS styling. To help you work with media queries, Dreamweaver CC (2015.1 release) offers the new *Visual* Media Queries interface, which should be visible at the top of the document window when you are in Live view.

Introducing the Visual Media Queries interface

The Visual Media Queries (VMQ) interface allows you to identify and interact with media queries instantly using the cursor.

1   If necessary, click the "Show Visual Media Queries bar" icon at the top of the document window to display the toolbar.

The toolbar displays two media queries settings for this document.

2   Position the cursor over the first media query.

A tooltip appears, identifying that the media query is set for a max-width of 480 pixels.

3   Position the cursor over the second media query.

The second media query is set for a max-width of 769 pixels. The interface displays the existing settings using numbers and colors so you can see the specifications instantly. You can use the cursor to activate or switch between each media query.

VMQ enables you to see the differences

Media queries enable your webpage and its content to adapt to a variety of different types of screens and devices. They do this by loading custom style sheets created just for specific screen sizes, devices, or even orientations. Later, you'll learn more about media queries, how they work, and how to create them. For now, let's just review how the Visual Media Queries (VMQ) interface works.

The VMQ interface identifies all media queries defined on the page or within style sheets linked to it. The media queries are displayed in color based on their specifications.

Media queries that define only a minimum width are displayed in green.

Media queries that define only a maximum width are displayed in purple.

Media queries that define both minimum and maximum widths are displayed in blue.

The Dreamweaver workspace is fully responsive and will display all the defined CSS styling appropriate to the screen size and orientation. To display the styling associated with a specific media query, simply double-click its representative display in the VMQ.

4 Click the cursor to the left of the number 480 in the VMQ interface.

The document window narrows instantly to 480 pixels. The content adapts to the window size based on the applicable CSS styles.

5 Click the cursor to the left of the number 769 in the Visual Media Queries interface.

The document window widens to 769 pixels. To return to full size, you can drag the Scrubber to the right edge of the window or double-click in the gray area to the right of the Scrubber.

6 Double-click in the gray area on the right side of the Scrubber.

The document window opens to the full size of the workspace.

If you examine the current layout and compare it to our chosen site design, the Blog Post layout is not similar enough to be easily adaptable. The same is true of the other responsive starter layouts. Perhaps the Bootstrap templates offer a closer fit.

Introducing Bootstrap

The Bootstrap templates are predefined layouts using the Bootstrap framework. Bootstrap is a set of open-source tools that help you quickly build websites and web applications that are fully responsive.

Created by Twitter, Bootstrap was released to the public in 2011 and quickly became one of the most popular frameworks in use. It has now been incorporated into Dreamweaver.

Before you begin this exercise, you should define a new site based on the lesson05 folder, as described in the "Getting Started" section.

1 Select File > New.

The New Document dialog appears.

Note: Don't click directly on the number itself; Dreamweaver may open an editing window instead.

2 Select Starter Templates > Bootstrap Templates in the New Document dialog.

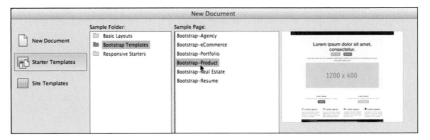

The Sample Page window displays six templates based on the Bootstrap framework. A preview of the layout appears when you select the template name.

3 Select each layout option and compare the preview to the proposed site design.

None of the templates are close enough to the proposed design to warrant trying to use one as the basis for the new site. Instead, you'll see what all the hype about Bootstrap is all about by using it to create your own template from scratch.

4 Select the New Document tab in the New Document dialog.

5 Select HTML in the Document Type window.

6 Select the Bootstrap framework.

7 For Bootstrap CSS, select Create New.

8 Deselect the Design option Include a Pre-built Layout.

9 Click the triangle beside the Customize option to expand it.

The Customize options allow you to change the number of columns, the gutter width, or the predefined screen sizes. For this layout, you will leave the default settings as they are, but if you use Bootstrap in the future you should make sure these numbers reflect the needs of your site and its visitors.

10 Click Create.

A new, untitled document appears in the document window.

11 Select File > Save.
Name the file **mylayout.html** and click Save.

Although the file is entirely empty, lots of things are already going on. You can see that the VMQ interface displays at least six media queries and that the Related files interface shows one CSS and two JavaScript files. The next thing to do is to add some basic structure.

Creating a layout with Bootstrap

Underlying all the power and flexibility of Bootstrap is a basic grid system of rows and columns. This concept harks back to the earlier days of web design, before the advent of CSS, when we would use tables to cobble together our layouts. The only way to impose order on our webpages was to organize our text and pictures into table rows and cells.

No, we're not going back to the bad old days. Tables were not responsive. Although they could scale up or down in size, they would not automatically adapt to the screen and knew nothing about mobile devices. Instead, the rows and columns of Bootstrap have been carefully engineered to work in most modern browsers and devices.

The first step in Bootstrap is to identify the basic grid structure you need to build, or impose, on the proposed site design. This should be quite easy when you examine the mockup. Start by marking up the content that would be grouped together in rows, as in the following figure.

Next, identify the columns within the content. Remember that the columns are divvied up in the rows you already created.

You will use the Insert panel to build this structure.

1 If necessary, open **mylayout.html** in Split view.
   Click in the Live view window.

Note: If you are an experienced user of Dreamweaver, you may expect to see your cursor inserted in the document window. Live view does not enable direct editing of your text and images as in Design view. You will learn the proper techniques for creating and editing text in Live view later in this lesson.

The <body> element is selected in the window.

2 Display the Insert panel. If it's not visible on the screen, you can select it from the Window menu.

3 In the Insert panel, select **Bootstrap Components** from the drop-down menu.

The panel displays a list of 26 main items and over 80 sub-items supported by the framework. Although the list is not exhaustive, it's a good start. Whatever you can't find in the Insert panel can always be added by hand manually in the Code window.

4 Click the **Container** item at the top of the panel.

Note: If you instead prefer to create a site that automatically scales to every screen width, use the Container-fluid item in the panel.

This option inserts in the page a fixed-width `<div>` element that in Bootstrap is, by default, 1170 pixels wide in a full-screen browser on a desktop computer. On smaller screens or devices, this container will display at various smaller fixed widths.

Once you've established your overall container, you can start creating the row and column scheme devised earlier, but first you will target the default page width.

Note: To see all the media queries, the document window will have to be at least 1100 pixels in width.

5 Click the *Small* media query (min-width 768 pixels) in the VMQ.

The document window resizes to match the dimensions of the media query. Targeting the width first determines what classes are automatically assigned by the Bootstrap framework when you add columns to your rows.

6 Click the **Grid Row with Column** item in the Insert panel.

The Insert Row with Columns dialog appears.

7 Click the **Nest** option.
Enter **1** in the No. of Columns to Add field.
Click OK.

In the Code window, you can see that Dreamweaver inserted two <div> elements, one with a class of row and the other with a class of col-sm-12, nested one inside the other in the initial container. Since the *Small* media query is targeted, the class says sm. *Medium* classes will say md, and *Large* classes will say lg.

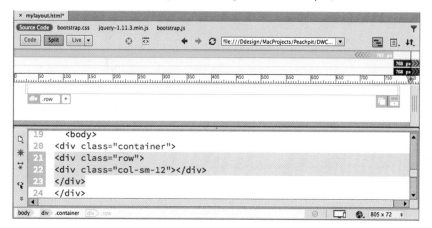

The structure doesn't look very remarkable, but this is the key to the power of Bootstrap. These classes apply to these elements predefined styles that will allow them to adapt to different screens and devices. By adding more classes or manipulating the existing ones, you can provide different formatting as desired.

As complex and elaborate as Bootstrap is, one aspect of this scheme is easy to understand. If you remember from the New Document dialog, when you created the page, the Bootstrap specifications called for 12 columns in the grid. The class col-sm-12 speaks to this grid by telling the <div> to be *12 columns* wide on *small* devices. A small device is considered to be a tablet at least 768 pixels wide. But don't let that fool you. It's important to know that some Bootstrap classes, like this one, are inherited and continue to format even on larger devices.

As we work through this layout and the upcoming lessons, you will learn how to add to the main components other Bootstrap classes that will specify their behavior in each environment you wish to support. Let's add the next row to the structure.

8 Click the **Grid Row with Column** item again.

The Insert Row with Columns dialog appears. The first row should still be selected.

9 Select **After**.

Enter **1** for the number of columns.

Click OK.

Insert row with columns

Insert row:

Before   After   Nest

No. of columns to add:

1

Help   Cancel   OK

A new row is created, inserted after the first. The second is a duplicate of the first and will eventually hold the navigation menu. You'll add that later, but now let's create the next row.

10 Repeat step 8.

In the Insert Row with Columns dialog, select After, and this time, for the number of columns, enter **3**.

Click OK.

```
25   <div class="col-sm-12"></div>
26   </div>
27   <div class="row">
28   <div class="col-sm-4"></div>
29   <div class="col-sm-4"></div>
30   <div class="col-sm-4"></div>
31   </div>
32   </div>
33
34      <!-- jQuery (necessary for Bootstrap's JavaScript plugins) -->
```

body   div   .container   div   .row   805 x 161

A new row appears with three nested `<div>` elements. The new elements have a class of `col-sm-4`. Because 4 divides into 12 three times, the new elements form three columns that divide the available space into three equal parts. Later, you will modify these classes to change the widths and the relationships of these elements to one another. But let's finish the layout first. There's one more row needed for the page footer.

11 Repeat steps 8 and 9 to create a row with one column.

A new row is added for the last row, which will hold the footer. The basic Bootstrap structure has been created for the site design.

12 Save the file. If you are continuing to the next exercise, leave **mylayout.html** open, but close all other open documents.

In the upcoming exercises you will modify the basic layout to add HTML5 elements and content placeholders for the site template.

Adding HTML5 elements to Bootstrap

As you can see from the previous exercise, Bootstrap relies heavily on the <div> element. There's nothing wrong with this technique, since the framework can't intuit the purpose of the elements in the rows and columns and automatically add the appropriate tags. But as a generic container, the <div> element conveys no semantic value or other information to search engines or other web applications.

Once you have created your basic structure, it makes sense to go back and swap out these generic structures with ones that more closely match your intended usage or content model. Dreamweaver makes it easy to edit structural elements.

1 If necessary, launch Dreamweaver CC (2015.1 release) or later. Open **mylayout.html** from the lesson05 folder.

The file has a basic Bootstrap structure containing four rows, three with one column and one with three columns.

2 Select Split view so that the workspace displays the Code and Live view windows at the same time.

The Bootstrap borders, rows, and columns should be visible in the Live view window.

3 Click in the first row of the layout and examine the tag selector at the bottom of the document window.

Dreamweaver selects one of the elements in the row and displays the blue heads-up display (HUD) interface.

Depending on where or how you click, you could select the row itself or the column nested within it. You can determine which element is selected by looking at the class name displayed in the HUD or tag selectors: `div.row` indicates that you have selected a row, whereas `div.col-sm-12` means you have a column selected. The selected element will be highlighted in blue in the tag selectors.

4   Click the tag selector for `div.row`.

5   Press Ctrl+T/Cmd+T to activate the Quick Tag Editor.

The Quick Tag Editor appears, populated by the code for the row element. If you recall from the original page diagram, this element should be designated as an HTML5 `<header>`.

6   Edit the element code as highlighted:
    `<header class="row">`

7   Press Enter/Return twice to complete the change.

The structure is now updated to use the new element.

8   Click in the second row, and select the `div.row` tag selector.

9   Press Ctrl+T/Cmd+T.
    Edit the element code as highlighted:
    `<nav class="row">`

10 Press Enter/Return twice to complete the change.

11 Repeat steps 8–10 to edit the third row as highlighted:
    `<article class="row">`

This row also contains three columns: one main element and two sidebars.

12 Click in the first column of the `article.row`.

The first `div.col-sm-4` element in the row should be selected. We'll refer to this element as Sidebar 1 throughout the book.

13 Press Ctrl+T/Cmd+T.
Edit the element as highlighted:
`<aside class="col-sm-4">`

14 Repeat steps 12–13 to edit the second column as highlighted:
`<section class="col-sm-4">`

15 Edit the third column as highlighted:
`<aside class="col-sm-4">`

We'll refer to this element as Sidebar 2.

16 Edit the fourth row as highlighted:
`<footer class="row">`

17 Save the file.

The layout has now been updated to use HTML5 elements. In the next lesson, you'll learn how to add some basic content and to format various elements.

Review questions

1 Does Dreamweaver provide any design assistance for beginners?

2 What advantages do you get from using a responsive starter layout?

3 What does the Visual Media Queries (VMQ) interface do?

4 What do the colors in the VMQ signify?

5 How does the Scrubber work in conjunction with the VMQ?

6 Why should you consider using Bootstrap for your next website?

7 True or false: You have to use one of the six predefined templates if you want to use Bootstrap.

8 Why should you replace the <div> elements created by Bootstrap with HTML5 semantic elements?

Review answers

1   Dreamweaver CC (2015.1 release) provides three basic layouts, five responsive starter layouts, and six Bootstrap templates.

2   Responsive starter layouts help you jumpstart the design of a site or layout by providing a finished layout complete with predefined CSS and placeholder content.

3   The VMQ interface provides a visual representation of the existing media queries in a file and allows you to create new media queries and interact with them in a point-and-click interface.

4   The colors displayed indicate whether the media query is defined with min-width specifications, max-width specifications, or a combination of both.

5   The Scrubber allows you to quickly preview the page design at varying screen sizes to test the predefined media queries and pertinent styling.

6   Bootstrap is one of the most popular frameworks for building responsive websites. It provides a comprehensive set of tools and components that allow you to build a site that adapts automatically to various screen sizes and devices in a fraction of the time you would need otherwise.

7   False. Dreamweaver provides tools and a workflow that allow you to easily build your own Bootstrap layout from scratch.

8   The <div> element conveys no semantic value or other information to search engines and other applications. Semantic elements may improve your ranking by making it easier for search engines to identify your site structure and content.

6 WORKING WITH A WEB FRAMEWORK

Lesson overview

In this lesson, you'll learn how to do the following:

- Insert and format new content and components into a Bootstrap-based layout

- Use the CSS Designer to identify applied CSS formatting

- Create advanced CSS background and gradient effects

- Access and use web-hosted fonts

This lesson will take about 3 hours and 30 minutes to complete. If you have not already done so, download the project files for this lesson from the Lesson & Update Files tab on your Account page at www.peachpit.com, store them on your computer in a convenient location, and define a new site in Dreamweaver based on this folder, as described in the "Getting Started" section of this book. Your Account page is also where you'll find any updates to the lessons or to the lesson files. Look on the Lesson & Update Files tab to access the most current content.

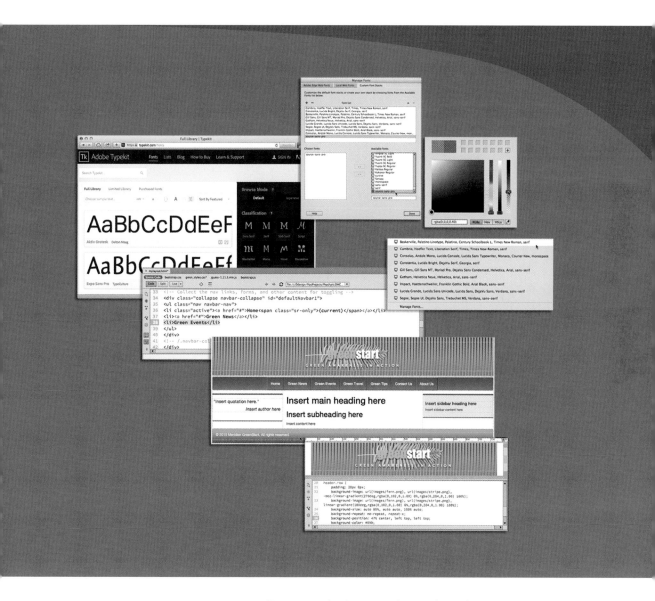

Dreamweaver has incorporated many advanced functions and components from various web frameworks, such as jQuery and Bootstrap, to speed up and simplify the process of developing fully functional, mobile-friendly websites, much of it without having to write a single line of code.

Creating header content

If you start at the top of the webpage and work down, the first element to address is the `<header>`. If you follow the site design mockup as your guide, the `<header>` is composed of several components, including the company name, the motto, the logo, and a graphical background.

This effect could be reproduced by using a single image, but that image would have to be quite large. A single image would be the least flexible option, not to mention the least accessible. Instead, we'll stretch your CSS skills by building a composite design combining text and multiple background effects. This technique will allow the design to be more adaptable to various devices, such as cellphones and tablets. Let's start by adding the text.

1   If necessary, open **mylayout.html** from the lesson06 folder in Split view, with Live view enabled.

2   Click the first row of the Bootstrap structure.
    Select the `div.col-sm-12` tag selector.

3   Open the Insert panel.
    Select the HTML tab from the drop-down menu.

    The HTML tab provides an easy way to insert all sorts of standard HTML elements.

4   In the Headings drop-down menu, select **H2**.

The position-assist interface appears. This interface enables you to choose where the new element will be inserted: before, after, nested within the current selection, or wrapped around the selection.

5 Select **Nest**.

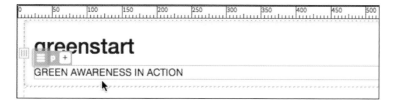

A new <h2> element appears within the <div> filled with placeholder text. Text can now be edited directly in Live view, but you need to know a simple trick to make it editable.

6 Double-click the placeholder text.

The blue HUD disappears and is replaced by a plain orange box, indicating that the content of the <h2> is now in text-editing mode.

7 Select the text and type **greenstart** in all lowercase.

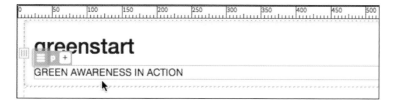

The company name replaces the placeholder text. Now let's add the company motto.

8 Press Enter/Return to create a new line.
   Type **GREEN AWARENESS IN ACTION** in all uppercase.

The motto appears in a new <p> element, but the change is not permanent yet. Looking at the Code window you will not see the text you just typed. If you press the ESC key or click in the Code window, the new text may be discarded altogether.

● **Note:** Exiting editing mode may take a moment. Be patient.

9 Click the cursor just outside the orange editing box.

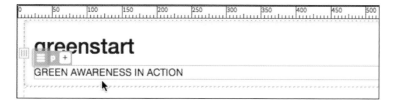

The orange box disappears. The heading and the motto are now a permanent part of the header.

10 Save the file.

The text has been entered but still needs to be formatted. Text and structural elements are formatted using cascading style sheets. The main tool for creating, editing, and troubleshooting these style sheets is the CSS Designer. Before you start styling your new webpage and content, it will help to familiarize yourself with how the CSS Designer functions.

Working with the CSS Designer

In the upcoming exercises in this lesson, you'll learn how to use the CSS Designer to inspect the existing CSS and create new rules to complete the basic site template design. Before you proceed, it's vital to your role as a designer to understand and identify any existing structure and formatting of a page so that you can effectively complete your tasks.

It's always a good idea when using any predefined components or frameworks to take a few minutes to examine the underlying HTML and CSS to understand what role they perform in the current document. It will also be a good opportunity to familiarize yourself with the CSS Designer and how to use it properly.

1 Open **mylayout.html** from the lesson06 folder in Live view, if necessary.

2 Choose Window > Workspace Layout > Design.
   Choose Window > CSS Designer to display it, if necessary.

The CSS Designer has four windows that display different aspects of the CSS structure and styling: *Sources, @Media, Selectors,* and *Properties.* The latest version of CSS Designer also features two distinct modes: *All* and *Current.* At this moment you should ensure that the All mode is enabled.

3 Click the All button in the CSS Designer, if necessary.

Note: CSS Designer should be a default component of the Design workspace, but sometimes users close panels unintentionally. Dreamweaver will remember any customizations you perform to the interface. If necessary, you can open it by selecting Window > CSS Designer.

The Sources window now displays all style sheets embedded or linked to the page. You should see two notations: ALL SOURCES and bootstrap.css.

4 Select ALL SOURCES in the Sources window.

The @Media and Selectors windows display all the media queries and selector names defined in any listed style sheet. The All mode will be very helpful in tracking down a specific rule and where it's defined. By selecting an item in either window, the CSS Designer will identify its location by highlighting its source in bold.

Note: The Current mode limits the display to only the CSS affecting the element selected in the document window.

5 Select the rule `a:active, a:hover` in the Selectors window.

Note that the name bootstrap.css in the Sources window and GLOBAL in the @Media window are now bolded. The bolding indicates that `a:active`, `a:hover` is defined in the bootstrap.css style sheet as a global rule. This behavior works even in the other windows.

6   Select the first (`min-width 768`) media query in the @Media window. Observe the changes in the CSS Designer display.

Note that bootstrap.css is still selected but the Selectors window now shows only one name: `.lead`. This indicates that only one rule is defined within the selected media query.

7   Select the `.lead` rule in the Selectors window.

The Properties window displays the CSS properties defined in the rule. Depending on its configuration, you may not see which property or properties are set.

8   If necessary, select the Show Set option in the Properties window.

When Show Set is enabled, the Properties window displays only the properties modified by the rule. In this case, the `.lead` rule sets the font-size property to 21 px.

You may also notice that the Properties window has a gray background color. This indicates that the properties are non-editable. If you look at the Sources window, you can see that the **bootstrap.css** style sheet is marked as `(read only)`. Since the page is based on the Bootstrap framework, Dreamweaver prevents you from modifying and potentially damaging its predefined styling. The styling contained within it is very complex and full of interdependencies. It's recommended that any changes be made in your own custom style sheet.

At the moment, there is no custom style sheet. Before you can style the structure or content of the new page and site, you'll have to add a new editable style sheet. You can create the style sheet directly in the CSS Designer.

9 Click the Add CSS Source icon ✚ in the CSS Designer.

A drop-down menu appears that allows you to create a new CSS file, attach an existing CSS file, or define a style sheet embedded within the page itself.

10 Choose **Create A New CSS File** from the drop-down menu.

The Create A New CSS File dialog appears.

11 Type **green_styles.css** in the Create a New CSS File dialog. Click OK to create the style sheet reference.

When you click OK, a reference to the new style sheet is added to the CSS Designer Sources window. The CSS file has not actually been created yet, but a link has been added to the <head> section of the page and the file will be created automatically as soon as you create your first custom rule.

12 Click **green_styles.css** in the Sources window.

The @Media and the Selectors windows are both empty. This means there are no CSS rules yet. You have a blank slate on which you can make any design additions or modifications. Since you will not change the Bootstrap CSS, this style sheet will be the means you use to make the structure and content bend to your wishes.

13 Select the text "greenstart" in the `<header>` element.

14 Click the Current button.

Observe the CSS Designer.

The windows in the CSS Designer change, displaying the media queries and selectors that format the selected element. A close inspection of the Sources window tells you that only the **bootstrap.css** file holds any of these rules. Then, a look at the Selectors window shows you the names of the rules that provide some sort of styling to the <h2> element itself or to its surrounding structure.

> **Note:** Remember you learned in Lesson 3, "CSS Basics," that some HTML elements have default styling. Default properties will not be shown in the CSS Designer.

15 Select each rule in the Selectors window, starting at the top of the list. Observe the Properties window as each rule is highlighted, but keep your eyes peeled for other changes in the workspace.

As you inspect each rule, you will see the Properties window change to display the formatting applied by each one. Did you notice that as you clicked each rule Live view highlighted the specific elements affected by the rule within the layout?

As you can see, CSS Designer can be used in a variety of ways to identify the styling applied to a specific element as well as to identify the element affected by a specific rule. It can also help you create and name the CSS rules.

Working with Type

In this exercise, you will learn how to create new selectors that will format text within the `<header>` element.

Note: When the Current button is selected, the CSS Designer allows you to edit only existing properties or add new properties to existing CSS rules.

1 Select the All button again in the CSS Designer.

When All is selected you can create new rules. Since **bootstrap.css** is locked, you need to select a different location for your new rule.

2 Select **green_styles.css** in the Sources window.

3 Click the Add New Selector icon ➕.

```
Files  Insert  Assets  CSS Designer  CC Libraries                    ▾≡
                        [ All ][ Current ]
+  −   Sources                        +  −   Properties
ALL SOURCES                                            ☑ Show Set
bootstrap.css ( Read Only )
green_styles.css
+  −   @Media
GLOBAL
Select a CSS source and click on the + sign to add a
media query.
+  −   Selectors
🔍  Add Selector
.row .col-sm-12 h2
```

The selector name .row .col-sm-12 h2 appears in the Selectors window. By default, Dreamweaver tries to create selector names using specific class or id attributes whenever they are present. This might be a good technique in a different layout, but this one is based on Bootstrap grid structures, meaning that the class names are not as useful as they might be in another situation.

For example, a selector written this way would affect <h2> elements inserted into the first, second, and fourth rows. To target the styling more narrowly, a bit of tweaking is required.

4 Edit the selector as shown: header.row h2
Press Enter/Return twice to complete the selector.

```
+  −   Selectors
🔍  Filter CSS Rules
header.row h2
```

This new name will target only <h2> headings that are inserted into <header> elements with a class of row. Note that the Properties window has a white background, indicating that this rule is fully editable.

5 Deselect the Show Set option in the Properties window.

Note: The Properties window is a list of CSS properties. You can also scroll up or down to the desired category.

Only when Show Set is deselected does the Properties window display the list of all available CSS specifications. The list is organized into five categories, which can be accessed quickly by clicking their icons: Layout 🖿, Text 🅃, Border ☐, Background ▨, and More ▪▪▪. To focus the display on a particular category, you can use the category icons at the top of the Properties window.

6 Click the Text category icon .

The Properties window focuses on the Text properties. You'll set some basic styling now and come back to this element later when you add more styling to the header.

7 Click the Set Color icon to open the Color Picker pop-up window.

The color picker enables you to select colors in several ways. You can choose a color by sight by using the various visual tools or by entering the color by number, using RGB, Hex, or HSL values.

8 Select Hex and enter **#00FF00** in the color field. Press Enter/Return to close the color window.

The text changes color to a bright green.

9 Click the value field to the right of the **font-family** property.

A pop-up window appears showing nine groups of typeface names and several design categories, such as sans-serif and monospace. We'll explore and learn more about how to use fonts later, but for the moment let's just pick one of the predefined font groups.

10 Select the group `Impact, Haettenschweiler, "Franklin Gothic Bold", "Arial Black", sans-serif`

The <h2> is now formatted by the font Impact.

Defining values

Values can be expressed in one or two parts in the Properties window. When the value comes in two parts, numeric values are entered on the left side and the measurement system (px, em, %) is entered, or selected, on the right. Single-part values (center, left, right, and so on) can be selected from the right side of the field or entered manually.

Predefined values (center, middle, top) or measurement systems can be selected from a hinting menu that pops up when Show Set is deselected. When Show Set is selected, the hinting menu does not appear at all and all values must be entered in full, manually.

You may enter the value and measurement system all at once at any time by double-clicking the field and typing them in using the keyboard.

11 Double-click the **font-size** property value field, enter **350%**

T Text	
color	: ◻ #00FF00
font-family	: Impact, Haettenschweiler, Franklin Goth...
font-style	:
font-variant	:
font-weight	:
font-size	: `350%`
line-height	:

As you learned in Lesson 3, font sizes based on percentage are factored from the size of the body element.

12 In the **text-align** property, select `center`.

font-size	: 350%	
line-height	:	
text-align	: ▤ ▤ ▤ ▤	⊘ 🗑
text-decoration	: ◻ ⊻ T T̄	
text-indent	: `center`	

The text moves to the center of the <header>. The text is hard to read in such a bright color, but a drop shadow can improve the legibility.

13 In the **text-shadow** property, enter the following specifications:

```
h-shadow: 0px
v-shadow: 5px
blur: 5px
color: rgba(0,0,0,0.4)
```

A drop shadow appears behind the heading.

The last task is to format the letters in "start" in white. This will require a custom class.

Creating Custom Classes

CSS styling can be applied to any distinct element, such as div, h1, p, a, and so on. When you want to apply formatting to a string of text that has no tag of its own, you need to use the <span> tag. When the styling can't be targeted using the structure of the code itself, the use of a class attribute is warranted.

In this exercise, you will create a custom class to apply white to a portion of the logo.

1   Double-click the text "greenstart" to enter text-editing mode in Live view.

The blue HUD is replaced by the orange editing box.

2   Select the letters "start".

3   Press Cmd+T/Ctrl+T to activate the Quick Tag Editor.

The Quick Tag Editor appears. It should default to Wrap tag mode.

4   Type <span> and press Enter/Return twice to complete the tag.

▶ **Tip:** If you know what class you want to add to the <span> tag, you can also add it directly in the Quick Tag Editor.

The blue HUD, displaying the span tag, replaces the editing box. There is no existing formatting to call on, so you'll have to create a new class.

5   Click the Add Class/ID icon ⊞ in the HUD for the span tag.

6   Type .logowhite to create a new class name.

After you type the leading period (.) to start the class name, Dreamweaver will display a list of existing classes for you to choose from. As you continue to type, the list is filtered to names that match. When you are done typing, the list will disappear, indicating that this class name doesn't already exist.

7 Press Enter/Return to create the class.

● **Note:** If green_styles.css does not appear in the source menu, select it manually.

A window appears allowing you to pick the style sheet and media query into which you can insert the new class. Since **bootstrap.css** is a read-only file, the menu should default to **green_styles.css**. At the moment, there are no media queries in **green_style.css**, so the class will be entered as a global style.

8 Press Enter/Return to complete the creation of the class `logowhite`.

9 Select **green_styles.css** in the Sources window.
Select `.logowhite` in the Selectors window.

10 Select the Text category icon [T] in the Properties window.

11 In the **color** property, enter #FFFFFF

The letters "start" appear in white. The logo is complete. Now, let's format the association motto. As with the heading, the process starts with a selection.

12 Select the text "GREEN AWARENESS IN ACTION" in the <header> element.

The blue HUD should appear around the <p> element.

13 If necessary, select the **green_styles.css** file in Sources.

14 Click the Add Selector icon ✚.

The name `.row .col-sm-12 p` appears in the Selectors window.

15 Change the selector to `header.row p`
Press Enter/Return twice to complete the name.

The new selector will target only <p> elements in the <header>.

16 Click the Text category in the CSS Designer, if necessary.

17 In the font-family property, select `"Lucida Grande", "Lucida Sans Unicode", "Lucida Sans", "DejaVu Sans", Verdana, sans-serif`.

18 In the **font-weight** property, enter bold

19 In the **text-align** property, select center.

20 In the **text-shadow** property, enter the following specifications:

```
h-shadow: 0px
v-shadow: 3px
blur: 5px
color: rgba(0,0,0,0.50)
```

21 In the **letter-spacing** property, enter .5em

The spacing between the letters expands.

22 In the **color** property, enter #FFFFFF

The motto now displays in white with a drop shadow. The styling of the header text is complete.

23 Save **mylayout.html**.

Next, you'll learn how to add background effects to the element.

Adding a background image

In this exercise, you will add the first background image to the <header> element and then use CSS to adjust its size and position.

1 If necessary, open **mylayout.html** from the lesson06 folder and switch to or activate Live view.

2 Select or open the CSS Designer.

3 Click the first row of the Bootstrap structure.
Select the header.row tag selector.

4 Click the All button in the CSS Designer.

5 Select **green_styles.css** in the Sources window.

When **green_styles.css** is selected, the Selectors window displays only the rules that appear in that file.

6 Click the Add Selector icon ➕.

The selector name `.container .row` appears in the Selectors window. As you saw earlier, this name is too generic to be useful here. It would format every element with the class of `row`, which includes all four rows of the layout. In this case, you want to format only the `<header>`.

7 Edit the selector name to say `header.row`
Press Enter/Return as needed to complete the name.

This new selector appears in the CSS Designer and will specifically target only the header row. The first thing you should do is add a little breathing room above and below the header text. In the past, designers would often set a fixed height to elements like this. But the trend is to stay away from hard measurements so that the design can be more responsive and adaptable. One technique is to add padding to an element, which allows it to expand naturally.

8 Click the Layout category icon ▇.

9 In the padding property, enter **20px 0px**

The header increases in height 40 pixels in total.

If you remember from Lesson 3, you can abbreviate CSS values using shorthand. This property applies 20 pixels of padding to the top *and* bottom of the header. Now, let's insert a background image.

10 Click the Background category icon ![icon].
In the **background-image** section, click in the URL field.

11 Click the Browse icon ![icon] next to the URL field.

12 In the Select Image Source dialog, navigate to the default images folder.

13 Select **fern.png** and click Choose/Open.

Background images repeat both vertically and horizontally by default. This image is too tall to repeat vertically but, depending on your screen size, two ferns appear left to right.

14 In the **background-repeat** property, choose the `no-repeat` option.

The background image now appears once in the `<header>` element, aligned to the left side. The background specifications can also control the size and alignment of background images.

15 In the **background-size** property, select % from the **height** (right side) value field.

When you set the measurement system, the value defaults to zero (0). If only one value is set, the other value is set to `auto` by default. For the background-size property, a percentage value scales the image based on the size of the parent element. In the Properties window you can enter the value via the keyboard or by using the mouse.

16 Position the cursor over the height value field.
Drag to the right to increase the value to **80%**.

The image will scale to 80 percent of the height of the <header> element.

17 In the **background-position** property, select `center` from the **horizontal** (left side) and **vertical** (right side) value fields.

The image appears centered vertically, but it seems slightly off-center horizontally.

18 In the **background-position** property, select % from the **horizontal** (left side) field.

The field defaults to zero (0).

19 Click the field and drag to the right to increase the setting to **47%**.

The fern image is now visually centered vertically and horizontally in the <header>.

20 Save the file.

In addition to the background image, you can also apply other background effects, such as solid colors and even gradients. Since gradients are a new CSS3 specification, it's recommended that you always add a solid color to the background to support browsers or devices that don't support gradients.

Adding other background effects

In this exercise, you will add both a `background-color` and a `background-gradient` to the <header> element.

1 If necessary, open **mylayout.html** in Live view and open the CSS Designer.

2 Click the All button in the CSS Designer.
Select **green_styles.css** in the Sources window.

3 Select the `header.row` rule.
In the **background-color** property, enter **#090**

The background color of the header changes to green. This color setting is a fallback option, which will display if the browser doesn't support CSS gradients. Next, let's create the gradient background for the newer applications and devices.

4 In the **background-image** property of the `header` rule, click the gradient color picker ⬜.

Tip: If you find the process of dragging to set the values too difficult, you may enter them via the keyboard by double-clicking the field.

Note: Hexadecimal colors can be written in shorthand, like #090, when the numbers are in matched pairs, such as #009900. Be aware, however, that any time you enter such shorthand expressions Dreamweaver may arbitrarily rewrite them in full or swap them with RGB values.

Note: When you set colors using hexadecimal formats in gradients, Dreamweaver will change them to RGBa notations automatically.

CSS3 gradients are code-intensive effects, but Dreamweaver's gradient color picker makes their specification both fast and easy. The default gradient has two color stops.

5 Set **#060** as the **top** gradient color stop.

Set **#0C0** as the **bottom** gradient color stop.

Set the Linear Gradient Angle to **180** degrees.

Press Enter/Return to complete and apply the gradient.

The gradient is applied, but there's a problem. The effect is centered vertically and horizontally behind the fern image but does not fill the entire header from edge to edge. Background gradients are treated as background *images*. Since there's already a background image applied to the element, the gradient uses the same size and positioning specifications that were applied to the fern.

CSS3 allows you to apply multiple background images to an element. It even allows you to apply individual specifications to each effect. Unfortunately, although the CSS Designer can apply both a gradient and an image to the background, it provides only one set of size and positioning specifications. But don't worry. Whenever the CSS Designer lets you down, you can always resort to Code view.

6 Right-click the `header.row` rule in the Selectors window.

Choose **Go to Code** from the context menu.

Dreamweaver switches to Split view, inserts the cursor in the Code view window, and focuses on the `header.row` rule in the style sheet. Note that the `background-image` property shows specifications for both the fern image and the gradient in one declaration. A comma separates the two properties.

Tip: Don't forget to add the comma (,) between each specification. They won't work properly without it.

Note: CSS properties in your code may appear in a different order than that pictured.

If you examine the `background-size` and `background-position` properties, you'll see but a single specification in each. To add a second value for the gradient, you just have to add a comma at the end of each declaration and then enter the desired values.

7 Add the following highlighted values to these existing properties:

`background-size: auto 80%, 100% auto;`

`background-position: 47% center, left top;`

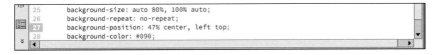

8 Select Show Set in the Properties window.

Observe the `header.row` rule and all the specifications displayed in the CSS Designer.

The Properties panel displays the background image and gradient but shows only one set of specifications for the size and position. You can edit the original set using the CSS Designer, but you'll have to continue to edit any others in Code view, manually.

▶ **Tip:** In some cases, you may need to refresh the document window display manually to see the effects of the CSS.

9 Choose File > Save.

The fern remains formatted as before, but the gradient now fills the entire header.

Incompatible Code

When you finish defining the gradient background for the header, you might see an error message appear above the document window.

Dreamweaver reports when specific code elements are not fully standardized or supported in various browsers or applications. In this case, the program is advising you that CSS gradients have not been fully adopted by all browsers and may display poorly or not at all.

Be sure to read the message and follow the links to learn more. When you are finished, you can clear the message by clicking the ✖ on the right side of the window.

Now that you've learned how to edit the rule manually, there's nothing stopping you from taking this effect one step further by adding a third background effect to create the vertical stripes, as shown in the mockup.

10 Right-click the `header.row` rule.

A context menu appears.

11 Select Go To Code from the menu.

The Code view window appears in Split view focused on the first `header.row` rule in the linked style sheet.

The reference to **fern.png** appears first in the `background-image` property, the gradient in the second. To get the stripes to appear between these two effects, you'll have to insert the new specifications between them. Be sure to separate each new specification with a comma.

● **Note:** The `stripe.png` image is identical to the one created using Adobe Generator in Lesson 4, "Web Design Basics."

12 Modify the following properties:
```
background-image: url(images/fern.png), url(images/stripe.
png), -webkit-linear-gradient(270deg,rgba(0,102,0,1.00)
0%,rgba(0,204,0,1.00) 100%);
background-image: url(images/fern.png), url(images/stripe.
png), linear-gradient(180deg,rgba(0,102,0,1.00) 0%,
rgba(0,204,0,1.00) 100%);
background-repeat: no-repeat, repeat-x;
background-size: auto 80%, auto auto, 100% auto;
background-position: 47% center, left top, left top;
```

13 Choose File > Save All.

The stripes appear and repeat horizontally across the header. By using a small graphic that repeats across the element, you are minimizing the size of the graphics that must be downloaded to create this effect. Best of all, if the graphic doesn't download at all, the gradient background is still displayed. In the odd chance that neither the graphic nor the gradient is displayed, the header will display the solid green color applied in step 1.

The basic design of the `<header>` element for desktop or GLOBAL environments is now complete. The text, logo, and background effects will require some custom specifications for smaller screens, but we'll address that task in Lesson 7, "Designing for Mobile Devices." Instead, let's turn our attention to the next component on the page: the horizontal navigation menu.

Creating a navigation menu

The site mockup we used in Lesson 5 sports a horizontal navigation menu with seven links. We don't have seven pages to link to yet, but you can create simple placeholders for the final content; we'll add actual functioning links in Lesson 12, "Working with Navigation." Let's create a menu to match the pages outlined in the thumbnails created in Lesson 4, and then style it to match the site color scheme.

Note: The site design mockup is included in the file set for Lesson 6. Feel free to open GreenStart_mockup.html to refresh your memory of the design and components.

1 If necessary, open **mylayout.html** in Live view.

2 Select the second row of the Bootstrap layout.

  The Element HUD appears.

3 Display the Insert panel.
  Select the Bootstrap Components category.

  The Bootstrap Components category offers two types of navigational elements: complete navigational menubars, or *navbars,* and standalone navigational menu components. In this situation, you'll use one of the complete navbars. Since the component already has its own built-in responsive structure and formatting, one of the existing layout elements will have to be removed to prevent conflicts, along with some other tweaks.

4 Select the `div.col-sm-12` tag selector.

This `<div>` element is inserted as a responsive Bootstrap element. The class `col-sm-12` formats the element to occupy all 12 columns in the grid, or the entire width of the container. The Bootstrap navbars are designed to be responsive, so this element is redundant and may cause undesirable interference with the navbar itself. You will replace this element with the navbar.

5 In the Navbar item drop-down menu, click **Basic Navbar**.

The position-assist dialog appears.

6 Click **Nest**.

A predefined Bootstrap navbar appears nested in the `<div>`, which can now be removed. The easiest way to delete an element is by using the Remove Tag command.

7 Switch to Split view. If necessary, select Source Code in the Referenced File display.

The Remove Tag command works only in Design view or Code view.

8 In Code view, locate and insert the cursor after the tag `<div class="col-sm-12">`.

```
26    </header>
27    <nav class="row">
28    <div class="col-sm-12">
29    <nav class="navbar navbar-default">
30    <div class="container-fluid">
31    <!-- Brand and toggle get grouped for better mobile display -->
```

9 Right-click the `div.col-sm-12` tag selector.
Select Remove Tag from the context menu.

The `<div>` is removed from the layout without affecting the navbar.

The navbar remains composed of two separate navigation menus with drop-down components and a search field with a button. It would be a rare situation that you would want or need all of these items.

In this case, you need only a single set of seven links. Any element that's not needed should be deleted. The safest method to select and delete HTML elements is via the tag selector interface.

10 In Live view, click the Dropdown menu on the right side of the navbar in Live view.

The HUD appears, focusing on the **a** tag. Observe the tag selector interface. Can you identify the parent element to the right side menu?

11 Select the `ul.nav.navbar-nav.navbar-right` tag selector.

The entire menu on the right side of the navbar is selected, displaying the HUD.

12 Press Delete.

The menu is removed. Next, you'll remove the search field and button.

13 Click the search field or button.

As before, the HUD appears, identifying the selected element. If you examine the tag selectors, you should be able to track down the parent structure. It helps to know that search fields need to be inserted in HTML `<form>` elements.

14 Select `form.navbar-form.navbar-left` in the tag selector interface and press Delete.

The search field and button are removed. The current design doesn't call for a drop-down menu. If you need one later, it's a simple matter to add one back. Drop-down menus are usually built from a sub-list inserted into an existing menu item.

15 Click the Dropdown menu and observe the tag selectors.

Dreamweaver will focus on the **a** tag in the parent `<li>`. In Live view, the drop-down menu should open, displaying the sublinks contained within the menu. Deleting the parent will remove the entire structure.

16 Select `li.dropdown` and press Delete.

The drop-down menu is removed, leaving two links and the word Brand. At first you might think that the word is simply another link in the remaining menu. But a quick look using the tag selectors and you will see the reality.

17 Click one of the Link items in the menu, and then click the word Brand. Examine the tag selectors.

If you compare the structures, you should see that the Link items are contained within `nav.nav.navbar-nav`, while the word Brand is actually in `nav.navbar-header`. In Bootstrap, the Brand element is intended to be used as a stand-in for your logo and to provide a handy link back to your home page. Like the other elements, it's unneeded in this layout. You need to remove the text as well as the link markup.

18 Select the `a.navbar-brand` tag selector and press Delete.

All the unneeded components have now been removed. Next, you will replace the generic link placeholders with ones that match the site design and learn how to make new Link items.

19 Double-click the first menu item.
Select the text "Link" and change it to **Home.**

20 Change the remaining Link item to **Green News** and save the file.

The two predefined links now match the menu items from the design mockup, but you still need to create five more items. The good thing about using an unordered list for the menu is that Dreamweaver makes it easy to insert new list items.

Adding new items to a navigation menu

In this exercise, you will learn how to insert new items in the navigation menu. Links can be added in any view mode, although the techniques differ.

1 In Live view, click the *Green News* link.
Select the `li` tag selector.

2 Choose Window > Insert to display the Insert panel.
In the HTML category, click the **List Item** option.

The position-assist interface appears.

3 Click **After**.

A new list item appears with placeholder text.

▶ **Tip:** Double-click to edit the text element. Click outside the orange editing box to finalize the content.

4 Select the placeholder text *Content for li Goes Here*. Type **Green Events** to replace it.

The new item appears beside the previous ones, but it's not formatted like the other links. You might be able to figure out what's wrong using Live view, but in this case, the problem can be identified faster in Code view.

5 Click the `<li>` tag selector for the new link item and switch to Code view. Observe the menu items and compare the first two to the new one.

```
33   <!-- Collect the nav links, forms, and other content for toggling -->
34   <div class="collapse navbar-collapse" id="defaultNavbar1">
35   <ul class="nav navbar-nav">
36   <li class="active"><a href="#">Home<span class="sr-only">(current)</span></a></li>
37   <li><a href="#">Green News</a></li>
38   <li>Green Events</li>
39   </ul>
40   </div>
41   <!-- /.navbar-collapse -->
42   </div>
```

Can you identify the difference? In fact, there are a few. For one thing, the first item features a class of `active` as well as a `<span>` element containing text intended for screen readers (`class="sr-only"`). But the only thing the first two share that the last item lacks is the hyperlink placeholder markup `<a href="#">`.

Since this is the only meaningful difference between the list items, you can rightly assume that the `<a>` markup is conveying at least part of the menu styling. To make *Green Events* look like the other menu items, you have to add a hyperlink to it, too, or at least a similar placeholder.

6 Select the text "Green Events" in Code view. In the Property inspector Link field, type # and press Enter/Return.

```
37   <li><a href="#">Green News</a></li>
38   <li><a href="#">Green Events</a></li>
39   </ul>
40   </div>
41   <!-- /.navbar-collapse -->
42   </div>
```

▶ **Tip:** If the Property inspector is not visible, you can display it by selecting Window > Properties. You can then dock it to the bottom of the program window.

The <a href="#"> notation is added to the text so that the menu item now features the same markup as the others.

7 Switch to Split view.

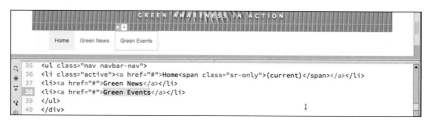

The new item looks like the others. New menu items can also be added by typing.

8 In Live view, insert the cursor at the end of the text "Green Events" and press Enter/Return to create a new line.

It may not be apparent in Live view, but Dreamweaver is creating a new <li> element in the background. But unlike using the Insert panel, this method doesn't add any placeholder text.

9 Type **Green Travel** and select the text.
Click just outside the orange editing box.

The HUD appears focused on the new *Green Travel* item.

10 In the Property Link field, enter # and press Enter/Return.

The new *Green Travel* link is complete. You can also add menu items in Code view.

11 Switch to Code view.

In this view, you can choose from several methods for creating a new list item. For example, you can type out the entire element manually, use the Insert panel as in step 2, or use copy and paste.

12 Insert the cursor in the *Green Travel* link.
Select the `li` tag selector.

By using the `<li>` element, Dreamweaver selects the link markup as well as the text.

13 Choose Edit > Copy or press Ctrl+C/Cmd+C.

14 Press the right arrow key.

The cursor moves to the end and outside the current `<li>` element. Although there's no need to insert a new line in the code, it keeps the markup consistent and easier to read.

15 Press Enter/Return to insert a new line.
Choose Edit > Paste or press Ctrl+V/Cmd+V.

```
38    <li><a href="#">Green Events</a></li>
39    <li><a href="#">Green Travel </a></li>
40    <li><a href="#">Green Travel </a></li>
41    </ul>
```

A duplicate version of the *Green Travel* list item appears.

16 Select the duplicate text *Green Travel*.
Type **Green Tips** to replace it.

The new menu item is complete and already contains the link # placeholder.

17 Using any of the methods describe above, create two more menu items for the links *Contact Us* and *About Us*.

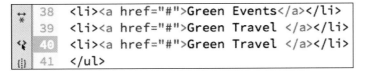

```
36    <li class="active"><a href="#">Home<span class="sr-only">(current)</span></a></li>
37    <li><a href="#">Green News</a></li>
38    <li><a href="#">Green Events</a></li>
39    <li><a href="#">Green Travel</a></li>
40    <li><a href="#">Green Tips</a></li>
41    <li><a href="#">Contact Us</a></li>
42    <li><a href="#">About Us</a></li>
43    </ul>
```

18 Save the file. If necessary, switch to Split view.

There are seven items in the menu now. Before you can format the menu, though, you'll have to correct some inconsistencies in its basic structure. These differences entail the attributes class `active` and the screen reader text (`sr-only`) noted earlier. Let's discard both of them.

Cleaning up Bootstrap components

Your newly modified Bootstrap menu has some inconsistent code structures in the new menu. In this exercise, you'll clean up these inconsistencies.

1   If necessary, open **mylayout.html**.
    Switch to Split view.

2   Examine the code of the horizontal menu.

    The menu is constructed using an unordered list with seven list items. In Live view you can see that the *Home* link is formatted differently from the rest. The most obvious difference between this link and the others is the class attribute `active`.

3   Select and delete the attribute ~~class="active"~~ from the first `<li>` element in Code view.

    Once the class is deleted from the *Home* link, the formatting of the button will match the others. The last step is to remove the screen reader text.

4   Select and delete the element ~~`<span class="sr-only">(current)</span>`~~ from the first `<li>` element.

5   Save the file.

All the links in the menu are now formatted identically. It's common when using predefined or third-party components that you will have to modify the original structure and formatting to conform to your own content or project requirements.

Hyperlink pseudo-classes

The <a> element (hyperlink) provides five states, or distinct behaviors, that can be modified by CSS using what are known as pseudo-classes. A pseudo-class is a CSS feature that can add special effects or functionality to certain selectors, such as the <a> anchor tag:

- The a:link pseudo-class creates the default display and behavior of the hyperlink, and in many cases is interchangeable with the a selector in CSS rules. But the a:link is *more* specific, and will override specifications assigned to a less-specific selector if both are used in the style sheet.

- The a:visited pseudo-class formats the link after it has been visited by the browser. This resets to default styling whenever the browser cache, or history, is deleted.

- The a:hover pseudo-class formats the link when the cursor passes over it.

- The a:active pseudo-class formats the link when the mouse clicks it.

- The a:focus pseudo-class formats the link when accessed via keyboard as opposed to mouse interaction.

When used, the pseudo-classes must be declared in the order listed above to be effective. Remember, whether declared in the style sheet or not, each state has a set of default formats and behaviors.

Styling a navigational menu

Menus typically exhibit two basic behaviors, or looks: a static, or default, state and a rollover, or hover, state. All the formatting is controlled by CSS.

1   Open **mylayout.html** in Live view, if necessary.
    Maximize the program to fill the computer display.
    The document window should be wider than 1024 pixels.

    The navigation menu was created from a Bootstrap component and comes with basic predefined styling provided by the Bootstrap default style sheet, which is locked. Any styles you create will be added to the **green_styles.css** file. The new styles will reset or override the predefined specifications or create new ones from scratch. The first step is to add a background color to the entire menu.

2   Select any menu item. Examine the tag selectors to identify the structure of the menu.

    The menu is built by inserting an <a> element within an unordered list. The list is contained within the nav.row element you created originally using Bootstrap components. But the formatting is coming from some aspect of the menu you inserted. To create a background color for the entire navbar, you first need to identify the rule that applies the current formatting.

Note: You will notice that the row and the navbar feature <nav> elements and classes named "nav," which could create some confusion. When identifying elements for styling, make sure you select the correct one.

3 Click the Current button in the CSS Designer.

The Selectors window displays a list of rules that are applying some sort of styling to the navbar or menu items.

4 Select the Show Set option, if necessary.

5 Start at the top of the Selectors list and click each rule. Examine the properties assigned by each, and look for any that assign background colors or background gradients.

The very first rule applies a background color of `transparent`. Although this is the correct property, you can see that the background of the navbar has some sort of shading or gradient. Keep looking.

Next, you will come across a rule that formats the `a:hover` and `a:focus` states of the menu links. Although this is a valid background property, the `a:hover` and `a:focus` selectors will format only the actual hyperlinks themselves. There still has to be another rule that formats the entire navbar. Keep looking.

Finally, over 20 rules down the list you will find `.navbar-default`, which applies a background color of `#f8f8f8`. To reset the styling and apply a background to match the site design, you have to make a new rule that has equal or greater specificity.

6 Select the `nav.navbar.navbar-default` tag selector.

The HUD appears around the entire navbar.

7 In the CSS Designer, click the All button.
Select **green_styles.css** in the Sources window.
Click the Add Selector icon ➕.

A suggested selector name appears in the window.

8 Edit the name to:

`nav.row .navbar.navbar-default`

9 Press Enter/Return twice to complete the selector.

10 In the CSS Designer, deselect Show Set.

11 In the Background category, enter **#069** in the **background-color** property.

The background color changes from light gray to dark blue. The background-color property covers the older browsers; now let's add some advanced styling.

12 In the **background-image** property, click the gradient color picker.

13 Set **#069** as the **top** gradient color stop.
Set **#08A** as the **bottom** gradient color stop.
Set the Linear Gradient Angle to **180** degrees.
Press Enter/Return to complete and apply the gradient.

The gradient background supersedes the solid background color. The new background color is nice, but it makes the menu buttons hard to distinguish. They could use some definition of their own, like adding some borders.

14 Select one of the menu items.

The HUD displays the a tag.

15 In the CSS Designer, click the Current button and enable the Show Set option again.

Check the list of rules again for ones that set borders. When you are finished, you'll find that there are a few that apply borders to the entire navbar, but none that do so for the menu items themselves. You could apply rules to either the <li> or the <a> element in this structure, but in this case it makes more sense to create a rule to format the <a> element.

16 Click the All button.
In **green_styles.css**, create a new selector named
`nav.row.nav.navbar-nav > li > a`

By adding `nav.row` to the selector, it will override the default formatting and specifically target only this `nav` element. It will also preclude the rule from unintentionally formatting other menus you may insert in the layout later.

17 Add the following properties to the new rule:

```
border-top: solid 1px #0AE
border-right: solid 1px #037
border-bottom: solid 1px #037
border-left: solid 1px #0AE
```

● **Note:** The greater-than symbols you see in the selector name indicate that the rule is targeting only the immediate children of the preceding element rather than any descendant.

By alternating the border colors this way, it produces a three-dimensional effect on the menu buttons.

The main feature of the navigation menu is the hyperlink. It features five distinct states: link, visited, hover, active, and focus, in that order. See the sidebar "Hyperlink pseudo-classes" for a full description of hyperlink behaviors and states.

When links appear in the body of a webpage, the link and visited states are usually formatted separately, but in a menu you want them to be identical. The selector created in step 16 already targets the default **a** state of the hyperlink. But you'll need to add the *visited* reference to the name to cover both behaviors.

18 Double-click the name `nav.row .nav.navbar-nav > li > a`.

The selector name becomes editable.

19 Select the entire name and copy it.

● **Note:** Don't forget the comma between selectors.

20 Insert the cursor at the end of the selector, type `:link,` and press Ctrl+V/Cmd+V to paste the copied selector.

21 At the end of the new name, type `:visited` and press Enter/Return as needed to complete the name.

The new selector targets the link and visited states of the menu items. Check your selector name to make sure you did not accidentally add spaces to the pseudo-classes.

Note: It's not required to add the :link markup to the default link name, but it increases the specificity of the rule.

22 Deselect the Show Set option.

In the Text category, enter **#FFC** in the **color** property.

The link names appear in light yellow.

The :hover pseudo-class is responsible for styling links whenever the cursor is positioned over them. Normally, you'll see this behavior simply as the cursor turning into the pointer icon, but for this dynamic menu let's apply different background and text colors to create a rollover effect.

23 Click the Add Selector icon **+**. Select the new name and press Ctrl+V/Cmd+V to replace it with selector you copied in step 19.

24 At the end of the name, type **:hover**

Press Enter/Return twice to create the new selector.

25 In the **background-image** property, click the gradient color picker.

26 Set **#069** as the **top** gradient color stop.

Set **#08A** as the **bottom** gradient color stop.

Set the Linear Gradient Angle to **0** degrees.

Press Enter/Return to complete and apply the gradient.

The new gradient is a mirror image of the one created in step 12.

27 In the Text category, enter **#FFF** in the **color** property.

You can test the effect in Live view.

28 Position the cursor over any of the menu items.

The gradient background flips vertically and the link color displays in white, providing a good contrast from the default menu state. Now, let's add the yellow border that divides the header from the menu.

29 Create a new Selector named `nav.row`

In the **border-top** property, enter `5px solid #FD5`

A yellow border appears above the menu.

30 Select File > Save All.

The navigation menu is nearly complete. The last step is to center the menu horizontally within the navbar itself.

Centering the navigation menu

Bootstrap allows you to create complex menu and navigation components with a minimum of effort, but it doesn't offer unlimited styling options. For one thing, the framework offers two basic alignment options for horizontal menus: aligned to the left or justified across the entire structure. Aligning the menu to the center of the navbar, as in our site design, will require you to step away from the framework defaults and create your own custom styling.

The first step is to set a fixed width on the menu.

● **Note:** The menu width is derived from the Bootstrap CSS, which sets a maximum of 750 pixels for the menu before it collapses to an icon. You will work with mobile design in Lesson 7.

1 Create a new selector in **green_styles.css** named `nav.row .nav.navbar-nav`

2 In the **width** property, enter `715px`

This width allows the menu to fit on one line but still function properly in the responsive structure. Now that you have set the element width, you can center it using a simple CSS trick.

3 In the **margin** property, enter the shorthand:
`0px auto`

The shorthand applies zero pixels of margin to the top and bottom of the menu and equal amounts of spacing to the left and right. This setting should center the element, but the menu isn't moving. When styling doesn't work as expected, use CSS Designer to identify the issue.

4   Click the Current button in CSS Designer.
    Select the COMPUTED option in the Selectors window.

5   Select Show Set and examine the properties styling the menu.

Some properties are displayed in gray and some in white, indicating which items are editable and which are not. One of the uneditable Bootstrap rules sets a `float:left` property. We can cancel it out using the rule created in step 1.

6   Select the `nav.row .nav.navbar-nav` rule.

When the Show Set option is enabled you can still edit the properties and values in the CSS Designer or even create new ones. When Show Set is enabled you don't see a list to choose from, so you have to know what property you want to enter in the open field.

7   Insert the cursor in the empty field in the Properties window.

8   Type `float` and press the Tab key.

Note how the hinting menu filters as you type. As with the HTML hinting menu, feel free to select the property using your mouse or keyboard.

9   Type or select **none** in the value field.

The menu centers in the navbar. There's one last tweak you need to make. If you look closely at the second row, you will see that there is space below the navbar. If you examine the rules affecting this element, you will find a bottom margin of 20 pixels applied via one of the Bootstrap rules: `.navbar`.

10 Create a selector named `nav.row .navbar`
    Create a new property **margin-bottom** and enter **0px**

The space below the navbar is removed. The navigation placeholder is now complete.

11 Select File > Save All.

The next task is to fill in the content area. First, you'll insert new placeholder content in the left `<aside>` element.

Building semantic content

The left column of the `<article>` element will be used for environmentally themed quotations. In the past, you might display quotations like any other paragraph, but to follow web standards under HTML5 you'll want to build these quotations using semantic elements. Unlike normal paragraph text, the value of a quotation is usually based on the perceived reputation of the author or source. HTML provides several elements designed specifically to identify this type of content.

1   If necessary, open **mylayout.html** in Live view.

2   Click the first column of the third row.
    Examine the tag selectors.

    The current structure is based on an `<aside>` element with the class of `col-sm-4`. First, we'll insert the placeholder for the quotation and then wrap it with a semantic structure.

3   Open the Insert panel and select the HTML category.

4   Click the **Paragraph** item.
    Select **Nest**.

    A `<p>` element appears in the column with placeholder text.

5   Select the placeholder text *This is the content for Layout P Tag* and delete it.

6 Type **"Insert quotation here."** and press Enter/Return to create a new paragraph.

7 Type **Insert author here** and click outside the orange box to complete the elements.

Semantically, quotations should be based on the `<blockquote>` element. You need to put both paragraphs into the `blockquote`, but unfortunately, you can't select two elements at once in Live view.

8 Select the p tag selector for the first paragraph.
Select Split view.

The first paragraph is selected entirely.

9 In the Code view window, hold the Shift key and click at the end of the second paragraph.

Both paragraphs are selected in Code view.

10 Press Ctrl+T/Cmd+T to activate the Quick Tag Editor.

The Quick Tag Editor appears in Wrap tag mode.

11 Type `blockquote`

12 Press Enter/Return twice to close the Quick Tag Editor and complete the element.

When it's completed, the default styling of the `<blockquote>` element automatically formats the content, indenting the text on the left and right.

Such indentation is typical of material quoted within a term or research paper, and may be desirable in the main content area, but it's totally unnecessary in the `<aside>` element. You'll need to create a new CSS rule to format these elements.

13 If necessary, click the All button.

Create a new selector in **green_styles.css**:

```
article.row aside blockquote
```

The Show Set option should still be active from the previous exercise.

14 Create the following properties in the new rule:

```
margin: 0px 0px 20px 0px
padding: 0px
```

Typically, a blockquote should contain a quotation, either alone or in one or more paragraphs, and an element providing the source or citation. Like `<blockquote>`, the `<cite>` element provides the correct semantic structure in this application.

● **Note:** The Quick Tag Editor features three modes: Edit tag, Wrap tag, and Insert HTML. When you select an element using the tag selector, the Quick Tag Editor should default to Edit mode. Press Ctrl+T/ Cmd+T again to switch modes.

15 In Code view, select the second paragraph.

Select the p tag selector.

16 Press Ctrl+T/Cmd+T to edit the tag.

Replace the p tag with `cite` and press Enter/Return twice to complete the edit.

▶ **Tip:** An alternate method is to right-click the tag selector and access the Quick Tag Editor from the context menu.

If you look carefully, you can see that the opening quotation mark in the first paragraph is indenting the first line of text slightly, leaving the text in the two paragraphs misaligned. A technique used by professional typesetters actually *outdents* such items to produce a *hanging* quotation mark.

17 Create a new selector in **green_styles.css**:

```
article.row aside blockquote p
```

18 Create the following properties:

```
margin: 0px 0px 5px 0px
padding: 0px .5em
text-indent: -0.5em
```

You can see now that the two lines of text are aligned, while the quotation mark is shifted to the left slightly. The effect on multiline quotations will be quite appealing.

Now you'll create a new rule to style the author name.

19 Create a new selector: `article.row aside blockquote cite`

20 Create the following properties in the new rule:

```
display: block
padding: 0px 10px
font-style: italic
text-align: right
```

The quotation placeholder is complete and semantically designed. To remain semantically correct, each new quotation should be inserted into its own `<blockquote>` element. The last thing you need to do is add the top and bottom borders shown in the site design.

21 Create a new selector: `article.row aside`

This rule will format both the left and right columns at once.

22 Add the following properties to the new rule:

```
border-top: solid 5px #069
border-bottom: solid 3px #069
margin: 1em 0px
padding: 1em 0px
```

green_styles.css

+ −   @Media : GLOBAL

+ −   Selectors

🔍 Filter CSS Rules

article.row aside blockquote

article.row aside blockquote p

article.row aside blockquote cite

article.row aside

··· More

border-top	:	solid 5px #069
margin	:	1em 0px
padding	:	1em 0px
border-bottom	:	solid 3px #069
add property	:	*add value*

Both `<aside>` elements display blue borders on the top and bottom.

23 Select File > Save All.

The placeholder for the first column is complete. Let's address the center section of the `<article>` element next.

Inserting main content placeholders

The layout will feature the main content in the center column. Content is usually introduced with HTML heading elements. In the past, typically only one `<h1>` would appear on each page. With the new semantic element, some designers are actually using `<h1>` elements to introduce each major section or article. For this design, you'll start with one `<h1>` and use more when warranted.

1 Click the second column in the third row.

The HUD appears focused on the `<section class="col-sm-4">` element.

2 Using the Insert panel Heading drop-down, insert an H1 nested in the center column.

3 Select the placeholder text.
Type **Insert main heading here** to replace the text.

4 Press Enter/Return to create a new line.
Type **Insert subheading here** and press Enter/Return.

5 Type **Insert content here** and click outside the orange editing box.

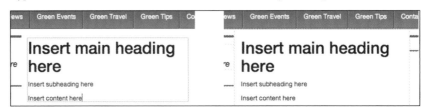

You have now created one heading and two new placeholder paragraphs. You need to make the first paragraph an `<h2>`.

6 Click the first paragraph "Insert subheading here".
The HUD appears focused on the p element.

7 In the Property inspector, select Heading 2 from the Format drop-down menu.

The paragraph is converted to an <h2> element. The placeholders for the center content area are complete. You'll format them later.

8 Save the file.

Now, let's add placeholders and formatting to the right column.

Tip: If the Property inspector is not visible, you can display it by selecting Window > Properties. Most people like to dock it to the bottom of the document window.

Creating custom element classes

The right column of the layout will contain materials related to the main content. As you can see from the site design, the element has a background color. You already have a rule that formats both <aside> elements, but in this case, the background will apply only to the right column. When you need to target styling to a specific element and there's no structural difference between it and other similar elements, a custom CSS class is warranted. First, we need to add a class attribute to the element. There are several ways you can do this, but using the HUD in Live view is fast and easy.

1 Open **mylayout.html** in Live view.

2 Select the third column of the third row.

The HUD appears focused on the aside element with a class of col-sm-4. At the moment, this structure is identical to the first column.

3 Click the Add Class/ID icon ⊞ in the HUD.

A blank text field appears beside the existing class col-sm-4.

4 Type .sidebar2 and press Enter/Return.

A dialog appears allowing you to insert the new class into an existing style sheet and media query. If **green_styles.css** does not appear in the source menu select it manually.

5 Press Enter/Return to complete the operation.

If you look at the **green_styles.css** reference in the CSS Designer, you will see the new class .sidebar2. The class will allow you to apply styling to the right column that differs from the left.

6 Select `.sidebar2` in the Selectors window.
Create the following properties:

```
background-color: #CFC
padding: 0px 10px
```

A light green background color appears in the right column. Let's add the placeholder text.

7 Using the Insert panel, add an <h2> element to the right column using the Nest option.

8 Select the placeholder text.
Type **Insert sidebar heading here** to replace it.

9 Press Enter/Return to create a new paragraph.
Type **Insert sidebar content here** on the new line.

10 Create a new selector, `.sidebar2 h2`

11 Create the following properties in the new rule:

```
margin-top: 10px
margin-bottom: 5px
padding: 0px 10px
font-size: 130%
line-height: 1.4em
```

12 Create a new selector, `.sidebar2 p`

13 Create the following properties in the new rule:

```
margin-bottom: 5px
padding: 0px 10px
line-height: 1.3em
```

14 Save all files.

The right column is complete. Before we move on to the <footer>, we need to adjust the spacing of the three columns in the main content row. Currently, the three columns are equal in width, but in the site design the left and right columns are narrower than the center one. Since the widths are determined by the pre-defined Bootstrap, changing the relationship of these elements is simply a matter of changing their class names.

Reading no writing

The Bootstrap style sheet is formatted as a read-only file to prevent you from making any accidental changes to the framework's complex styling. From time to time as you work in your pages, a warning message may appear at the top of the screen indicating that the file is read-only. You can dismiss the message by clicking the ⊗ icon on the right side. It also provides an option to make the file writable. You're advised to resist the temptation.

Managing Bootstrap component width

Bootstrap is based on a 12-column vertical grid system. Elements inserted into a layout conform to this grid by occupying some fraction of it. The amount of space an element uses is typically represented by a number that appears in the class attribute. For example, the three columns all have a class of `col-sm-4`. Since 4 divides into 12 three times, each column occupies one-third of the screen. By adjusting these class names, you should be able to change the width of each element.

1 Open **mylayout.html** in Live view, if necessary.

   At the moment, the three columns have the same class name and are equal in width.

2 Click the first column of row three.

   The HUD appears. Depending on where you click, it may focus on any of the elements contained with the first column.

3 If necessary, select the `aside.col-sm-4` tag selector.

   You can edit the class name directly in the HUD.

4 Double-click the class name .col-sm-4 in the HUD.
Change the name to .col-sm-3

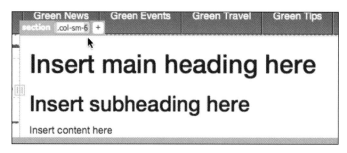

The width of the first column narrows. The other columns shift to the left, leaving open space on the right side of the third row. The right column should be the same width as the left one.

5 Click the third column.
Select the aside.col-sm-4 tag.sidebar2 selector.

6 Change the class name to .col-sm-3

The right column narrows. In total, the entire row is now occupying only 10 of the 12 columns in the grid. You can leave these settings this way, add more space between the columns, or simply add the space to the main content section.

7 Select the second column.
Select the section.col-sm-4 tag selector.
Change the class name to .col-sm-6

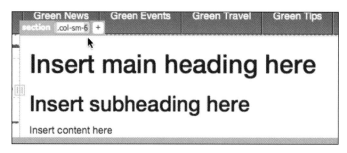

The center column widens to take up the empty space.

8 Save the file.

Later, you will learn more about how you can control the responsive behavior of your layout using Bootstrap classes. This will enable your layout to adapt to various screen sizes and devices automatically.

The last tasks remaining to complete the basic layout are to insert some new place-holder text and to format the footer.

Inserting HTML entities

In this exercise, you will insert a generic copyright statement that includes an HTML entity and format the footer.

1 Open **mylayout.html** from the lesson06 folder, if necessary.

The file contains a four-row Bootstrap layout with various placeholder contents and formatting, but the fourth row is still empty.

2 Click the fourth row of the layout.

The HUD appears focused on the `div` element displaying a class of `.col-sm-12`.

The site design shows the footer containing a copyright symbol. This character is one of many that you might want to use in your website but that you can't type directly using the keyboard. To insert a copyright character, you will use an HTML entity. But before you can insert the copyright character, you first need to insert a paragraph element to hold it.

3 Choose Insert > Paragraph to nest a new paragraph into the footer.

Dreamweaver inserts a `<p>` element into the footer, complete with placeholder text. To insert the entity, you will have to switch to Design or Code view. This particular command does not work in Live view.

4 Switch to Split view.
Locate the `<footer>` element and the new placeholder text in Code view.

5 Select the placeholder text "*This is the content for Layout P Tag*" and delete it.

6 Choose Insert > HTML > Character > Copyright.

The copyright symbol © appears at the insertion point. Dreamweaver creates the copyright character using the named entity `&copy;` in the code. Since the cursor is already inserted in this location, let's finish the footer placeholder text.

7 Press the spacebar to insert a space.
Type **2015 Meridien GreenStart. All rights reserved.**

```
        © 2015 Meridien GreenStart. All rights reserved.

65    <div class="row">
66    <div class="col-sm-12">
67    <p>&copy; 2015 Meridien GreenStart. All rights reserved.</p>
68    </div>

body    div   .container   footer   .row   div   .col-sm-12
```

> ◆ **Warning:** You may discover that you can sometimes insert special characters directly. This is not a recommended practice.

> ● **Note:** Many entities can be created with named or numbered entities. Some applications do not support named entities. Always check to make sure you can use a specific character.

> ▶ **Tip:** Modify the copyright date as necessary when you create a new page or update the content.

8 In **green_styles.css** in the CSS Designer, create a new selector named `footer`

9 Create the following properties:

```
padding: 1em 0px
background-color: #090
```

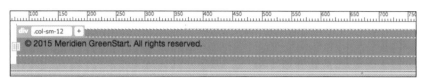

10 Deselect the Show Set option.

11 In the **background-image** property, click the gradient color picker.

12 Set **#060** as the **top** gradient color stop.
Set **#0C0** as the **bottom** gradient color stop.
Set the Linear Gradient Angle to **0** degrees.
Press Enter/Return to complete the gradient.

The footer displays a gradient that shifts from light to dark green.

13 Change the `color` property to `#FFC` in the `footer` rule.

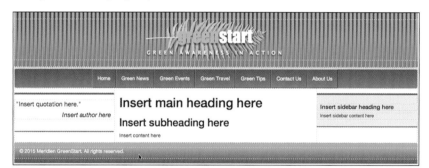

14 Save all files.

You've completed the basic structure and added placeholders to all the elements. You've even formatted some of the elements and content. The last task you'll accomplish will be to implement a global theme for the site design that will establish the basic design and usage of type within the site.

Creating global type styles

Most of the content of your site will be represented in text. Text is displayed in the web browser using digitized typefaces. Based on designs developed and used for centuries on the printing press, these typefaces can evoke all sorts of feelings in your visitors, ranging from security to elegance to sheer fun and humor.

Some designers may use multiple typefaces for different purposes throughout a site. Others select a single base typeface that may match their normal corporate themes or culture. CSS gives you tremendous control over page appearance and the formatting of text. In the last few years, there have been many innovations in the way typefaces are used on the web. The following exercises describe and experiment with these methods.

Face versus font: Know the difference?

People throw the terms *typeface* and *font* around all the time as if they were interchangeable. They are not. Do you know the difference? *Typeface* refers to the design of an entire family of letterforms. *Font* refers to one specific design. In other words, a typeface is usually composed of multiple fonts. Typically, a typeface will feature four basic designs: regular, italic, bold, and bold-italic. When you choose a font in a CSS specification, you usually choose the regular format, or font, by default.

When a CSS specification calls for italic or bold, the browser will normally load the italic or bold versions of the typeface automatically. However, you should be aware that many browsers can actually generate italic or bold effects when these fonts are not present or available. Purists resent this capability and go out of their way to define rules for italic and bold variations with specific calls to italic and bold versions of the typefaces they want to use.

Using Edge Web Fonts

The first choice for most web designers is selecting the base typeface that will display their content. In this exercise, you will see how easy it is to use web fonts to apply a global site typeface by editing a single rule. There's no need to be intimidated about using web fonts—everything you need to implement this technology is built right into Dreamweaver CC.

1   If necessary, open **mylayout.html** in Live view.

2   In the CSS Designer, select **green_styles.css**.
    Create a new selector named **body**

3   In the Properties window, deselect the Show Set option, if necessary.

    The window now displays all CSS specifications.

4   Click the Text category icon T.

    The window display focuses on CSS Properties for text.

> **Note:** Edge Web Fonts and other types of hosted fonts are rendered properly in Dreamweaver only in Live view with an active Internet connection.

5 Click to open the **font-family** property.

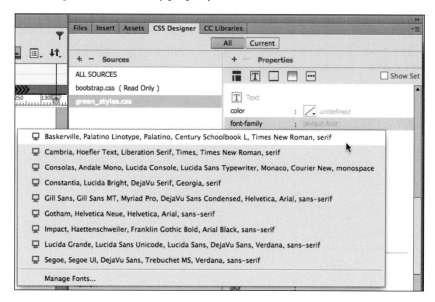

A window appears showing nine predefined Dreamweaver font groups, or *stacks*. You can select one of these or create your own. Are you wondering why you don't see the entire list of fonts installed on your computer?

The answer is a simple but ingenious solution to a problem that has nagged web designers from the very beginning. Until recently, the fonts you see in your browser were not actually part of the webpage or the server; they were supplied by the computer browsing the site.

Although most computers have many fonts in common, they don't always have the same fonts. So, if you choose a specific font and it isn't installed on the visitor's computer, your carefully designed and formatted webpage could immediately and tragically appear in Courier or some other equally undesirable typeface.

For most people, the solution has been to specify fonts in groups, or *stacks*, giving the browser a second, third, and perhaps fourth (or more) choice to default to before it picks for itself (egads!). Some call this technique *degrading gracefully*. Dreamweaver CC (2015.1 release) offers nine predefined font groups.

As you can see, the predefined font stacks are pretty limited. If you don't see a combination you like, you can click the Manage Fonts option at the bottom of the Set Font Family pop-up menu and create your own.

But before you start building your own group, remember this: Go ahead and pick *your* favorite font, but then try to figure out what fonts are installed on your visitors' computers, and add them to the list too. For example, you may prefer the font Hoefelter Allgemeine Bold Condensed, but the majority of web users are unlikely to have it installed on their computers. By all means, select Hoefelter as your first choice; just don't forget to slip in some of the more tried-and-true, or *web-safe*, fonts, such as Arial, Helvetica, Tahoma, Times New Roman, Trebuchet MS, Verdana, and, finally, a design category like serif or sans serif.

In the last few years, a new trend has been gaining momentum to use fonts that are actually hosted on the site or by a third-party service. The reason for the popularity is obvious: Your design choices are no longer limited to the dozen or so fonts from which everyone can choose. You can choose among thousands of designs and develop a unique look and personality that was nearly impossible in the past. But you can't use just *any* font.

Licensing restrictions prohibit many fonts from web-hosted applications altogether. Other fonts have file formats that are incompatible with phones and tablets. So it's important to look for fonts that are designed and licensed for web applications. Today, multiple sources exist for web-compatible fonts. Google and Font Squirrel are two such sources, and they even provide some free fonts for the budget-minded. Luckily, as a subscriber to Adobe Creative Cloud, you have access to two new services: Adobe Typekit and Adobe Edge Web Fonts.

Web-hosted fonts offer a vast variety of design options.

Typekit is a web-hosted subscription service that offers both print and web fonts. You can subscribe to the service even if you don't have Creative Cloud, but as a subscriber you can access many of the available fonts for free. Adobe Edge Web Fonts is a free service that provides only web fonts, hence its name, and is powered by Typekit. The best thing about Edge Web Fonts is that you can access it directly inside Dreamweaver.

6 At the bottom of the font stack window, click Manage Fonts.

The Manage Fonts dialog gives you three options (tabs) for using web fonts: Adobe Edge Web Fonts, Local Web Fonts, and Custom Font Stacks. The first two tabs provide access to a new technique for using custom fonts on the web. Adobe Edge Fonts supports the Edge Web Fonts service to access hundreds of fonts in multiple design categories right inside the program. Local Web Fonts allows you to define the use of fonts that you can buy or find free on the Internet. Custom Font Stacks enables you to build font stacks using either the new web-hosted fonts, various web-safe fonts, or a combination of both. For the site's base font, let's pick one from Edge Web Fonts.

The tab for Adobe Edge Web Fonts displays samples of all the fonts available from the service. You can filter the list to show specific designs or categories of fonts.

7 In the Manage Fonts dialog, select the option "List of fonts recommended for Headings."

The window shows a list of fonts that are typically used for headings and titles. Some designers like to use the same font for both headings and paragraph text.

8 Select the option "List of fonts recommended for Paragraphs," directly below the option for "Headings."

Only one font is displayed: Source Sans Pro. Since this font works well for headings and paragraph text, it's a perfect choice for the site's base font. By applying it to the body rule, it will automatically be applied to headings and paragraphs throughout the site.

9 Click the font sample displayed in the Manage Fonts dialog. Click Done to close the panel.

A blue checkmark appears on the sample of Source Sans Pro. Once you click Done, Dreamweaver will add the font to the CSS Designer interface and write any code needed in your page to use it in your CSS specifications.

10 Click the **font-family** property again.

When the Font Stack dialog opens you will see source-sans-pro at the bottom of the list.

11 Select `source-sans-pro`.

12 In the **font-weight** property, select 400.

Source Sans Pro appears in the font-family property for the body rule. In most cases, the change in the layout will be instantaneous. The entire page, both headings and paragraph text, should now display Source Sans Pro. If you did not see the font style change, Dreamweaver may have not updated the Live view display.

13 If necessary, click the Refresh icon ↻ above the document window.

If this step doesn't display the new font, you may not have a live connection to the Internet at this moment. Because Edge Web Fonts are hosted on the Internet, you won't be able to see them until you establish a live connection or upload this page to a live web server. You will learn how to upload pages to the Internet in Lesson 17, "Publishing to the Web."

14 Save all files.

As you can see, using Edge Web Fonts on your website is really easy. But don't be fooled into thinking they're any less problematic than old-fashioned font stacks. In fact, even if you want to use Edge Web Fonts as your primary font source, the best practice would be to include them in a custom font stack of their own.

Introducing web-hosted fonts

The latest trend around the Internet is the increasing popularity of custom type-faces. For years, we've been stuck with the familiar but faded presence of the same web-safe fonts gracing most of our websites: Arial, Tahoma, Times New Roman, Trebuchet MS, Verdana, and so on. To use a less common typeface, your options were to chance fate and flirt with font substitution or to render the custom typeface as a graphic (and all that entails).

If the concept of web fonts is new to you, you're not alone. At the time of this writing, "web fonts" had only been in existence a little over five years and only starting to gain widespread popularity for the last two.

The basic concept is relatively simple: The desired font is copied to your website or linked to it from a common web server. Then, the browser loads the font and caches it, as needed.

Here are some handy links to learn more about the new trend in web fonts:

- Adobe Edge Web Fonts: http://html.adobe.com/edge/webfonts
- Adobe Typekit: https://typekit.com

Here are some other font services:

- Google Web Fonts: www.google.com/fonts
- Font Squirrel: www.fontsquirrel.com
- MyFonts.com: www.myfonts.com/search/is_webfont:true/fonts

Building font stacks with web fonts

If you're lucky, your web-hosted fonts will display every time for every user. But luck can run out and it's better to be safe than sorry. In the last exercise, you accessed and selected an Edge Web Font and applied it to the base font of the body rule. In this exercise, you'll build a custom stack anchored on your chosen web font to provide the necessary fallback support for safety's sake.

1   Open **mylayout.html** in Live view, if necessary.

2   In the CSS Designer, select the body rule.

3 In Text category, select the **font-family** property.

The Font stack dialog appears.

4 Choose Manage Fonts.

5 In the Manage Fonts dialog, click the Custom Font Stacks tab.

6 In the Available Fonts list, locate **Source Sans Pro**.

Click the << button to move the font to the Chosen Fonts list. If you cannot find the font in the list, you can type the name in the text field at the bottom of the dialog and press the << button.

7 Repeat step 6 to add **Trebuchet MS**, **Verdana**, **Arial**, **Helvetica**, and **sans-serif** to the Chosen Fonts list.

Feel free to add more web or web-safe fonts to your list as desired. If any fonts you want to use are not installed on your computer, type the names into the text field and then add them to the stack using the << button.

8 Click Done.

9 In the **font-family** property, select your new custom font stack.

The page display should not change; Source Sans Pro is still the primary font in the list. But the new font stack, based on the new Edge Web Font, will ensure that your text will be formatted in all contingencies.

10 In the **font-size** property, enter **14px**

Setting the size of the body rule is a common practice for many web designers. This is designed to reset the base font size to a size that should be optimum. You can adjust the size as necessary using media queries for various devices and screen sizes.

11 Save all files.

Now you've learned how to specify the look of your text content. Next, you'll learn how to control the size of the text.

Specifying font size

Font size can convey the relative importance of the content on the page. Headings are typically larger than the text they introduce. In your working document, the content is divided into three areas: the main content and the two sidebars. In this exercise, you will learn how to manage the size of the text in both areas to add emphasis as desired.

1 Open **mylayout.html** in Live view, if necessary.

2 Insert the cursor in the text "Insert main heading here."

If you look at the Selectors window, you will see that you have not yet created a rule to format this heading. Let's create one now.

3   Create a new selector in **green_styles.css** named
`article.row section h1`

Since the <h1> element is the main heading of the page, you should design it to stand out from the rest of the text and headings. This can be done in a variety of ways, using color, size, or a great typeface.

4   Add the Edge Web Font **Patua One** as you did in the previous exercise.

5   Create the following properties for the h1 rule:

```
margin-top: 0px
margin-bottom: 15px
font-family: patua-one
font-size: 300%
line-height: 1.4em
```

Note: In this rule formatting the h1, you added only a single font. You may think you should have to build a custom font stack, but you don't. That's because the stack created earlier will be inherited by default if this font doesn't display properly.

Insert main heading here

Insert subheading here

Insert content here

The main heading reformats and increases in size.

The sidebars contain text that is related to, but not semantically as important as, the main content. Reducing the size of this content provides a visual distinction to the layout. You created rules earlier in this lesson to format these items.

6   In **green_styles.css,** select the rule `article.row aside`.

7   Create the following property: `font-size: 95%`

The text in the right column has resized, but the quotation placeholder in the left column has not changed. When a rule does not format an element, it means one or more other rules are conflicting with it. This will be a common problem when you use predefined templates or frameworks, like Bootstrap. You can use the CSS Designer to troubleshoot the conflict.

8   Click the text "Insert quotation here" in the left column.

The HUD appears, focused on the p element.

9 Examine the list of rules and identify any that format font-size properties.

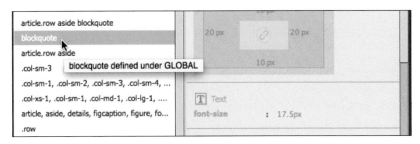

A `blockquote` rule in the **bootstrap.css** file is applying a font-size property of 17.5px and applied a 5px gray border on the left. To override this rule, you have to create a similar or more specific selector in **green_styles.css**.

10 In **green_styles.css**, create the selector: `article.row blockquote`

11 Create the following property in the new rule:

```
font-size: 100%
border: none
```

The new property resets the size of the blockquote and its contents to the default font size. That means the property you created in step 7 can function properly now. The basic page layout for desktop media is complete.

12 Save all files.

Congratulations. You created a workable basic page layout for your project template and learned how to insert additional components, placeholder text, and headings; modified existing CSS formatting; and created new rules. In upcoming lessons, you will continue to work on this file to tweak the CSS and Bootstrap structure to make it work on all mobile devices and then set it up as the primary site template.

Review questions

1 Why should you insert images into the element as a background property?

2 What is the advantage of using Bootstrap components in your layout?

3 Can you edit the styling of a Bootstrap element directly?

4 How does the CSS Designer assist in troubleshooting your website layout?

5 If a character does not appear on your keyboard, such as a copyright symbol, how is it possible to use this element on your webpage?

6 Can you use any font to create a font stack?

7 Why should you consider using web-hosted fonts?

Review answers

1 By inserting graphics as a background image you leave the container free for other content and gain additional flexibility when designing for mobile devices.

2 Bootstrap components are built to be responsive out of the box, allowing you to create complex structures that support a variety of screen sizes and devices with minimum effort.

3 No. The Bootstrap style sheet is locked, but you can easily create styles in your own style sheet to format or override default styling.

4 The CSS Designer serves as a CSS detective, allowing you to investigate what CSS rules are formatting a selected element and how they are applied.

5 HTML provides code entities for all characters that you may want to use on your webpage but that you cannot type from the keyboard. Many are available directly from Dreamweaver's insert menu.

6 Technically, yes, you can declare any font name in your CSS rules. However, normally the font will load only if the visitor has that font installed on their computer. Today, many designers are hosting custom fonts on their own sites or using third-party font hosting services. But if you use third-party fonts on your site, be sure to check that they're licensed for web use.

7 Web-hosted fonts provide thousands of uniquely designed typefaces, many of them free, that can enhance the design and personality of your website.

7 DESIGNING FOR MOBILE DEVICES

Lesson overview

In this lesson, you'll edit and adapt cascading style sheets (CSS) and CSS3 media queries in Dreamweaver for mobile devices and learn how to:

- Edit and manipulate a Bootstrap framework to adapt to different types of mobile devices

- Create and edit a media query for mobile and handheld devices, such as tablets and smartphones

- Select and target CSS rules within specific media queries

- Configure page components to work with mobile devices

- Preview this page in Dreamweaver

 This lesson will take about 2 hours to complete. If you have not already done so, download the project files for this lesson from the Lesson & Update Files tab on your Account page at www.peachpit.com. Store them on your computer in a convenient location, and define a new site based on the lesson07 folder, as described in the "Getting Started" section of this book. Your Account page is also where you'll find any updates to the lessons or to the lesson files. Look on the Lesson & Update Files tab to access the most current content.

The trend toward designing sites to respond automatically to mobile devices and smartphones continues to grow exponentially. Dreamweaver has powerful tools to get your site mobile-ready.

Responsive design

The Internet was never conceived for smartphones and tablets. For the first decade, the most difficult challenge a programmer or developer had to worry about was the size and resolution differences between 13- and 15-inch computer monitors. For years, resolutions and screens sizes only got *larger*.

Today, the chances that some or all of your visitors are using a smartphone or tablet to access your site are increasing day by day. Statistics show that in 2014, more people were using mobile devices to access the Internet than using desktop computers, and that number has been increasing steadily ever since.

Mobile-first design

One concept that is starting to gain traction today is known as "mobile-first" design. It assumes that sites that aren't optimized for phones and tablets will shed users and traffic in this new environment.

This technique actually starts with a design for mobile devices, such as smartphones, and then adds content and structure for larger devices and computers. In some cases, the site content is actually minimized so that it loads and performs in an optimal fashion, then other content can be injected using JavaScript and databases for computers and more powerful devices. In the end, the decision to design for desktop or mobile first should be based on your site's demographics and analytics.

How your site deals with smartphones and mobile devices depends on whether you're adapting an existing site or developing a new one from scratch. For an existing site, you first have to create a basic design for the site's main components. Then, you have to work through each page, one at a time, to individually assess existing components—like images and tables—that do not inherently adapt to the specific environment.

For new websites, the typical approach is to build in the adaptability as you create the overall design, and then build each page to achieve maximum flexibility. In either case, to support a truly mobile design, be aware that some site components may need to be replaced, left out of the final design altogether, or swapped out live by JavaScript or by the media query itself. For the time being, there is no single solution to all responsive issues, and many solutions are still in development.

Whether you design for desktop or mobile first, you still need to learn how to build designs that respond to all devices. To help web designers adapt pages and content to this changing landscape, two basic tools were created: *media type* and *media query*. These functions enable browsers to identify what size and type of device is accessing the webpage and then load the appropriate style sheet, if one exists.

Media type properties

The media type property was added to the CSS2 specifications and adopted in 1998. It was intended to address the proliferation of non-computer devices that were able to access the web and web-based resources at that time. The media type is used to target customized formatting to reformat or optimize web content for different media or output.

● **Note:** In Lessons 4 and 5, you created the basic design for the website as it should appear on a standard desktop computer display based on the screen media type.

In all, CSS includes ten individually defined media types, as shown in **Table 7.1**.

Table 7.1 Media type properties

PROPERTY	INTENDED USE
all	All devices
aural	Speech and sound synthesizers
braille	Braille tactile feedback devices
embossed	Braille printers
handheld	Handheld devices (small screen, monochrome, limited bandwidth)
print	Documents viewed onscreen in print preview mode and for printing applications
projection	Projected presentations
screen	Primarily for color computer screens
tty	Media using a fixed-pitch character grid, such as teletypes, terminals, or portable
tv	Television-type devices (low resolution, color, limited-scrollability screens, sound available)

Although the media type property works fine for desktop screens, it never really caught on with browsers used on cellphones and other mobile devices. Part of the problem is the sheer variety of devices in all shapes and sizes. Add to this smorgasbord an equally diverse list of hardware and software capabilities, and you've produced a nightmare environment for the modern web designer. But all is not lost.

Media queries

A media query is a newer CSS development that provides code in the webpage that allows it to interactively determine what formatting to use based on not only what kind of device (media type) is displaying the page, but also on what dimensions and orientation it's using. Once the browser knows the type or size of the device it has encountered, it reads the media query to know what resources to load to format the webpage and content. This process is as fluid and continuous as a precision dance routine, even allowing the user to switch orientations during a session and have the page and content adapt seamlessly without other intervention. The key to this ballet is the development of style sheets optimized for specific browsers, specific devices, or both.

Media query syntax

Like the CSS it controls, a media query requires a specific syntax to work properly in the browser. It consists of one or more media types and one or more expressions, or media features, which a browser must test as true before it applies the styles it contains. Currently, Dreamweaver supports 22 media features. Others are being tested or are still under development and may not appear in the interface, but you can add them manually to the code, if necessary.

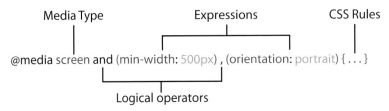

The media query creates a set of criteria to determine whether or not a specific set of rules contained within it is applied in a webpage.

You can create media queries in a variety of ways. For example, they can be designed to work exclusively—by completely resetting the existing styling—or in tandem—by inheriting some styles and modifying specifications only as necessary. The latter method requires less CSS code and is typically more efficient. We will favor that method in the upcoming exercises and for the sample site design.

To learn more about media queries and how they work, check out www.w3schools.com/cssref/css3_pr_mediaquery.asp.

Adapting Bootstrap layouts to different screen sizes

The GreenStart site design was based on a predefined Bootstrap layout that was created to be responsive out of the box. The Bootstrap framework provides a very complex style sheet complete with numerous media queries and CSS rules to accommodate a wide variety of browsers and devices. Using a framework like Bootstrap shortens the development time and allows you to concentrate on your content, instead of on technical issues.

In Lesson 6, you fleshed out a Bootstrap layout with placeholder content based on your site design. This content will form the foundation of the site template, which you will use later to build pages for your site. At the moment, the page is partially responsive. In this exercise, you will learn how to tap into Bootstrap's built-in styles and media queries to make the page fully responsive.

Working with the responsive Scrubber

Before you can learn how to manipulate the Bootstrap framework for various screen sizes, it helps to identify how the current layout responds to changing screen sizes. New to Dreamweaver CC (2015.1 release) is the Scrubber tool. It enables you to change the width of your document viewport so you can interact with the style sheets and media queries defined in the page and actually simulate different device widths right inside Dreamweaver. In the past, to change the viewport you had to manipulate the whole program interface, dragging the edge of the document window or program to see a reaction in the page.

1 If necessary, define a site based on the lesson07 folder as described in the "Getting Started" section at the beginning of the book.

2 Open **mylayout.html** from the lesson07 folder in Live view.

3 Maximize the program to fill the entire display; the program window should be displayed at a minimum of 1200 pixels in width to display and test all the media queries contained in the Bootstrap CSS.

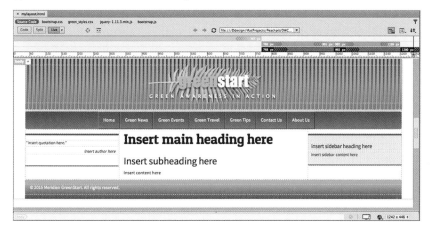

The page displays the basic site design, complete with text placeholders and graphical treatments for the header and footer.

4 Drag the Scrubber to the left to decrease the width of the document window.

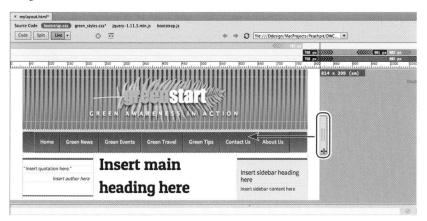

Tip: Dreamweaver displays the current screen size just below the VMQ interface as you drag the Scrubber.

As the window narrows, the layout adapts to the changes. At first, the columns in the main content area share the row side by side. When the screen narrows below 767 pixels, the layout completely changes and all the elements stack vertically one atop the other and the navigation menu collapses to an icon. The collapse coincides with the beginning of the final media query displayed in the VMQ interface at the top of the document window.

5 Stop dragging the Scrubber when the width reaches 320 pixels. Observe how the structure and content reacts to this screen width.

This is the width of the original iPhone and one of the narrowest phone screens you will want to support.

6 Drag the Scrubber to the right to increase the width of the document window.

As the window widens, the content and structure resume their original styling. As you can see, the Bootstrap structure that you created is already fairly responsive, although there are a few things you will probably want to tweak.

For example, as the page narrows the content continues to divide the space into the three-column layout. When the page narrows below 900 pixels, it gets unappealingly tight. Although the columns adjust properly for the tighter space, you may want to change the basic structure or content. One technique designers use in this situation is to hide content when there's no room for it or when it doesn't make sense to show it in a specific way or in a specific screen size.

Since the first column is intended for quotations and other inspiring messages, it's not essential to the purpose of the page or the site. Hiding it is one solution to the issue. Luckily, Bootstrap provides a simple solution.

Hiding Bootstrap elements

In this exercise, you will learn how to use predefined Bootstrap styles to hide unwanted content on small screens.

1 If necessary, open **mylayout.html** from the lesson07 folder in Live view.

2 Make sure the Scrubber is positioned fully to the right side of the document window and the program is wider than 900 pixels.

The change can be made when the screen is at any width, but displaying the correct window size makes it easier to select the desired elements and styling.

3   Click the Small media query in the VMQ.

The Scrubber jumps to the media query displayed in the VMQ. The three columns appear very tight at this width; headlines and text break into short lines, which may adversely affect readability.

4   Click the first column of the third row.
    Select the `aside.col-sm-3` tag selector.

The HUD appears focused on the `<aside>` element.

Bootstrap provides various CSS styles to format elements at specific screen sizes. The framework classifies these sizes as *large* (desktop screens larger than 1200 pixels), *medium* (screens from 992 to 1199 pixels), *small* (screens from 768 to 991 pixels), and *extra-small* (screens 767 pixels and below).

The class assigned to the `<aside>` (`col-sm-3`) styles the element for small screens. The styling will be inherited for larger screen sizes, but for smaller screen sizes there is no styling applied so the elements revert to CSS defaults. To hide the element on small screens, you need to add a second predefined Bootstrap class.

5   Click the Add Class/ID icon in the HUD.

    A text field appears in the HUD.

6   Type `.hidden-sm` and press Enter/Return to complete the class.

Note: As you type the class, a hinting menu will appear. This hinting menu is responsive to the screen width and the media query selected and may not show classes pertinent to other media queries.

A hinting list appears as you type. After you select the class, Dreamweaver assigns it to the element. The element disappears from the layout.

7 Drag the Scrubber to the right to the Medium Bootstrap media query (992 to 1199 pixels).

The `<aside>` element reappears. A second class appears on the element. This class is designed to hide elements on small screens. If the document width is from 768 to 991 pixels, the first column will disappear from the row. At 992 pixels, it reappears. Let's see what happens on extra-small screens.

8 Drag the Scrubber to the left until the document window is less than 767 pixels wide.

The `<aside>` disappears and then reappears back in the layout when the page drops below 767 pixels in width. Did you notice how the quotations reappeared at the top of the document in the Extra Small media query? The class `hidden-sm` hides the element only on small screens.

Hiding the element on small screens solves the original spacing issue when you have three columns. But on extra-small screens, the position of the element creates a new problem. It appears at the top of the page, pushing the main content down the screen where it may not even be visible on smaller devices. You could hide the element again on extra-small screens, but this is a problem that calls for a more imaginative solution.

Mobile-ready vs. mobile-optimized

Hiding elements, such as the first sidebar, is not an ideal solution in all situations. If you find yourself hiding an inordinate amount of content, or you see that you have a large number of visitors via phones and tablets, you may want to consider creating a separate, mobile-*optimized* site.

A mobile-optimized site is often hosted on a subdomain, such as *mobile .yourdomain.com*, and contains pages designed specifically for mobile devices. These sites not only reduce page size, they may also select, or filter, content appropriate for the specific device. For example, some sites remove images, tables, video, and other large elements that don't scale down very well.

Obviously, producing two or more completely different sites can drastically increase design and maintenance costs, especially if the content changes on a regular basis. It's also not the best plan for optimizing your search engine ranking.

Instead, another option is to create your website based on an online database or content management system (CMS), such as Drupal, Joomla, or WordPress. A CMS can dynamically create pages as needed based on a template and style sheets with no additional effort. These systems enable you to design mobile-optimized templates that can automatically adapt to various devices and be programmed to deliver only content appropriate for those devices.

On sites that aren't made with a CMS, you may have to figure out a different solution. Hiding elements is good in some situations. But hiding an element doesn't prevent it from downloading. A hidden video or image still takes up valuable bandwidth on your visitors' devices and may cost them in minutes or data charges. Some designers take a mobile-first strategy and actually remove the undesirable content entirely from the page, making the pages and site work optimally on mobile devices. Then, they use JavaScript or other techniques to *inject* videos or large images into the layout but only on screens or devices that can handle it.

In this case, the quotations are not too large or unwieldy to display; they just appear in the wrong place at the wrong time, or screen size.

In situations like this, Bootstrap may offer a better alternative than hiding the element: You can *move* it. To learn how to rearrange the elements in your layout you'll first have to remove the `hidden-sm` class.

9 Select the `aside.col-sm-3.hidden-sm` tag selector.

The HUD appears focused on the `<aside>` element.

10 Click the Remove Class/ID icon ✖ for the `hidden-sm` class.

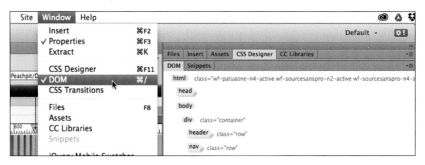

The class is removed from the element.

11 Save the file.

Before you can solve this "mobile" design challenge, you'll have to adjust the way you think about how elements are ordered and structured. You have to discard old-fashioned notions of form and function.

Creating a mobile-first structure

In this exercise, you will change the basic structure of the layout to create a mobile-first structure.

1 Open **mylayout.html** in Live view.

2 Make sure the document window is wider than 767 pixels and that the Scrubber is positioned at the right side of the window.

3 Drag the Scrubber to the Extra Small media query (767 pixels or less).

The content of the layout stacks vertically. The quotations appear at the top.

To build the mobile-first scheme, you have to adjust the current layout by moving the quotations to a location that will be more appropriate on extra-small screens. Then, by using a Bootstrap function, you will adjust the display of the elements for small screens before finally restoring the original design for larger screens and devices.

The process starts by moving the first column to a different position in the code structure. You could move the elements in Code view, but in this case you'll use a new tool: the DOM viewer.

4 If necessary, open the DOM viewer by selecting Window > DOM. Resize the window as necessary to see the document structure.

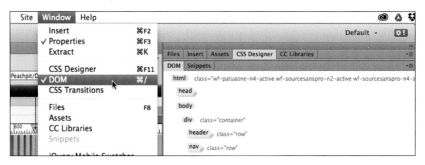

DOM stands for Document Object Model. It offers a schematic view of your HTML code, displaying the elements that compose its structure in a graphical interface. But it's not just a pretty picture. You can also use the DOM viewer to insert, delete, and move elements.

5 Select the `aside.col-sm-3 .hidden-sm` tag selector.
Observe the DOM panel display.

The `<aside>` element is highlighted. The diagram shows the parent `<article>` element and its three children. Notice that the child elements are indented in the structure. To move an element, simply drag it to the proper location.

6 Drag the first `<aside>` element below the `<section>` element.

A green line appears indicating where the element will be inserted. If done properly, the element will appear below the `<section>` and indented at the same level. The quotations now appear below the main content. The new arrangement puts the important content where it belongs on extra-small screens, but it has created a new problem on larger screens.

● **Note:** Dragging elements in the DOM viewer requires a careful eye and a steady hand. It's easy to mess up the first few times you try. Take your time and check the code to make sure you put the element in the right spot. You can undo any errors by pressing Ctrl+Z/Cmd+Z.

7 Drag the Scrubber to, or click, the Small media query (768 to 991 pixels).

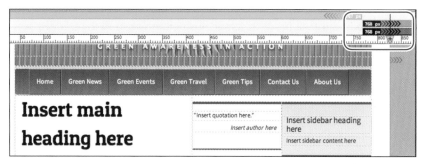

When the Scrubber moves into the Small media query, the three-column layout reappears, but now the quotations are displayed to the right of the main content. To restore the original look of the layout, you have to use a special Bootstrap function that is supplied within the predefined CSS.

8 If necessary, select the `aside.col-sm-3` tag selector for the quotations' column.

9 Using the HUD, add the following class:

`.col-sm-pull-6`

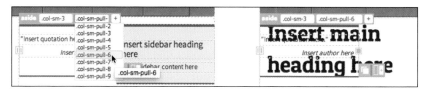

The `pull` function shifts the quotations back to the left side of the row, but it's overlapping the main content. To correct this problem, you can use a `push` function to move the main content back to the right.

10 Click the `<h1>` element.
Select the `section.col-sm-6` tag selector.
Add the class `.col-sm-push-3`

The main content section moves back to the center. All three columns are back in their original locations, but with an important *mobile-first* difference.

11 Drag the Scrubber to the left until the document window is narrower than 767 pixels.

Below 767 pixels the content displays in a single column again. The quotations appear below the main content. Through some Bootstrap magic you have created a layout that automatically adapts to mobile screens by shifting elements to more appropriate positions depending on the size of the screen.

12 Save the file.

Although you have solved one of the original challenges, the three columns still look a bit too tight on small screens. It would look better and less crowded in a two-column layout.

Manipulating column widths in Bootstrap

The great thing about Bootstrap is that it makes it easy to change the widths of columns at different screen sizes. In this exercise, you will create a two-column layout on small screens and then switch back to three columns at larger sizes.

1 Open **mylayout.html** in Live view if necessary.

2 Click the Medium screen media query (992 to 1199 pixels) in the VMQ.

The Scrubber jumps to the selected media query. It may stop at the beginning or end of the screen range, but the CSS applies to the entire range, so it doesn't really matter where it stops. The important concept here is that setting the screen to the correct size before you begin allows you to see the results immediately.

Before you can change the layout, you have to understand how it was created in the first place. In Lesson 5, "Creating a Page Layout," you built the three-column layout by manipulating the default Bootstrap class `col-sm-4` applied to each element in the row. The number indicates how many grid columns the element will use. By changing the number "4," you manipulated the widths of the columns to take space away from the `<aside>` elements and give more to the main content.

You may have noticed that the class has the letters `sm` in the name. This indicates that it applies to the Small media query. Some Bootstrap classes limit styling to a specific range of screen sizes, while others are designed to have their styles inherited. In this instance, column widths are inherited in the larger screens sizes.

To change the number of columns displayed in different screen sizes, you simply have to change the existing classes or add additional ones. Since you want to keep the current layout on larger screens, the first change will be a minor one.

▶ **Tip:** Press Enter/
Return to complete
each new class.

3 Click the quotation placeholder.

Select the `aside.col-sm-3 .col-sm-pull-6` tag selector for the first column.

4 In the HUD, edit the class name as highlighted:

`.col-md-3`

This change makes the class start formatting on Medium screens. You'll have to change the `pull` function too.

5 In the HUD, edit the class name as highlighted:

`.col-md-pull-6`

This change pulls the element into the first column for medium screens. You need to make the same changes for the other columns.

6 Change the classes for the main content element to:

`.col-md-6` and `.col-md-push-3`

7 Change the class for Sidebar 2 to:

`.col-md-3`

Nothing changes. The layout remains the same as before, which means the new classes are doing their job. The layout is ready now for medium and larger screens. But let's check out what happens on smaller screens.

8 Click the Small screen media query.

The document window resizes. The layout reformats into a single column, as it had done for the extra-small screens. This is because none of the Bootstrap classes are currently formatting these elements. To create the new column layout, you'll need to add new classes to each element.

9 Click in the main content window.

Select the `section.col-md-6.col-md-push-3` tag selector.

On small screens, you want two columns on the first line and Sidebar 2 on the second line. You'll split the first line, with one-third for the quotations and two-thirds for the main content.

10 Add a new class to the `section`:

`.col-sm-8`

The main content section resizes to two-thirds of the screen width. Let's push the column to the right side of the row.

11 Add a new class to the `section`:

`.col-sm-push-4`

The column shifts to the right side of the row. Next, you'll deal with the quotations column.

12 Select the tag selector `aside.col-md-3.col-md-pull-6` for Sidebar 1. Add a new class to the `aside`:

`.col-sm-4`

The column occupies four column grids but is still aligned to the right.

13 Add a new class to the `aside`:

`.col-sm-pull-8`

The column shifts back to the left edge, but Sidebar 2 is obscuring the first row. Nothing is formatting this column, and since it isn't floating it's trying to rise up to take the place of the other two elements. You can get it back into the mix by adding the proper class.

14 Select the `aside.col-md-3.sidebar2` tag selector and add the following class:

`.col-sm-8`

The new class resizes the column. It now matches the width of the main content area and has shifted below it. The column is aligned to the left. Let's match the alignment of the main content column.

15 Add the following class:

`.col-sm-push-4`

Sidebar 2 aligns to the main content section. The styling of the new structure is complete. Let's see how it responds now to different screen sizes.

16 Drag the Scrubber left and right to test the styling at different screen widths.

On small and extra-small screens, the layout looks fine. When the Scrubber hits the medium media query, the elements shift back to one row, but there's a problem. Sidebar 2 was OK originally, but now it appears far to the right edge of the screen. To get it back into the layout, you need to add a `push` function.

17 Add the following class to Sidebar 2:

`.col-md-push-0`

Sidebar 2 now fits back into the layout.

18 Drag the Scrubber left and right and observe the layout.

The layout shifts from one, to two, to three columns interactively as you change the width of the window. The layout works perfectly now, responding to all screen sizes smoothly. Overall, the structure looks fine, but the content could use a few tweaks on smaller screens. When the screen width gets to the smallest size, the logo in the header seems too big and actually extends beyond the edges of the screen.

19 Save the file.

In the remaining exercises, you will learn how to style elements at different screen sizes by creating a custom media query and adding CSS rules to it.

Working with media queries

As you learned earlier, a media query is a method you can use to target styling to specific screen sizes, orientations, and devices. The Bootstrap framework provides predefined style sheets and JavaScript to make the underlying page structure responsive out of the box. In most cases, you only have to add your own style sheets and media queries to deal with conflicts with your page content or with specific design requirements. Whenever you start a project with predefined resources, it's a good idea to inspect the basic structure and the elements that format it.

Identifying media queries

The `<header>` is made up of several elements and CSS effects. Take a moment to identify the styling that has already been created for mobile devices and what it does.

1 If necessary, launch Dreamweaver CC (2015.1 release) or later. Maximize the program to fill the entire screen.

2 Open **mylayout.html** from the lesson07 folder in Live view.

3 Choose Window > CSS Designer, if necessary, to display the panel.
Click the All button.

● **Note:** If your screen is too small to display the CSS Designer in two columns, you will still be able complete the exercise.

4 Adjust the CSS Designer to display in two columns while maintaining a screen width of 1024 pixels or wider, if possible.

Setting up the CSS Designer in two columns makes working with and editing CSS easier.

5 Select ALL SOURCES.

6 Examine the @Media window and note the existing media queries.

The window shows a list of media queries for a variety of screen sizes and applications.

7 Click the first few media queries and observe the Sources window display.

The bootstrap.css file is highlighted in bold, indicating that the selected media query is defined within that file. In fact, there are over 60 media queries defined. The nature of a predefined framework is to anticipate all the needs and usage of basic HTML elements as well as any provided components and format them to work in any foreseeable environment or application. The rest is up to you.

8 Click in the <header> element.
Click the Current button.

The list of media queries is shorter, showing only the styles affecting the `<header>` element.

9 Drag the Scrubber to the left. Observe the text "Green Awareness in Action." When the words break to two lines, stop dragging the Scrubber.

The motto breaks to two lines at approximately 425 pixels. Also note that the logo is filling the screen from left to right. If you added a new rule to adjust the formatting of this element, it would apply to the element at all screen sizes. That's because CSS rules are applied to all screen states unless limited by a media query. Since the Bootstrap media queries are locked, you'll need to create a new one in the **green_styles.css** file.

10 Drag the Scrubber to the right until the motto appears on one line, approximately between 426 to 438 pixels.

The motto should still be displayed on one line. Dreamweaver allows you to create a new media query right in the document window.

11 Click the Add Media Query icon at the top of the Scrubber.

> **Note:** If your text doesn't display on one line, keep dragging to the right until it does and then adjust the media query accordingly.

Mac   Windows

Note: If *green_styles.css* does not appear in the pull-down menu automatically, select it manually.

A Media Query Definition dialog appears. The max-width field is already populated with the pixel position of your Scrubber, between 426 to 438 pixels. The min-width field is empty. That means this media query will apply to screens starting at this width and smaller. Using the minimum-width property means that none of the styles contained within it will affect any devices wider than that designated. Make sure that the file name **green_styles.css** appears in the source pull-down menu.

12 Click OK to create the media query.
If necessary, open the CSS Designer.

13 Click the All button.
Click **green_styles.css** in the Sources panel.

Note: The purpose of the media query is to keep the motto on one line. Your pixel position may differ from the one described here or pictured in subsequent screen shots. Substitute your measurement in the following exercises, as necessary.

Mac   Windows

A new (`max-width`) media query has been added to the style sheet. You will use this media query to tweak the header and other elements on small screens.

14 Save all files.

Adding rules to a media query

CSS rules contained within a media query are used to reset or reformat elements based on the size, orientation, or type of device displaying your webpage. In this exercise, you will add rules to the new media query.

1 Open **mylayout.html** in Live view, if necessary.

2 Ensure the program is maximized to the full extent of the computer display.

3 Adjust the CSS Designer to display in two columns while maintaining a screen width of 1024 pixels or wider, if possible.
Click the All button.

4 Click the new media query displayed in the VMQ interface (max-width 426 pixels).

The Scrubber repositions to 426 pixels. The motto should display in one line.

5 Drag the Scrubber to 320 pixels.

This is the width of the iPhone classic and probably the smallest device you will have to support. The motto breaks to two lines.

6 Click the motto "GREEN AWARENESS IN ACTION."

The motto is highlighted, displaying the HUD focused on the p tag. When adding new rules, it's vital that the rule be inserted into the correct style sheet and media query. The following technique will ensure that your rules get into the proper location every time in the CSS Designer.

7 Select **green_styles.css** in Sources.
Select (max-width:426px) in @Media.
Click the Add Selector icon ✚ in Selectors.

The selector .row .col-sm-12 p appears in the Selectors window.

8 Edit the selector name to header.row p and press Enter/Return as needed to complete the name.

9 Add the following property to the new rule:

`letter-spacing: .1em`

The motto narrows to fit on one line.

10 Drag the Scrubber to the right.
Observe the header.

The motto remains narrow until the screen width exceeds 426 pixels. Then it expands to its original settings.

11 Save all files.

Now you can adjust the logo.

Copying and pasting CSS properties

In this exercise, you will learn how to create CSS styling by copying and pasting properties from one rule to another.

1 Drag the Scrubber to 320 pixels.
Click in the <header> element and select the header.row tag selector.

2 Click the All button in the CSS Designer, if necessary.

The <header> has a complex set of properties creating the background effects. Writing a new rule to tweak the <header> on small devices might be a challenge for some designers. But instead of writing the new rule from scratch, you'll use a feature of the CSS Designer that will make the job fast and simple.

3 Select **green_styles.css** in Sources.

The Selectors window shows all the rules contained in the file. To narrow down the list to the rules affecting the <header>, use the Current button.

4 Click the Current button.

The selectors list shows only the rules affecting the <header> in **green_style.css**. The header.row rule is at the top of the list.

5 Select header.row in Selectors.

When the rule is selected, **green_styles.css** is bolded, indicating where the rule is located. The Properties window displays the current settings. The CSS Designer enables you to copy some or all of the styles within one rule and paste them into a new or existing rule.

6 Right-click the header.row rule.

A context menu appears. Note the options for copying some or all of the properties in the rule.

7 Select Copy Styles > Copy Background Styles.

8 Click the All button.

The All button must be selected to create new rules.

9 Select **green_styles.css** in Sources.
Select (max-width:426px) in @Media.
Click the Add Selector icon ✚ in Selectors.
The name .container .row appears in the Selectors window.

10 Edit the name to header.row and press Enter/Return as needed to complete the selector.

The new selector appears in the window. The Properties window is empty. The new rule has no styling applied to it.

11 Right-click header.row in Selectors.
In the context menu, select **Paste Styles**.

● **Note:** Select Show Set to see the pasted styles, if necessary.

The background styles you copied in step 6 and 7 are pasted into the new rule. The Properties window is populated with the background styling from the original `header.row` rule.

There are now two rules formatting the `<header>`. Since the original rule still formats the element even at the smaller sizes, there's no need to keep any property that isn't going to change. You need only the ones that will reset the logo's size. Let's delete the redundant properties.

12 Select the new `header.row` rule and select the Show Set option in Properties, if necessary.

The Properties window displays the background specifications that were copied and pasted into the new rule. Beside the fields that allow you to add or edit CSS properties, each setting in the window also provides options to disable or delete the value.

13 Position the cursor over the **background-color** property.

When the cursor moves over the property, Dreamweaver highlights it. The Disable icon ⃠ and the Delete icon 🗑 appear to the right.

14 Click the Delete icon 🗑.

The background-color property is removed.

15 Delete all background properties except **background-size**.

The new rule now styles only the background size. At the moment, the setting is still identical to the one in the original rule. You can use this last property to reformat the `<header>` on extra-small screens, but remember that it contains multiple settings to format the different parts of the background.

16 Right-click the rule `header.row`.

Select **Go to Code** from the context menu.

Dreamweaver switches to Split view and loads **green_style.css** in the Code window. The window is focused on the `header.row` rule in the media query `@media (max-width: 426px)`.

17 Edit the declaration as highlighted:

`background-size: 95% auto, auto auto, 100% auto;`

Note: Switching the emphasis of the settings to the width instead of the height allows the logo to adapt better to the narrowing screen width.

```
136    }
137    header.row {
138        background-size: 95% auto, auto auto, 100% auto;
139    }
140    }
```

Live view updates the `<header>` display, scaling the logo to fit the width of the screen. The new settings will prevent the logo from getting too big on the smaller screens.

18 Save all files.

The last step is to tweak the text styles to fit the content better on smaller screens.

Completing the mobile design

In this exercise, you'll wrap up the mobile design by overriding some of the existing rules to make the text fit better on the smaller window.

1 Open **mylayout.html** in Live view.
Adjust the screen width to 400 pixels to activate the new media query.

The logo and headings in the `<article>` element seem too large for the smaller screen. They take up too much space.

2 Open the CSS Designer, if necessary.
Select **green_styles.css** > `(max-width:426px)` > `header.row`

You can adjust all the text sizes in the `<header>` with a single property.

3 Create the following properties:

```
padding: 10px 0px
font-size: 80%
```

The logo text and motto scale down in size along with the height of the `<header>`.

4 Create a new rule: `article.row section h1`
Add the following properties:

```
padding-top: 15px
font-size: 185%
line-height: 1.1em
text-align: center
```

5 Create a new rule: `article.row section h2`
   Add the following properties:

   ```
   font-size: 150%
   line-height: 1.1em
   ```

The h1 and h2 headings now fit the smaller screens better.

6 Save all files.

The layout is complete and adapted to mobile screens. In the next lesson, you will turn this layout into a Dreamweaver template, which will allow you to create pages based on the site design quickly and easily.

More information on media queries

To learn more about media queries and how to work with them, check out the following links:

* Adobe: http://tinyurl.com/adobe-media-queries

* W3C Consortium: http://tinyurl.com/w3c-media-queries

* Smashing Magazine: http://tinyurl.com/media-queries-smashing

Congratulations, you've successfully modified a predefined mobile-ready layout and adapted it to your site design requirements. Although it's hard to imagine what amazing new features may come along, one thing you can be sure of is that Dreamweaver will continue to be at the forefront of web development. With support for media queries and other responsive techniques, the program continues to innovate and be a leader in the industry.

Review questions

1 What's the purpose of a media type?

2 What are media queries?

3 How do media queries target a specific device or screen size?

4 What's the difference between a mobile-ready and mobile-optimized site design?

5 Do you have to worry about CSS inheritance when using media queries?

6 In a mobile device, what happens to the webpage display if you rotate the device?

Review answers

1   A media type identifies what type of device is accessing the webpage, such as a screen, printer, Braille reader, and so on.

2   Media queries are a CSS3 specification for loading style sheets interactively, based on the size and other characteristics of the device viewing the webpage.

3   Media queries include a logical expression that instructs the browser what style sheet to load, based on screen and device characteristics.

4   Mobile-ready sites adapt the existing design to various screen sizes using media queries and custom style sheets. Mobile-optimized sites build duplicate sites using subdomains and content created especially for each environment.

5   Yes. But bear in mind that media queries can be written to format exclusively or in conjunction with other media queries or style sheets. By allowing a base set of styles to be inherited, you can save on the total amount of CSS that needs to be created by the designer and downloaded by the user.

6   By rotating the device, you are changing the width of the screen and its orientation. Both factors can be used to load various style sheets or rules to format the page components and content differently.

8 WORKING WITH TEMPLATES

Lesson overview

In this lesson, you'll learn how to work faster, make updating easier, and be more productive. You'll learn how to do the following:

- Create a Dreamweaver template
- Insert editable regions
- Produce child pages
- Update templates and child pages

 This lesson will take about 1 hour to complete. If you have not already done so, download the project files for this lesson from the Lesson & Update Files tab on your Account page at www.peachpit.com, store them on your computer in a convenient location, and define a new site based on the lesson08 folder as described in the "Getting Started" section of this book. Your Account page is also where you'll find any updates to the lessons or to the lesson files. Look in the Lesson & Update Files tab to access the most current content.

Dreamweaver's productivity tools and site-management capabilities are among its most useful features for a busy designer.

Creating a template from an existing layout

Note: Create a new site based on the lesson08 folder before beginning the lesson.

A template is a type of master page from which you can create related child pages. Templates are useful for setting up and maintaining the overall look and feel of a website while providing a means for quickly and easily producing site content. A template is different from your completed pages; it contains areas that are editable and other areas that are not. Templates enable a workgroup environment in which page content is created and edited by several team members while the web designer controls the page design and the specific elements that must remain unchanged.

Although you can create a template from a blank page, converting an existing page into a template is far more practical and also far more common. In this exercise, you'll create a template from your existing layout.

1 Launch Dreamweaver CC (2015.1 release) or later.

2 Open **mylayout.html** from the lesson08 folder. Switch to Design view.

Note: Design view will often not display the layout accurately in the document window, and some of the responsive styling may not work as expected.

The first step in converting an existing page to a template is to save the page as a template. Most of the work creating a template must be completed in Design or Code view. The template options will not be accessible within Live view.

3 Choose File > Save as Template.

The Save As Template dialog appears.

Tip: Adding the suffix "temp" to the filename helps to visually distinguish this file from others in the site folder display, but it's not a requirement.

4 If necessary, choose lesson08 from the Site pop-up menu. Leave the Description field empty. Type **mygreen_temp** in the Save As field. Click Save.

Note: A dialog may appear, asking about saving the file without defining editable regions; just click Yes to save anyway. You'll create editable regions in the next exercise.

An untitled dialog appears, asking whether you want to update links.

Templates are stored in their own folder, Templates, which Dreamweaver automatically creates at the site root level.

5 Click Yes to update the links.

Since the template is saved in a subfolder, updating the links in the code is necessary so that they will continue to work properly when you create child pages later. Dreamweaver automatically resolves and rewrites links as necessary when you save files anywhere in the site.

Although the page still looks exactly the same, you can identify that it's a template by the file extension **.dwt** displayed in the document tab, which stands for Dreamweaver template.

A Dreamweaver template is *dynamic*, meaning that the program maintains a connection to all pages within the site that are derived from the template. Whenever you add or change content within the dynamic regions of the template and save it, Dreamweaver passes those changes to all the child pages automatically, keeping them up-to-date. But a template shouldn't be completely dynamic. Some sections of the page should contain areas where you can insert unique content. Dreamweaver allows you to designate these areas of the page as *editable*.

Inserting editable regions

When you create a template, Dreamweaver treats all the existing content as part of the master design. Child pages created from the template would be exact duplicates, and all the content would be locked and uneditable. This setup is great for repetitive features of the design, such as the navigation components, logos, copyright, contact information, and so on, but the downside is that it stops you from adding unique content to each child page. You get around this barrier by defining *editable regions* in the template. Dreamweaver creates two editable regions automatically, one for the `<title>` element and another for metadata or scripts that need to be loaded in the `<head>` section of the page; you have to create the rest.

First, give some thought to which areas of the page should be part of the template and which should be open for editing. At the moment, three sections of your current layout need to be editable: both `<aside>` elements and the main content area.

1   Open **mygreen_temp.dwt** from the lesson08 templates folder in Design view, if necessary. Maximize the program window to fill the entire screen.

2   Insert the cursor in the heading text *Insert main heading here*. Click the `section` tag selector.

    Dreamweaver selects the entire `<section>` element.

3   Choose Insert > Template > Editable Region.

Note: The template workflow currently works only in Design and Code views. You will not be able to perform any of these tasks in Live view.

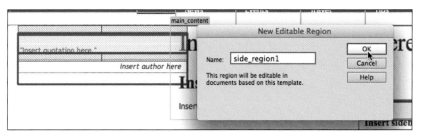

4 In the New Editable Region dialog, type **main_content** in the Name field. Click OK.

Each editable region must have a unique name, but no other special conventions apply. However, keeping the name short and descriptive is a good practice. The name is used solely within Dreamweaver and has no other bearing on the HTML code. In Design view, you will see the new region name in a blue tab above the designated area identifying it as an editable region. In Live view, the tabs are orange.

You also need to add an editable region to Sidebar 1 and Sidebar 2. Each of these sidebar regions contains text placeholders that you can customize on each page.

5 Insert the cursor in the left column. Click the `aside` tag selector.

6 Choose Insert > Template > Editable Region.

7 In the New Editable Region dialog, type **side_region1** in the Name field. Click OK.

8 Insert the cursor in the right column.
Click the `aside` tag selector.

9 Choose Insert > Template > Editable Region.

10 In the New Editable Region dialog, type **side_region2** in the Name field.
Click OK.

11 Save the file.

Once you have set up the visible components of the template, you should turn your attention to areas that are hidden from most visitors.

Inserting metadata

A well-designed webpage includes several important components that users may never see. One such item is the *metadata* that is often added to the <head> section of each page. Metadata is descriptive information about your webpage or the contents it contains that is often used by other applications, like the browser or a search engine.

Adding metadata—for instance, a piece of data such as *title*—is not only a good practice, it's vital to your ranking and presence in the various search engines. Each title should reflect the specific content or purpose of the page. But many designers also append the name of the company or organization to help build more corporate or organizational awareness. By adding a title placeholder with the company name in the template, you will save time typing it in each child page later.

1 If necessary, open **mygreen_temp.dwt** in Design view.

2 In the Document Title field of the Property inspector, select the placeholder text *Untitled Document*.

Many search engines use the page title in the listings of a search result. If you don't supply one, the search engine will pick one of its own. Let's replace the generic placeholder with one geared for this website.

▶ **Tip:** The Document Title field is available in the Property inspector only when you are in Design or Code views.

3 Type **Meridien GreenStart Association - Add Title Here** to replace the text. Press Enter/Return to complete the title.

▶ **Tip:** If the Property inspector is not visible, you can display it by selecting Window > Properties.

Along with the title, the other piece of metadata that usually appears in these search results is the page *description*. A description is a type of summary of a page that succinctly describes the contents in 25 words or less. Over the years, web developers have tried to drive more traffic to their sites by writing misleading titles and descriptions or outright lies. But be forewarned—most search engines have become wise to such tricks and will actually demote sites that use these tactics.

To achieve the highest ranking with the search engines, make the description of the page as accurate as possible. In many cases, the contents of the title and the description metadata will appear verbatim in the results page of a search.

4 Choose Insert > HTML > Description.

An empty Description dialog appears.

5 Type **Meridien GreenStart Association - add description here**. Click OK.

Dreamweaver has added the two metadata elements to the page. Unfortunately, only one of them was implemented properly in the template.

6 Switch to Code view. Locate and examine the `<title>` tag in the code and the surrounding markup.

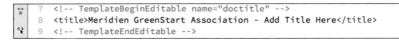

```
7    <!-- TemplateBeginEditable name="doctitle" -->
8    <title>Meridien GreenStart Association - Add Title Here</title>
9    <!-- TemplateEndEditable -->
```

In most cases, the `<title>` will appear around line 8. Notice how the title appears between two comments that delineate an "editable" portion of the template named `"doctitle"`.

7 Locate and examine the `<meta>` tag containing the `"description"` and the surrounding markup.

```
21   <!-- TemplateBeginEditable name="head" -->
22   <!-- TemplateEndEditable -->
23   <meta name="description" content="Meridien GreenStart Association - add description here">
24   </head>
25     <body>
```

You should find the description near the end of the `<head>` section, around line 23. This element is not contained in an *editable* section of the template. This means that this metadata will be locked on all child pages, and you will not be able to customize it for that page.

Luckily, Dreamweaver comes to the rescue by providing an editable section designed for metadata just like this. In this case, it can't even get any more convenient—you'll find it just above the description delineated by the HTML comment markup `<!-- TemplateBeginEditable name="head" -->`. To make the description metadata editable, you'll need to move it into this section.

8 Click the line number containing the entire description, or select the entire `<meta>` element using the cursor.

The `<meta>` tag and its contents should occupy a single line of the markup.

9 Press Ctrl+X/Cmd+X to cut this code into memory.

10 Insert the cursor at the end of the comment `<!--TemplateBeginEditable name="head"-->` (around line 21).

11 Press Enter/Return to insert a new line.

12 Click the line number of the new blank line. Press Ctrl+V/Cmd+V to paste the description `<meta>` element.

> **Note:** The new line is simply intended to make the markup easier to read. It's otherwise unnecessary.

```
21    <!-- TemplateBeginEditable name="head" -->
22 ▼  <meta name="description" content="Meridien GreenStart Association - add description here">
23    <!-- TemplateEndEditable -->
```

The description is now contained within the editable template region named `"head"`.

13 Choose File > Save.

You now have three editable regions—plus editable metadata for title and description—that you can change as needed when you create new child pages using this template.

14 Choose File > Close All.

Now it's time to learn how to use your new template.

Producing child pages

Child pages are the *raison d'être* for Dreamweaver templates. Once a child page has been created from a template, only the content within the editable regions can be modified in the child page. The rest of the page remains locked within Dreamweaver. It's important to remember that this behavior is supported only within Dreamweaver and a few other HTML editors. Be aware: If you open the page in a text editor, like Notepad or TextEdit, the code is fully editable.

Creating a new page

The decision to use Dreamweaver templates for a site should be made at the beginning of the design process so that all the pages in the site can be made as child pages of the template. In fact, that was the purpose of the layout you've built up to this point: to create the basic structure of your site template.

1 Launch Dreamweaver CC (2015.1 release) or later, if necessary.

  The template workflow functions only in Design and Code views. You can also access site templates from the New Document dialog.

2 Choose File > New, or press Ctrl+N/Cmd+N.

  The New Document dialog appears.

3 In the New Document dialog, select the Site Templates option.
  Select lesson08 in the Site list, if necessary.
  Select **mygreen_temp** in the Template For Site "lesson08" list.

4 Select the Update Page When Template Changes option, if necessary.
  Click Create.

  Dreamweaver creates a new page based on the template.

5 If necessary, switch to Design view.

  Typically, Dreamweaver defaults to the last document view (Code, Design, or Live) you were using for the new document. In Design view, you will see the name of the template file displayed in the upper-right corner of the document window. Before modifying the page, you should save it.

6 Choose File > Save.

  The Save As dialog appears.

7 In the Save As dialog, navigate to the site root folder.
Name the file **about_us.html**, and click Save.

The child page has been created. When you save the document in the site root folder, Dreamweaver updates all links and references to external files. The template makes it easy to add new content.

▶ **Tip:** The Save As dialog provides a handy button to take you to the site root with a single click. Feel free to use it in any exercise, as needed.

Adding content to child pages

When you create a page from a template, only the editable regions can be modified.

1 Open **about_us.html** in Design view, if necessary.

You'll find that many of the features and functionality of templates work properly only in Design view, although you should be able to add or edit content in the editable regions from Live view.

2 Position the cursor over each area of the page.

◆ **Warning:** If you open a template in a text editor, all the code is editable, including the code for the non-editable regions of the page.

When the cursor moves over certain areas of the page, such as the header, horizontal menu, and footer, the Locked icon ⊘ appears. These areas are uneditable regions that are locked and cannot be modified within the child page inside Dreamweaver. Other areas, like side_region1 and the main content section, can be changed.

3 Open the Property inspector, if necessary.

In the Title field, select the placeholder text *Add Title Here*.

Type **About Meridien GreenStart** and press Enter/Return.

4 In the `main_content` region, select the placeholder text *Insert main heading here*. Type **About Meridien GreenStart** to replace the text.

5 Select the placeholder text *Insert subheading here*.

Type **GreenStart - green awareness in action!** to replace the text.

6 In the Files panel, double-click **aboutus-text.rtf** in the lesson08 resources folder to open the file.

▶ **Tip:** To add a little editorial flair, use the command Insert > HTML > Character > Em Dash to replace the hyphen in the heading with a long dash.

Dreamweaver opens only simple, text-based file formats, such as .html, .css, .txt, .xml, .xslt, and a few others. When Dreamweaver can't open the file, it passes the file to a compatible program, such as Word, Excel, WordPad, TextEdit, and so on. The file contains content for the main content section.

7 Press Ctrl+A/Cmd+A to select all the text. Press Ctrl+C/Cmd+C to copy the text.

8 Switch back to Dreamweaver.

9 Insert the cursor in the placeholder text *Insert content here*.

Select the p tag selector.

10 Press Ctrl+V/Cmd+V to paste the text.

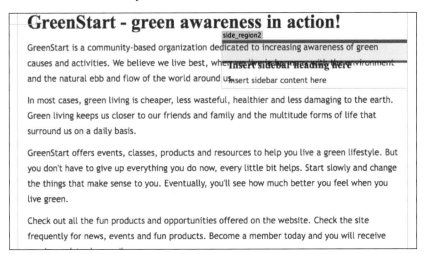

The placeholder text is replaced by the new content. You can also add content to the sidebar elements.

11 Open **sidebars08.html** in Design view from the site root folder.

The file contains content for each sidebar. The top half is composed of three environmentally themed quotations and the bottom half of environmental tips and news.

12 Insert the cursor in the first paragraph, and examine the tag selectors.

The tag selectors indicate a structure identical to what you created for the quotations column in Lesson 6, "Working with a Web Framework," but unformatted by the CSS. Let's use this content to replace the existing sidebar.

13 Click the `aside` tag selector.

The tag selector shows the same Bootstrap class structure used in the template.

14 Press Ctrl+X/Cmd+X to cut the entire element into memory.

15 Select the **about_us.html** document tab.

The child page appears in the document window again.

16 Insert the cursor into the first column.
Select the `aside` tag selector.

17 Press Ctrl+V/Cmd+V to replace the sidebar placeholder.

▶ **Tip:** You may find it difficult to identify and select Sidebar 2 because of the inaccurate way Design view renders the page. To achieve success, be sure to use the correct tag selectors.

The replacement content appears, formatted somewhat by the external CSS file.

18 Select the **sidebars08.html** document tab.

19 Repeat steps 12–17 to replace the Sidebar 2 placeholder.

All three editable regions have now been populated with content.

20 Close **sidebars08.html**.

Do not save the changes.

By not saving the changes, you preserve the content in the file if you want to repeat the exercise later.

21 Switch to Live view to preview the page.

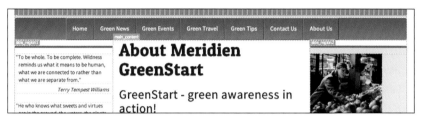

The CSS styling kicks in again and the page design and columns now render properly. Although you can't see the template name in the upper-right corner any more, the names of the editable regions now display in orange tabs above their corresponding element.

22 Save the file.

You have populated the editable regions with text and pictures, but they can hold any type of web-compatible content, including tables, video, banner ads, and more. From time to time, content inserted into a template will require some additional styling via CSS.

For example, notice that the images and text in the right column are touching the left and right edges of the column. If the element had no background color, this would not be an issue. But normally you would want the text and other content to be moved slightly off these edges.

Formatting content in editable regions

Often content inserted into the editable regions will need to have custom styling created for it to help it adapt to the layout itself or to various screen sizes that may be encountered. In this exercise, you will create some new rules to format the picture and text in Sidebar 2.

1 Open **about_us.html** in Live view, if necessary. Maximize the program window to the full size of the computer display. Ensure that the document window and Scrubber show the page at least 1024 pixels in width.

Before you create any CSS rules, you should examine the structure of the element you want to style.

2 Select the first image in Sidebar 2.

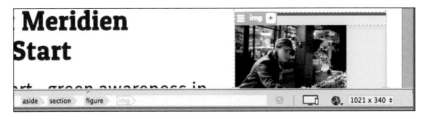

The HUD appears focused on the `img` tag. The image appears in a semantic structure using the `<section>` and `<figure>` elements.

3 In the CSS Designer, select the All button.
Select **green_styles.css** > GLOBAL.
Click the Add Selector icon ✚.

The selector `section figure img` appears in the Selectors window. This selector would format the image, but you'll want to limit the effect to Sidebar 2 to prevent unintended consequences.

4 Edit the selector name to say:

`.sidebar2 section figure img`

By adding the class `sidebar2` to the selector name, only images appearing in this specific structure will be targeted.

5 Create the following properties in the new rule:

```
margin: 0px auto
display: block
```

The images in Sidebar 2 align to the center of the column. Setting *auto* margins on the left and right forces elements toward the center. But this alone will not achieve the desired result. Images are considered inline elements, which ignore margin settings. Setting `display: block` allows images to honor the specifications.

6   Select the caption below the first image in Sidebar 2.

The HUD appears focused on the `figcaption` element.

7   Select **green_styles.css** > GLOBAL.
Click the Add Selector icon ➕.

The selector `section figure figcaption` appears in the Selectors window. Let's limit this selector as you did the previous one.

8   Edit the selector name to say:

`.sidebar2 section figure figcaption`

9   Create the following property:

`margin: 5px 10px 15px 10px`

The captions are now indented on the left and right and exhibit more space at the top and bottom. Other custom styling may be needed as you create more pages, but for now you're finished.

10 Save all files.

11 Choose File > Close All.

Once you have created child pages and added content, there will come a time when you need to add or change a menu item, update the header or footer, or otherwise modify the content in the base template.

Updating a template

Templates can automatically update any child pages made from that template. But only areas outside the editable regions will be updated. Let's make some changes in the template to learn how templates work.

1 Choose Window > Assets.

▶ **Tip:** The Template category in the Assets panel does not appear when a document is open in Live view. Switch to Design or Code view, if necessary, to access this category.

The Assets panel appears. If it appears floating freely in the document window, you can dock it with the CSS Designer panel. The Assets panel gives you immediate access to a variety of components and content available to your website.

2 In the Assets panel, click the Templates category icon 📄.
If no templates appear in the list, click the refresh icon **C**.

The panel displays a list of site templates and a preview window. The name of your template appears in the list.

3 Right-click **mygreen_temp** and choose Edit from the context menu.

The template opens.

4 In the navbar, select the text *Home*.
Type **Green Home** to replace the text.

5 In the vertical menu, select the text *Green News*. Type **Headlines** to replace the text.

6 Select and replace the text *Insert* with the word **Add** wherever it appears in the main_content, side_region1, and side_region2 editable regions.

7 Switch to Live view.

You can now clearly see the changes to the menu and content areas. In the template, the entire page is editable.

8 Save the file.

The Update Template Files dialog appears. The filename **about_us.html** appears in the update list.

9 Click Update.

The Update Pages dialog appears.

10 Select the Show Log option.

The window displays a report detailing which pages were successfully updated and which ones were not.

11 Close the Update Pages dialog.

Tip: If an open page has been changed during the update, it will be updated by Dreamweaver and show an asterisk in the document tab by its name.

12 Choose File > Open Recent > **about_us.html**. Observe the page, and note any changes.

The changes made to the horizontal menu in the template are reflected in this file, but the changes to the sidebars and main content areas were ignored, and the content you added to both areas earlier remains unaltered.

As you can see, you can safely make changes and add content to the editable regions without worrying that the template will delete all your hard work. At the same time, the boilerplate elements of the header, footer, and horizontal menu all remain consistently formatted and up-to-date, based on the status of the template.

13 Click the document tab for **mygreen_temp.dwt** to switch to the template file.

14 Switch to Design view.

15 Delete the word *Green* from the Green Home link in the horizontal menu. Change the word Headlines in the vertical menu back to **Green News**.

16 Save the template and update related files.

17 Click the document tab for **about_us.html**. Observe the page and note any changes.

The horizontal menu has been updated. Dreamweaver even updates linked documents that are open at the time. The only concern is that the changes have not been saved; the document tab shows an asterisk, which means the file has been changed but not saved.

If Dreamweaver or your computer were to crash at this moment, the changes would be lost; you would have to update the page manually or wait until the next time you make changes to the template to take advantage of the automatic update feature.

18 Save and close all files.

Dreamweaver's templates help you build and automatically update pages quickly and easily. In the upcoming lessons, you will use the newly completed template to create files for the project site. Although choosing to use templates is a decision you should make when first creating a new site, it's never too late to use them to speed up your workflow and make site maintenance faster and easier.

▶ **Tip:** Always use the Save All command whenever you have multiple files open that have been updated by a template. In most cases, it's better to update when your files are closed so that they are saved automatically.

Review questions

1 How do you create a template from an existing page?

2 Why is a template "dynamic"?

3 What must you add to a template to make it useful in a workflow?

4 How do you create a child page from a template?

5 Can templates update pages that are open?

Review answers

1   Choose File > Save as Template, and enter the name of the template in the dialog to create a .dwt file.

2   A template is dynamic because Dreamweaver maintains a connection to all pages created from it within a site. When the template is updated, it passes any changes to the locked areas of the child pages and leaves the editable regions unaltered.

3   You must add editable regions to the template; otherwise, unique content can't be added to the child pages.

4   Choose File > New, and in the New Document dialog, select Site Templates. Locate the desired template, and click Create. Or right-click the template name in the Assets > Template category, and choose New From Template.

5   Yes. Open pages based on the template are updated along with files that are closed. The only difference is that files that are open are not automatically saved after being updated.

9 WORKING WITH TEXT, LISTS, AND TABLES

Lesson overview

In this lesson, you'll create several webpages from your new template and work with headings, paragraphs, and other text elements to do the following:

- Enter heading and paragraph text
- Insert text from another source
- Create bulleted lists
- Create indented text
- Insert and modify tables
- Spellcheck your website
- Search and replace text

This lesson will take about 2 hours and 30 minutes to complete. If you have not already done so, download the project files for this lesson from the Lesson & Update Files tab on your Account page at www.peachpit.com, store them on your computer in a convenient location, and define a new site based on the lesson09 folder as described in the "Getting Started" section of this book. Your Account page is also where you'll find any updates to the lessons or to the lesson files. Look on the Lesson & Update Files tab to access the most current content.

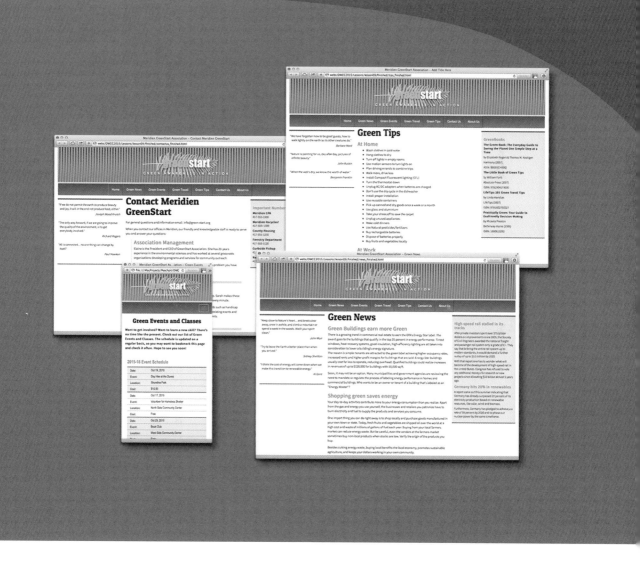

Dreamweaver provides numerous tools for creating, editing, and formatting web content, whether it's created within the program or imported from other applications.

Previewing the completed file

To get a sense of the files you will work on in the first part of this lesson, let's preview the completed pages in a browser.

1   Launch Adobe Dreamweaver CC (2015.1 release) or later, if necessary. If Dreamweaver is already running, close any open files.

2   If necessary, define a new site for the lesson09 folder, as described in the "Getting Started" section at the beginning of the book.
    Name the new site **lesson09**.

3   If necessary, press F8 to open the Files panel. Select lesson09 from the site drop-down list, and expand the site root folder.

    Dreamweaver allows you to open one or more files at the same time.

4   Open the lesson09/finished folder.

5   Select **contactus_finished.html**. Press Ctrl/Cmd, and then select **events_finished.html**, **news_finished.html**, and **tips_finished.html**.

    By pressing Ctrl/Cmd before you click, you can select multiple non-consecutive files.

6   Right-click any of the selected files.
    Choose Open from the context menu.

All four files open. Tabs at the top of the document window identify each file.

7 Click the **news_finished.html** tab to bring that file to the top, and switch to Live view if necessary.

● **Note:** Be sure to use Live view to preview each of the pages.

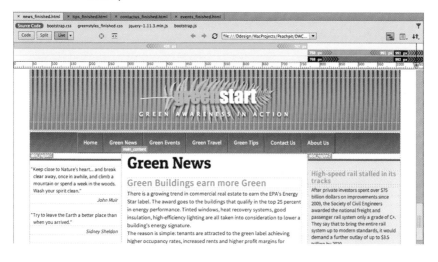

Note the headings and text elements used.

8 Click the **tips_finished.html** document tab to bring that file to the top.

Note the bulleted list elements used.

9 Click the **contactus_finished.html** tab to bring that file to the top.

Note how text elements are indented and formatted.

10 Click the **events_finished.html** tab to bring that file to the top.

Note the two HTML-based tables used. The design employs techniques that allow the tables to adapt to tablets and smartphones.

11 Drag the Scrubber to the left.

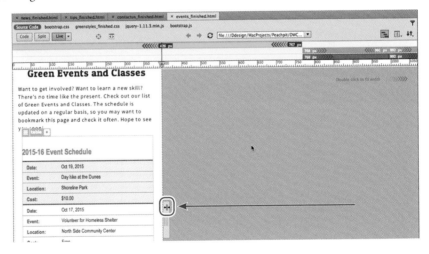

As the screen narrows, the media queries apply styles to reformat the content and layout. Note how the tables themselves drastically alter their appearance and structure to fit the smaller screens.

12 Choose File > Close All.

In each of the pages, there are a variety of elements used, including headings, paragraphs, lists, bullets, indented text, and tables. In the following exercises, you will create these pages and learn how to format each of these elements.

Creating and styling text

Most websites are composed of large blocks of text with a few images sprinkled in for visual interest. Dreamweaver provides a variety of means for creating, importing, and styling text to meet any need. In the following exercises, you will learn a variety of techniques for working with and formatting text.

Importing text

In this exercise, you'll create a new page from the site template and then insert heading and paragraph text from a text document.

1 Choose Window > Assets to display the Assets panel. Select the Templates category icon ▤. Right-click **mygreen_temp**, and choose New From Template from the context menu.

▶ **Tip:** The Assets panel may open as a separate, floating panel. To save screen space, feel free to dock the panel on the right side of the screen, as shown in Lesson 1, "Customizing Your Workspace."

A new page is created based on the site template.

2 Save the file as **news.html** in the site root folder.

3 If necessary, choose Window > Properties to display the Property inspector. In the Document Title field, select the placeholder text *Add Title Here*. Type **Green News** and press Enter/Return to complete the title.

4 In the Files panel, double-click **green_news.rtf** in the lesson09/resources folder.

Dreamweaver automatically launches a program compatible to the file type selected. The text is unformatted and features extra lines between each paragraph. These extra lines are intentional. For some reason, Dreamweaver swaps out single paragraph returns for <br> tags when you copy and paste them from another program. Adding a second return forces Dreamweaver to use paragraph tags instead.

This file contains four news stories. When you move the stories to the webpage, you're going to create semantic structures, as you did for the quotation placeholders. As explained earlier, semantic web design attempts to provide a context for your web content so that it will be easier for users and web applications to find information and reuse it, as necessary.

5 In the text editor or word-processing program, insert the cursor at the beginning of the text *Green Buildings earn more Green*. Press Ctrl+A/Cmd+A.

All the text is highlighted.

> ▶ **Tip:** When you use the clipboard to bring text into Dreamweaver from other programs, you must be in Design view if you want to honor the paragraph returns and other formatting.

6 Press Ctrl+C/Cmd+C to copy the text.
Close **green_news.rtf**.
Do not save any changes.

7 Switch back to Dreamweaver.
Switch to Design view.
Select the text *Add main heading here*.
Type **Green News** to replace it.

8 Insert the cursor in the placeholder heading *Add subheading here.*

9 Click the <h2> tag selector.
Press Delete.

10 Select the text *Add content here.*

11 Press Ctrl+V/Cmd+V to paste the text from the clipboard and swap out the placeholder text.

The text from **green_news.rtf** appears in the layout.

12 Save the file.

The four news stories were inserted as individual <p> elements. Although a human visitor would be able to distinguish where one story ends and another begins, there is no differentiation between them within the code. Adding semantic structures should be your goal whenever possible. This is encouraged not only to support accessibility standards but also to improve your SEO ranking at the same time.

Creating semantic structures

In this exercise, you will insert HTML5 `<article>` elements to contain the news stories.

1 If necessary, open **news.html** in Design view.
Click in the text *Green Buildings earn more Green.*
Select the p tag selector.

The entire <p> element is selected.

2 Hold the Shift key and click at the end of the text *Energy Waster?*

The first news story is selected.

3 Choose Insert > Article.

The Insert Article dialog appears. The dialog should default to the Wrap Around Selection mode. If it doesn't, select the option from the Insert pull-down menu in the dialog.

This dialog allows you to add custom IDs and classes to your element. At the moment, we don't have the need for one, so you can insert the new element as is.

4   Click OK to insert a new `<article>` element.

The new element appears in the tag selector interface wrapping the first news story.

5   Repeat steps 1–4 to create new `<article>` elements for the remaining three news stories.

When you're finished, you should have four new `<article>` elements, one for each news story.

6   Save **news.html**.

Creating headings

In HTML, the tags <h1>, <h2>, <h3>, <h4>, <h5>, and <h6> create headings. Any browsing device, whether it is a computer, a Braille reader, or a cellphone, inter-prets text formatted with any of these tags as a heading. On the web, headings are used to introduce distinct sections with helpful titles, just as they do in books, magazine articles, and term papers.

You are using one <h1> element per page as the primary page title. Any other headings used on the page should descend in order from the <h1>. Since each news story has equal importance, they all can begin with a second-level heading, or <h2>. At the moment, all the pasted text is formatted as <p> elements. Let's format the news headings as <h2> elements.

1   In Design view, select the text *Green Buildings earn more Green*.
    Choose **Heading 2** from the Format menu in the Property inspector, or press Ctrl+2/Cmd+2.

▶ **Tip:** If the Format menu is not visible, select the HTML mode of the Property inspector.

    The text is formatted as an <h2> element.

2   Repeat step 1 with the text *Shopping green saves energy*, *Recycling isn't always Green*, and *Fireplace: Fun or Folly?*

    All the selected text should now be formatted as <h2> elements. Let's create a custom rule for this element to set it off from the other headings with a unique style.

3   Insert the cursor in any of the newly formatted <h2> elements.
    Choose Window > CSS Designer to open the CSS Designer, if necessary.

4   Choose **green_styles.css** > GLOBAL.
    Click the Add Selector icon ➕.

    A new selector appears that targets the <h2> element but contains all the Bootstrap classes styling the parent elements too. There's no need for such a complex selector, so you should simplify these names whenever they appear.

5   Edit the selector to say:

    `article h2`

    This name will target only <h2> elements used in the main content area.

6   Create the following specifications:

    ```
    margin-top: 15px
    margin-bottom: 5px
    color: #090
    font-size: 170%
    font-weight: bold
    ```

● **Note:** By default, each heading tag—<h1>, <h2>, <h3>, and so on—is formatted smaller than the preceding tag. This formatting reinforces the semantic importance of each tag. Although size is an obvious method of indicating hierarchy, it's not a requirement; feel free to experiment with other styling techniques, such as color, indenting, borders, and background shading, to create your own hierarchical structure.

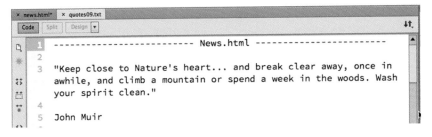

7 Save all files.

Adding other HTML structures

Descendant selectors are often sufficient for styling most elements and structures in a webpage. But not all the structural elements are available from the Insert menu or panel. In this exercise, you will learn how to build a custom HTML structure for a quotation and an attribution using the Quick Tag Editor.

1 Open **news.html** in Design view, if necessary.

2 In the Files panel, open **quotes09.txt**.

Since this is a plain-text file, Dreamweaver can open it. The file contains quotations you will insert in the pages that will be created in this lesson.

3 Select the text of the first quotation, excluding the author name.
Press Ctrl+X/Cmd+X to cut the text.

● **Note:** When pasting text into existing HTML structures, it is important not to accidentally delete or damage these structures.

4 Switch to **news.html**.
Select the first quotation placeholder.
Press Ctrl+V/Cmd+V.

The quotation has replaced the placeholder.

5 Switch to **quotes09.txt**. Select and cut the author name, John Muir.

6 Switch to **news.html**. Select the *Add Author Name* placeholder text and paste the text.

John Muir has replaced the author name placeholder. Since there was only one quotation placeholder in the template, you'll have to create the other quotation structures from scratch.

7 Switch to **quotes09.txt**. Select and cut the next two quotations and authors.

8 In **news.html**, insert the cursor anywhere in the first quotation. Click the `blockquote` tag selector. Press the right arrow key.

▶ **Tip:** In Design view, there may not be any visual indication of the cursor location, but you can see it if you use Split view.

The cursor moves to a position in the code after the `<blockquote>` element.

9 Press Ctrl+V/Cmd+V to paste the new quotations and authors.

The text appears, but it is not styled properly.

10 Using the cursor and the tag selector interface, compare the structure of the three quotations, and note the differences.

The new quotations and author names appear in two separate p elements. Part of the styling problem is due to the missing parent `blockquote` element. Dreamweaver has no menu option for adding this specific tag, but you can use the Quick Tag Editor to build all types of custom structures in a pinch.

11 Select the second quotation, including the author name, Sidney Sheldon.

Tip: Press Ctrl+T/Cmd+T to toggle between modes in the Quick Tag Editor, if necessary.

12 Press Ctrl+T/Cmd+T to activate the Quick Tag Editor.

The Quick Tag Editor appears. Since you have more than one element selected, it should default to Wrap mode.

13 Type `blockquote` and press Enter/Return twice to add the element as a parent to the two paragraphs.

The quotation text is now formatted properly, but the author name needs one more tweak: You need to change the tag applied to it. As with `blockquote`, there's no menu option for the `<cite>` tag.

14 Insert the cursor in the author name, Sidney Sheldon. Select the tag selector for the `<p>` element. Press Ctrl+T/Cmd+T to activate the Quick Tag Editor.

The Quick Tag Editor appears. Since you have only one element selected, it should default to Edit mode. If the correct mode is not visible, press Ctrl+T/Cmd+T until it is.

Note: In HTML5, the *cite* element is used to identify the attribution of a quotation.

15 Press the Backspace key to delete "p" from the selected tag. Type `cite`, and press Enter/Return twice to complete the change.

The author name now appears in a `<cite>` element and is styled identically to the other author.

16 Repeat steps 11–15 to create the blockquote structure for the third quotation in **news.html**.

All three quotations are now structured properly in the first column.

17 Save and close **news.html**.

When you close **news.html**, Dreamweaver may prompt you to save **green_styles.css**. It is vital that you remember to save changes to the style sheet, especially when the file itself is not open. If you forget, you will lose any styling that was created in the previous exercises.

18 Click Save if necessary.

19 Close **quotes09.txt**. Do not save changes.

Closing the text file without saving the changes will preserve the original content in case you want to repeat this exercise later.

Creating lists

Formatting should add meaning, organization, and clarity to your content. One method of doing this is to use the HTML list elements. Lists are the workhorses of the web because they are easier to read than blocks of dense text; they also help users find information quickly.

In this exercise, you will learn how to make an HTML list.

1 Choose Window > Assets to bring the Assets panel to the front.
In the Template category, right-click **mygreen_temp**.
From the context menu, choose New From Template.

● **Note:** The Template category is not visible in Live view. To create, edit or use Dreamweaver templates, you must switch to Design or Code view.

A new page is created based on the template.

2 Save the file as **tips.html** in the site root folder. Switch to Design view, if necessary.

3 In the Property inspector, select the placeholder text *Add Title Here* in the Document Title field. Type **Green Tips** to replace the text and press Enter/Return.

4 In the Files panel, double-click **green_tips.rtf** in the resources folder of lesson09.

The file will open outside Dreamweaver. The content consists of three individual lists of tips on how to save energy and money at home, at work, and in the community. As in the news page, you will insert each list into its own `<article>` element.

5 In **green_tips.rtf**, press Ctrl+A/Cmd+A.
Press Ctrl+X/Cmd+X to cut the text. Close but do not save changes to **green_tips.rtf**.

You have selected and cut all the text.

6 Switch back to Dreamweaver.
Select *Add main heading here.*
Type **Green Tips** to replace it.

7 Select and delete the <h2> *Add subheading here.*
Select *Add content here.*
Press Ctrl+V/Cmd+V.

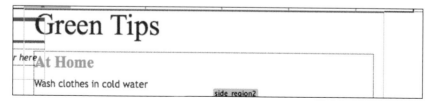

The text for all three lists appears.

8 Select the text starting at *At Home* and ending with *Buy fruits and vegetables locally.*

9 Choose Insert > Article.
Click OK in the Insert Article dialog.

The `<article>` element appears, wrapping the new list.

10 Select the text starting at *At Work* and ending with *Buy natural cleaning products.*

11 Choose Insert > Article.
Click OK in the Insert Article dialog.

12 In Dreamweaver, repeat steps 10 and 11 to create the third list and `article` structure.

All three lists now appear in their own `<article>` elements.

As you did with the titles of the news stories, apply HTML headings to introduce the list categories.

13 Apply `<h2>` formatting to the text *At Home*, *At Work*, and *In the Community*.

The remaining text is currently formatted entirely as HTML paragraphs. Dreamweaver makes it easy to convert this text into an HTML list. Lists come in two flavors: ordered and unordered.

14 Select all the `<p>` elements under the heading *At Home*.
In the Property inspector, click the Ordered List icon .

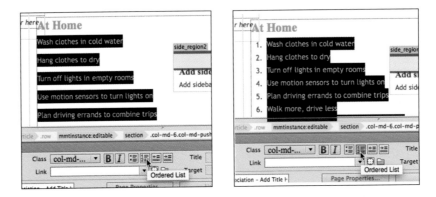

An ordered list adds numbers automatically to the entire selection. Semantically, it prioritizes each item, giving them intrinsic values relative to one another. This list doesn't seem to be in any particular order; each item is more or less equal to the next one, so it's a good candidate for an unordered list—used when the items are in no particular order. Before you change the formatting, let's take a look at the markup.

15 Switch to Split view. Observe the list markup in the Code section of the document window.

```
61  <ol>
62  <li>Wash clothes in cold water</li>
63  <li>Hang clothes to dry</li>
64  <li>Turn off lights in empty rooms</li>
65  <li>Use motion sensors to turn lights on</li>
```

The markup consists of two elements: <ol> and <li>. Note that each line is formatted as an <li> (list item). The <ol> parent element begins and ends the list and designates it as an ordered list. Changing the formatting from numbers to bullets is simple and can be done in Code or Design view.

Before changing the format, ensure that the formatted list is still entirely selected. You can use the <ol> tag selector, if necessary.

16 In the Property inspector, click the Unordered List icon ⊞.

All the items are now formatted as bullets.

If you observe the list markup, you'll notice that the only thing that has changed is the parent element. It now says `<ul>`, for *un*ordered list.

17 Select all the `<p>` formatted text under the heading *At Work*. In the Property inspector, click the Unordered List icon ⊞.

18 Repeat step 17 with all the text following the heading *In the Community*.

All three lists are now formatted with bullets.

19 In Dreamweaver, save and close **tips.html**.

▶ **Tip:** The easiest way to select the entire list is to use the `<ol>` tag selector.

▶ **Tip:** You could also change the formatting by editing the markup manually in the Code view window. But don't forget to change both the opening and the closing parent elements.

Creating indented text

Some designers still use the `<blockquote>` element in Dreamweaver, and elsewhere, as an easy way to indent headings and paragraph text. Semantically, the `<blockquote>` element is intended to identify whole sections of text quoted from other sources as in Sidebar 1. Visually, text formatted this way will appear indented and set off from the regular paragraph text and headings. But if you want to comply with web standards, you should leave this element for its intended purpose and instead use custom CSS classes when you want to indent text, as you will in this exercise.

1 Create a new page from the template **mygreen_temp**.
Save the file as **contact_us.html** in the site root folder.

2 Switch to Design view, if necessary.
Enter **Contact Meridien GreenStart** to replace the placeholder text *Add Title Here*.

3 In the Files panel, open **contact_us.rtf** from the lesson09/resources folder.

The text consists of five department sections, including headings, descriptions, and email addresses for the managing staff of GreenStart. You will insert each department into its own `<article>` element.

4 In **contact_us.rtf**, select all the text and cut it.
Close the file and do not save the changes.

5 In Dreamweaver, enter **Contact Meridien GreenStart** to replace the placeholder heading *Add main heading here*.

6 Select and delete the heading *Add subheading here*.

7 Select the text *Add content here* and press Ctrl+V/Cmd+V to paste the content.

All the content cut from **contact_us.rtf** appears.

8 Format the text *Association Management* as a Heading 2.

As before, you need to wrap each content group in an `<article>` element.

9 Click the h2 tag selector.
Hold the Shift key and select the rest of the text for this section.

10 Select Insert > Article.

Press Enter/Return in the Insert Article dialog to create the element.

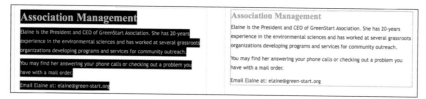

When the `<article>` element is created, the `<h2>` element formats in green as specified by the rule you created earlier.

11 Repeat steps 8–10 to structure and format the content for the *Education and Events, Transportation Analysis, Research and Development*, and *Information Systems* sections.

With all the text in place, you're ready to create the indent styling. If you wanted to indent a single paragraph, you would probably create and apply a custom class to the individual `<p>` element. In this instance, we want to indent the entire `<article>` element to produce the desired graphical effect.

First, let's assign a `class` attribute to the element. Since the class we want to use does not exist yet, you'll have to create it manually. This can be done in any view. In Design view it's best done in the Quick Tag Editor.

12 Insert the cursor anywhere in the *Association Management* `<article>` element. Click the `<article>` tag selector.
Press Ctrl+T/Cmd+T.

The Quick Tag Editor appears, displaying the `<article>` tag. The cursor should appear at the end of the tag name, but within the brackets.

13 Press the spacebar to insert a space.

The Code Hinting window appears, displaying the appropriate attributes for the `<article>` element.

14 Type **class** and press Enter/Return, or double-click the `class` attribute in the Code Hinting window.

Note how Dreamweaver automatically creates the attribute markup and provides a list of any existing `class` attributes as you type. Since the class you want to use doesn't exist yet, you'll type the entire name yourself.

15 Type **profile** as the class name.

Press Enter/Return as necessary to complete the attribute and close the Quick Tag Editor.

16 Select the `article.profile` tag selector. Choose **green_styles.css** > GLOBAL in the CSS Designer.

17 Click the Add Selector icon ✚.

A new selector name appears.

18 Edit the name to say:

```
article.profile
```

19 Enable the Show Set option, if necessary.

Enter the following property in the Properties window:

```
margin: 0px 25px 15px 25px
padding-left: 10px
```

As with margins, border specifications can be entered individually or all at once.

20 Enter the following specifications for the left and bottom borders:

```
border-left: solid 2px #CADAAF
border-bottom: solid 10px #CADAAF
```

Although the display is not as accurate as in Live view, you can still see the borders appear on the left and bottom of the `article` element. The borders help to visually group the indented text under its heading. In Live view the display is more accurate.

<img> **Tip:** When creating specifications manually, enter the property name in the field and press Tab. A value field will appear to the right. When Show Set is enabled, hinting may not appear in the values field.

21 Switch to Live view.

22 Insert the cursor anywhere in the *Education and Events* section. Click the `<article>` tag selector.

The HUD appears focused on the `article` element.

23 In the HUD, click the Add Class/ID icon [+] and type **.profile** in the text field.

As you type, a hinting menu will show the matching class names. Feel free to select the name from the list.

24 Repeat steps 22 and 23 to apply the `profile` class to the remaining `<article>` elements.

Each section is indented and displays the custom border.

25 Save all files.

Whenever you add new components or styling to a site, you need to make sure the elements and styling work well on all screen sizes and devices.

Making it responsive

In this exercise, you will test the new *profile* elements at multiple screen sizes and adapt them as needed.

1 If necessary, switch to Live view.

2 Drag the Scrubber to the left to make the document window narrower. Observe how the new components respond to the changing widths.

The `.profile` section looks fine until you get down to widths less than 450 pixels. At those sizes the left indent and border wastes too much space. You can fix this situation easily by simply adding alternate styling in the appropriate media query.

3   Restore the document window to its full width.

4   In the CSS Designer, choose **green_styles.css** > (max-width: 426px). Create the following selector:

```
article .profile
```

● **Note:** Insert the new rule in the custom media query you created in Lesson 8, if it is different than the one described in step 4.

5   Create the following properties in the new rule:

```
padding: 5px 0px
margin: 5px 0px
border-top: solid 10px #CADAAF
border-bottom: solid 4px #CADAAF
border-left-style: none
```

6   Save all files.
    Repeat step 2 to test the new styling.

Note: You may need to click the Refresh button to see the changes in the layout properly.

When the screen drops down to your custom media query, the `.profile` section expands nearly to the full width of the screen and drops the indents and the left border. Remember to test all new components at every screen size and orientation and make changes to the styling as needed.

Creating and styling tables

Before the advent of CSS, HTML tables were often used to create page layouts. Although tables are not good for page layout, they are very good, and necessary, for displaying many types of data, such as product lists, personnel directories, and timetables, to name a few.

Dreamweaver enables you to create tables from scratch, to copy and paste them from other applications, or to create them instantly from data supplied from other sources, such as database or spreadsheet programs, like Microsoft Access or Microsoft Excel.

Creating tables from scratch

Dreamweaver makes it easy to create tables from scratch. In this exercise, you will learn how to create an HTML table.

1 Create a new page from the **mygreen_temp** template. Save the file as **events.html** in the site root folder.

2 Enter **Green Events and Classes** to replace the *Title* placeholder text in the Property inspector.

3 In Design view, select the *Add main heading here* placeholder heading and type **Green Events and Classes** to replace it.

▶ **Tip:** Whenever you need to select complete elements, it's a good practice to use the tag selectors.

4 Select the *Add subheading here* placeholder heading and click the h2 tag selector. Press Delete.

5 Select the text *Add content here.*

6 Type the following text: **Want to get involved? Want to learn a new skill? There's no time like the present. Check out our list of Green Events and Classes. The schedule is updated on a regular basis, so you may want to bookmark this page and check it often. Hope to see you soon!**

7 Without moving the cursor position from step 6, choose Insert > Table.

The Table dialog appears.

Some aspects of the table may be controlled and formatted by HTML attributes, but others can be controlled entirely by CSS. Whenever possible, avoid using HTML to format tables. As with text formatting, HTML formatting is neither efficient nor flexible.

The only advantage HTML has is that the attributes continue to be well supported by all popular browsers, both old and new. When you enter values in this dialog, Dreamweaver still applies them via HTML attributes.

8 Enter the following specification for the table:

Rows: **2**
Columns: **4**
Width: **100%**
Border thickness: **1**

9 Click OK to create the table.

A four-column, two-row table appears below the main heading. Note that it fills the column from left to right. Let's wrap it in an `<article>` element.

10 Select Insert > Article.

The Insert Article dialog appears. The Insert drop-down menu should default to Wrap Around Selection.

11 Click OK to create the `<article>` element.

The table is ready to accept input.

Tip: While in a table cell in Design view, pressing the Tab key moves the cursor to the next cell on the right. Hold the Shift key when pressing the Tab key to move to the left, or backward, through the table.

12 Insert the cursor in the first cell of the table.

Type **Date** and press Tab to move into the next cell in the first row.

13 In the second cell, type **Event** and press Tab. Type **Location** and press Tab. Type **Cost** and press Tab.

Date	Event	Location Add sidebar heading here	Cost
		Add sidebar content here	

The cursor moves to the first cell of the second row.

14 In the second row, type **May 1** (in cell 1), **May Day Parade** (in cell 2), **City Hall** (in cell 3), and **Free** (in cell 4).

When the cursor is in the last cell, inserting additional rows in the table is easy.

15 Press Tab.

may want to bookmark this page and cha 100% (599) ▾ ___ region? to see you soon!

Date	Event	Add sidebar heading here	Cost
May 1	May Day Parade	Add sidebar content here City Hall	Free

A new blank row appears at the bottom of the table. Dreamweaver also allows you to insert multiple new rows at once.

16 Select the `<table>` tag selector at the bottom of the document window.

may want to bookmark this page and cha 100% (599) ▾ ___ region? to see you soon!

Date	Event	Add sidebar heading here	Cost
May 1	May Day Parade	Add sidebar content here City Hall	Free

ance:fileinstance body div … article … mmtinstance:editable section … article table tbody tr td

Properties

	Table	Rows 3	W 100 % ▾	CellPad	Align `<table width="100%" border="1">`
		Cols 4		CellSpace	Border 1

The Property inspector displays the properties of the current table, including the total number of rows and columns.

17 Select the number 3 in the Rows field.

Type **5** and press Enter/Return to complete the change.

Dreamweaver adds two new rows to the table.

The fields in the Property inspector create HTML attributes to control various aspects of the table, including table width, width and height of cells, text alignment, and so on. You can also add rows and columns to the table interactively using the mouse.

18 Right-click the last row of the table.

Choose Table > Insert Row from the context menu.

Another row is added to the table. The context menu can also insert multiple rows and/or columns at once.

19 Right-click the last row of the table.

Choose Table > Insert Rows or Columns from the context menu.

The Insert Rows or Columns dialog appears.

20 Insert 4 rows below the selection and click OK.

Four more rows are added to the table, for a total of 10 rows.

21 Save all files.

Copying and pasting tables

Although Dreamweaver allows you to create tables manually inside the program, you can also move tables from other HTML files or even other programs by using copy and paste.

● **Note:** Dreamweaver allows you to copy and paste tables from some other programs, such as Microsoft Word. Unfortunately, it doesn't work with every program.

1 Open the Files panel and double-click **calendar.html** in the lesson09/resources folder to open it.

Date	Event	Location	Cost
Oct 19, 2015	Day hike at the Dunes	Shoreline Park	$10.00
Oct 17, 2015	Volunteer for Homeless Shelter	North Side Community Center	Free
Oct 23, 2015	Book Club	West Side Community Center	Free
Oct 24, 2015	Halloween Haunted Hike	West Side Park	$10.00

This HTML file opens in its own tab in Dreamweaver. Note the table structure—it has four columns and numerous rows.

When moving content from one file to another, it's important to match views in both documents. Since you were working in Design view in **events.html**, you should use Design view in this file too.

2 Switch to Design view, if necessary.

3 Insert the cursor in the table.
Click the `<table>` tag selector.
Press Ctrl+C/Cmd+C to copy the table.

4 Click the **events.html** document tab.

5 Insert the cursor in the table.
Select the `<table>` tag selector.
Press Ctrl+V/Cmd+V to paste the table.

The new table element completely replaces the existing table. This workflow will work in Design and Code views. But you must match views in both documents before you copy and paste.

6 Save the file.

Styling tables with CSS

Currently, the formatting for the table is a mixed bag. Some is being supplied by HTML defaults and some by the Bootstrap framework. Whenever CSS styles conflict with HTML attributes, CSS wins. In the following exercise, you will create CSS rules to override any HTML styling.

1 If necessary, insert the cursor in the table. Select the `table` tag selector.

2 In the CSS Designer, choose **green_styles.css** > GLOBAL.
Create a new selector:

```
article table
```

3 In the CSS Designer Properties window, deselect the option Show Set, if necessary.

4 In the Type category, click to open the font-family property.
Select Manage Fonts, and create the following custom font stack:

```
Arial Narrow, Arial, Verdana, sans-serif
```

5 Create the following specifications for the new rule:

```
font-family: Arial Narrow, Arial, Verdana, sans-serif
font-size: 90%
width: 95%
border-bottom: 3px solid #060
margin-bottom: 2em
```

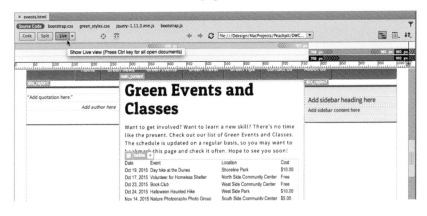

● **Note:** Feel free to enable the Show Set option when creating these specifications, as shown.

▶ **Tip:** Table styling may not appear properly in Design view. Switch to Live view to see the full effect of your CSS.

The table displays a dark green border at the bottom, and the content has been reduced in size and styled with Arial Narrow.

You have applied styling to one aspect of the table properties, but there are plenty of things you still need to address within this element. It's hard to see what's actually happening using Design view. It's a good idea to preview the page in Live view from time to time.

6 Save all files.

7 Switch to Live view and examine the page content.

In Live view everything looks better, but the data in the table appears a bit crowded, and if your screen is narrower than the one shown, the content may wrap to two lines. It could use some extra spacing and other highlighting. The rule article table you just created formats only the overall structure of the table. It can't control or format the individual rows and columns. In the next exercise, you will turn your attention to the inner workings of the table.

Styling table cells

Just as for tables, column styling can be applied by HTML attributes or CSS rules. Formatting for columns can be applied via two elements that create the individual cells: <th> for table header and <td> for table data.

It's a good idea to create a generic rule to reset the default formats of the <th> and <td> elements. Later, you will create custom rules to apply more specific settings.

1 Insert the cursor into the table.
In the CSS Designer, choose **green_styles.css** > GLOBAL.

2 Create a new selector:

```
article td, article th
```

This simplified selector will work fine. Since td and th elements have to be in tables anyway, there's really no need to put table in the selector name.

3 In the Properties window, select the Show Set option.

4 Create the following properties for the new rule:

```
padding: 4px
text-align: left
border-top: solid 1px #090
```

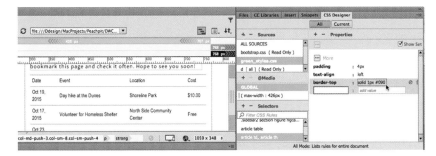

A thin green border appears above each row of the table, making the data easier to read. You may not be able to see the border properly unless you use Live view.

Long columns and rows of undifferentiated data can be tedious to read and hard to decipher. Headers are often used to help the reader identify data. By default, the text in header cells is formatted in bold and centered to help it stand out from the normal cells, but some browsers do not honor this default styling. So don't count on it. You can make the headers stand out by giving them a touch of color of your own.

5 Choose **green_styles.css** > GLOBAL.
Create a new rule: `article th`

Note: Remember that the order of the rules can affect the style cascade as well as how and what styling is inherited.

Note: The standalone <th> rule for the <th> element must appear after the rule styling th and td elements in the CSS or some of its formatting will be reset.

6 Create the following properties in the `article th` rule:

```
color: #FFC
text-align: center
border-bottom: solid 6px #060
background-color: #090
```

The rule is created, but it still needs to be applied. Dreamweaver makes it easy to convert existing `<td>` elements into `<th>` elements.

● **Note:** You cannot select more than one cell at a time in Live view.

7 Insert the cursor into the first cell of the first row of the table. In the Property inspector, select the Header option. Note the tag selector.

The cell background is filled with green.

When you click the Header checkbox, Dreamweaver automatically rewrites the markup, converting the existing `<td>` tags to `<th>` and thereby applying the CSS formatting. This functionality will save you lots of time over editing the code manually. If you switch to Design view, you can also convert multiple cells at one time.

8 Switch to Design view.

9 Click the second cell of the first row and drag to select the remaining cells in the first row. Or you can select an entire row at once by positioning the cursor at the left edge of the table row and clicking when you see the black selection arrow appear to the left of the row.

10 In the Property inspector, select the Header option to convert the table cells to header cells.

The whole first row is filled with green as the table cells are converted to header cells.

11 Save all files.

Controlling table display

Unless you specify otherwise, empty table columns will divide the available space between them equally. But once you start adding content to the cells, all bets are off—tables seem to get a mind of their own and divvy up the space in a different way. In most cases, they'll award more space to columns that contain more data, but that's not guaranteed to happen.

To provide the highest level of control, you'll assign unique classes to the cells in each column. But first you have to create the CSS rules. You can create them one at a time or all at once. If the rules already exist in the style sheet it makes it easier to assign them to the various elements later.

1 Choose **green_styles.css** > GLOBAL. Create the following new selectors:

```
article .date
article .event
article .location
article .cost
```

Four new rules appear in the Selectors window but contain no styling information. Even without styling, the classes can be assigned to each column. Dreamweaver makes it easy to apply classes to an entire column.

2 In Design view, position the cursor above the first column of the table until you see a black arrow. Click to select the entire column.

3 Choose `date` from the Class menu in the Property inspector.

The cells in the first column should display `th.date` or `td.date` in the tag selector interface.

4   Repeat steps 2 and 3 to apply the appropriate classes to each column.

Controlling the width of a column is quite simple. Since the entire column must be the same width, you only have to apply a width specification to one cell. If cells in a column have conflicting specifications, typically the largest width wins. Since you just applied a class to the entire Date column, settings will affect every cell at once. This will make it easier to get the table to adapt to any screen.

5   Add the following property to the rule `article .date`:

```
width: 6em
```

The Date column resizes, although the change may not be visible in Design view. The remaining columns automatically divvy up the space left over. Column styling can also specify text alignment as well as width. Let's apply styling to the contents of the Cost column.

6   Add the following properties to the rule `article .cost`:

```
width: 4em
text-align: center
```

The Cost column resizes to a width of 4 ems, and the text aligns to the center. Now if you want to control the styling of the columns individually, you have the ability to do so. Note that the tag selector shows the class names with each element, such as `th.cost` or `td.cost`.

7   Save all files.

Inserting tables from other sources

In addition to creating tables by hand, you can also create them from data exported from databases and spreadsheets. In this exercise, you will create a table from data that was exported from Microsoft Excel to a comma-separated values (CSV) file. As with the other content models, you will first create an `<article>` element in which to insert the new table.

1   In Design view, insert the cursor anywhere in the existing Events table. Select the `<article>` tag selector. Press the right arrow key.

The cursor moves after the closing `</article>` tag.

2   Without moving the cursor, choose File > Import > Tabular Data.

The Import Tabular Data dialog appears.

3   Click the Browse button and select classes.csv from the lesson09/resources folder. Click Open. Comma should be automatically selected in the Delimiter menu.

Note: Even if you apply a width that's too narrow for the existing content, by default a cell can't be any smaller than the largest word or graphic element contained within it.

Note: The event and location will be used later in the lesson.

4 Select the following options in the Import Tabular Data dialog:
Table width: **100%**
Border: **0**

The table width will actually be controlled by the table rule created earlier, but HTML attributes will be honored in browsers or devices that do not support CSS. Because this is the case, make sure that the HTML attributes you use don't break the layout.

5 Click OK.

A new table—containing a class (course) schedule—appears below the first. To conform to the structure you created for the first table, you should insert the new one into an `<article>` element.

6 Select the `table` tag selector for the new table.

7 Select Insert > Article.
Click OK to insert the `<article>` element.

The new table is inserted into the `<article>` element. Green lines appear between the rows, but the header cells are not styled the same as in the first table.

8 Select the first row of the Class schedule.
In the Property inspector, select the Header option.

The header cells now display in green with reversed text.

The new table has an extra column, and the text is wrapping awkwardly in the last three columns. You will fix this display by using the `.cost` class created earlier and by creating additional custom classes too.

9 Select the entire Cost column as you did in the previous exercise.
In the Property inspector, choose `cost` from the Class menu.

The two Cost columns are now the same width.

10 In the CSS Designer, right-click the rule `article .cost`.
Choose Copy All Styles from the context menu.

11 Create a new selector: `article .day`
Right-click the new selector and select Paste Styles from the context menu.

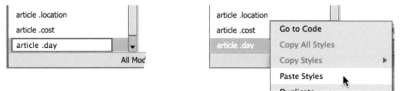

The new rule now has the same styling as the `article .cost` rule.

12 Repeat step 9 to apply the day class to the Day column in the Classes table.

Dreamweaver also provides an option for duplicating rules.

13 Right-click the rule `article .cost`.
Choose Duplicate from the context menu.
Enter `article .length` as the new selector.

14 Apply the `.length` class to the Length column in the Classes table, as in step 9.

By creating and applying custom classes to each column, you have the means to modify each column individually. We need to make two more rules: one to format the Class column and the other to format the Description column.

15 Duplicate the rule `article .date`. Enter `article .class` as the new rule name. Change the width to `10em`.

16 Duplicate the rule `article .event`.
Enter `article .description` as the new name.

17 Apply the `.class` class to the Class column.
Apply the `.description` class to the Description column.

All columns in both tables now have classes assigned to them.

18 Save all files.

Adding and formatting caption elements

The two tables you inserted on the page contain different information but don't feature any differentiating labels or titles. To help users distinguish between the two sets of data, let's add a title to each and a bit of extra spacing. The `<caption>` element was designed to identify the content of HTML tables. This element is inserted as a child of the `<table>` element itself.

1 Open **events.html** in Design view, if necessary.

2 Insert the cursor in the first table.
Select the `<table>` tag selector.
Switch to Code view.

By selecting the table first in Design view, Dreamweaver automatically highlights the code in Code view, making it easier to find.

3 Locate the opening `<table>` tag.
Insert the cursor directly after this tag.
Type `<caption>` or select it from the code-hinting menu when it appears.

4 Type **2015-16 Event Schedule** and then type </ to close the element.

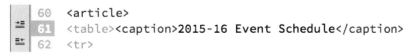

```
60   <article>
61   <table><caption>2015-16 Event Schedule</caption>
62   <tr>
```

5 Switch to Design view.

The caption is complete and inserted as a child element of the table.

6 Repeat steps 1 and 2 for the Classes table.
Type **2015-16 Class Schedule.**
Then, type </ to close the element.

7 Switch to Live view.

The schedule is updated on a regular basis, so you may want to bookmark this page and check it often. Hope to see you soon!

2015-16 Event Schedule			
Date	Event	Location	Cost
Oct 19, 2015	Day hike at the Dunes	Shoreline Park	$10.00
Oct 17, 2015	Volunteer for Homeless Shelter	North Side Community Center	Free

The captions are relatively small, and they're lost against the color and formatting of the table. Let's beef them up a bit with a custom CSS rule.

8 Choose **green_styles.css** > GLOBAL.
Create a new selector: `article caption`

9 Create the following properties for the rule `article caption`:

```
margin-top: 20px
padding-bottom: 10px
color: #090
font-weight: bold
font-size: 160%
line-height: 1.2em
```

The captions now appear sufficiently large and impressive above each table.

10 Save all files.

Formatting the tables and the captions with CSS has made them much easier to read and understand. Feel free to experiment with the size and placement of the caption and specifications affecting the tables.

Making tables responsive

The tables are finished and ready to go. They work fine for normal desktop displays and larger tablets, but the underlying page design is built to work seamlessly all the way down to smartphones. On the other hand, tables are notoriously ill-suited to smaller screens because they don't naturally adapt to them. To understand this concept, let's see how the current elements function on smaller screens.

1 If necessary, open **events.html** in Dreamweaver CC (2015.1 release) or later.

Design view doesn't provide an accurate rendition of the tables. Live view is a better choice, but the best option is to view the page in a browser.

2 Choose File > Preview in Browser.
Choose your favorite browser from the list.

The page opens in the browser, displaying all the colors, fonts, background images, and other CSS specifications set by the style sheet. To see how the tables will react to a smaller screen, just resize the browser window.

3 Drag the right edge of the browser window to the left to make it narrower. Watch carefully how the tables respond, or don't respond, to the changing environment.

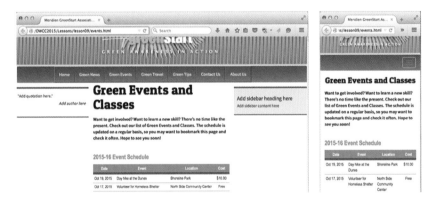

As the screen becomes narrower, the media queries will kick in and reformat the page and components to adapt to the smaller screen. Since the table widths are set to 95%, they mostly scale down with the page. But at the smallest sizes, the text within the table is trying to fit by wrapping in very narrow columns.

We need to rethink the whole concept of table design and display. You need to change the basic nature of the elements that compose tables so you can display them in a completely different way. During this process, you may sometimes find it easier to work in the CSS Designer; at other times you may want to enter the settings directly in Code view. Feel free to use whichever method feels more comfortable to you.

4 In Dreamweaver, switch to Live view and open the CSS Designer, if necessary. Click the custom media query in the VMQ you created in Lesson 7.

5 Choose **green_styles.css** > (max-width:426px) in the CSS Designer.

Your media query may differ from the one described. Choose the one you created in **green_styles.css**.

6 Create a new selector: article th, article td

7 Add the display: block property to the new rule.

The cells are now displayed vertically, stacking one atop the other.

This rule resets the default behavior of the table elements so that you can control their appearance on smaller screens. Some cells appear narrower than others because formatting is still being inherited from other parts of the style sheet. You'll have to create additional rules to override these specifications.

Note: Be sure that all subsequent rules and properties are added only to the custom media query.

8 Create a new rule: `article table`

Give the new rule the following properties:

```
margin-right: auto
margin-left: auto
```

With the data stacking vertically, it doesn't make much sense now to have a header row. We could set the header row to the `display:none` property to hide it, but that's not recommended for accessibility standards. The next best thing would be to simply format it to take up no space.

9 Create a new rule: `article th`

Give the new rule the following properties:

```
height: 0
margin: 0
padding: 0
font-size: 0
border: none
overflow: hidden
```

The header rows disappear visually but are still accessible to visitors using screen readers or other assistive devices. But now that they are invisible, you have to address the fact that there are no headers describing the data being displayed.

For this purpose, we'll resort to a new CSS3 property that can actually create labels based on the CSS class applied to the cell. Some of the latest CSS3 properties are not directly supported in the CSS Designer, but you can enter them manually in the Properties window or in Code view, and Dreamweaver may provide hinting support for them as well.

10 Create a new rule: `td.date:before`

11 Enable the Show Set option.

Enter the following property:value combo:

```
content: "Date: "
```

Notice that the label "Date: " appears in all the cells styled by the `date` class. You need to make a similar rule for each of the data elements.

12 Repeat steps 10 and 11 to create the following rules and properties:

Rule	Property: Value
`td.event:before`	`content: "Event: "`
`td.location:before`	`content: "Location: "`
`td.cost:before`	`content: "Cost: "`
`td.class:before`	`content: "Class: "`
`td.description:before`	`content: "Description: "`
`td.day:before`	`content: "Day: "`
`td.length:before`	`content: "Length: "`

Each data cell now shows the appropriate labels. CSS can also style the data and labels.

13 Create the following rule:

```
article .date,
article .event,
article .location,
article .cost,
article .class,
article .description,
article .length,
article .day
```

We typed this rule on multiple lines to make it easier to read, but you can enter it as one long string. As long as the styling for all the data cells is identical, you can combine all the selectors into a single rule, separated by commas. Remember to mind the punctuation and spelling carefully. Even a tiny error in the code can cause the formatting to fail. If you want the styling to be different in one or more of the elements, then create seven separate rules.

Next, let's apply some styling to the labels themselves to help make them stand out more distinctly.

▶ **Tip:** Creating long selectors may be easier to do in Code view. You can access the **green_styles.css** file by clicking its name in the Referenced file interface at the top of the document window.

Note: Although the formatting is identical for these classes at this point, you may want to adjust the styling for one or more items later. Making separate rules can add flexibility even though it adds to the amount of code that has to be downloaded.

14 Apply the following properties to the new rule or in each of the separate rules:

```
width: 100%
padding-left: 30%
position: relative
text-align: left
```

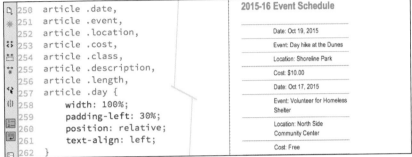

```
250    article .date,
251    article .event,
252    article .location,
253    article .cost,
254    article .class,
255    article .description,
256    article .length,
257    article .day {
258        width: 100%;
259        padding-left: 30%;
260        position: relative;
261        text-align: left;
262    }
```

The event and class entries are now indented, and all appear at the same width.

15 Create a new rule: `td:before`

Give the new rule the following properties:

```
width: 25%
display: block
padding-right: 10px
position: absolute
top: 6px
left: 1em
color: #060
font-weight: bold
white-space: nowrap
```

```
264    td:before {
265        width: 25%;
266        display: block;
267        padding-right: 10px;
268        position: absolute;
269        top: 6px;
270        left: 1em;
271        color: #060;
272        font-weight: bold;
273        white-space: nowrap;
274    }
```

The labels now appear separately from the data and are styled in boldface and dark green. The only thing left to do now is to differentiate one record from the next. One way is to simply add a darker border between each table row.

16 Create a new rule: `article tr`

Give the new rule the following property:

`border-bottom: solid 2px #060`

Using a CSS3 selector will add a little more pizzazz to the table.

17 Create a new rule: `tr:nth-of-type(even)`

Give the new rule the following property:

`background-color: #D4EAD4`

◆ **Warning:** Advanced selectors like `nth-of-type(even)` may not be supported by older browsers.

This CSS3-based selector actually applies the background only on even rows of the table.

Both tables are now slickly styled and responsive to any changes in the screen size. Although they look good in Live view, don't get complacent; it's vital to test the design in a variety of browsers and mobile devices too.

18 Save all files. Preview the page in the default browser. Test the media queries and the responsive table styling by changing the size of the browser window.

Congratulations! You've learned not only how to insert HTML tables into your web pages but also how to make them adapt to almost any screen environment. It's very likely that everything you tried in this exercise worked perfectly in both Dreamweaver and any browser you tested it in. But you have to remember that CSS3 is still fairly new and has not been fully adopted within the industry.

The good news is that most of the mobile devices we're targeting should support the various settings used in this exercise. And you can be sure Dreamweaver will stay current with the latest updates.

Spellchecking web pages

It's important to ensure that the content you post to the web is error free. Dreamweaver includes a robust spellchecker capable of identifying commonly misspelled words and creating a custom dictionary for nonstandard terms that you might use on a regular basis.

Note: Spellcheck runs only in Design view. If you are in Code view, Dreamweaver will switch to Design view automatically. If you are in Live view, the command will be unavailable.

1 Open **contact_us.html**, if necessary.

2 Switch to Design view.
Insert the cursor at the beginning of the heading *Contact Meridien GreenStart*. Choose Commands > Check Spelling.

Modify	Format	**Commands**	Site	Window	Help	
		Edit Command List...				
		Check Spelling			⇧F7	
ootstrap.js		Apply Source Formatting				

Spellchecking starts wherever the cursor has been inserted. If the cursor is located lower on the page, you will have to restart the spellcheck at least once to examine the entire page. It also does not check content locked in noneditable template regions.

The Check Spelling dialog highlights the word *Meridien*, which is the name of the fictional city where our GreenStart association is located. You could click the option Add To Personal to insert the word into your custom dictionary, but for now we will skip over other occurrences of the name during this check.

3 Click Ignore All.

Dreamweaver's spellchecker highlights the word *GreenStart*, which is the name of the association. If GreenStart were the name of your own company, you'd want to add it to your custom dictionary. However, you don't want to add a fictional company name to your dictionary.

4 Click Ignore All again.

Dreamweaver highlights the domain for the email address info@greenstart.org.

5 Click Ignore All.

Dreamweaver highlights the word *Asociation*, which is missing an "*s*."

6 To correct the spelling, locate the correctly spelled word (Association) in the Suggestions list and double-click it.

7 Continue the spellcheck to the end. Correct any misspelled words and ignore proper names, as necessary. If a dialog prompts you to start the check from the beginning, click Yes.

Dreamweaver will start spellchecking from the top of the file to catch any words it may have missed.

8 Click OK when the spellcheck is complete. Save the file.

It's important to point out that spellcheck is designed to find only words that are *spelled* incorrectly. It will not find words that are *used* incorrectly. In those instances, nothing takes the place of a careful reading of the content.

Finding and replacing text

The ability to find and replace text is one of Dreamweaver's most powerful features. Unlike other programs, Dreamweaver can find almost anything, anywhere in your site, including text, code, and any type of whitespace that can be created in the program. You can search the entire markup, or you can limit the search to just the rendered text in Design view or to just the underlying tags. Advanced users can enlist powerful pattern-matching algorithms known as *regular expressions* to perform sophisticated find-and-replace operations. And then Dreamweaver takes it one step further by allowing you to replace the targeted text or code with similar amounts of text, code, and whitespace.

In this exercise, you'll learn some important techniques for using the Find and Replace feature.

1 Select the **events.html** document tab, if necessary, or open it from the site root folder.

There are several ways to identify the text or code you want to find. One way is to simply type it in the Find field. In the Events table, the name *Meridien* was spelled incorrectly as *Meridian*. Since *Meridian* is an actual word, the spellchecker won't flag it as an error and give you the opportunity to correct it. So you'll use find and replace to make the change instead.

2 Switch to Design view, if necessary. Insert the cursor in the *Green Events and Classes* heading. Choose Edit > Find and Replace.

The Find and Replace dialog appears. The Find field is empty.

3 Type **Meridian** in the Find field.
Type **Meridien** in the Replace field.
Choose Current Document from the Find In menu, and choose Text from the Search menu.

4 Click Find Next.

Dreamweaver finds the first occurrence of *Meridian*.

5 Click Replace.

Dreamweaver replaces the first instance of *Meridian* and immediately searches for the next instance. You can continue to replace the words one at a time, or you can choose to replace all occurrences.

6 Click Replace All.

If you replace the words one at a time, Dreamweaver inserts a one-line notice at the bottom of the dialog that tells you how many items were found and how many were replaced. When you click Replace All, Dreamweaver closes the Find and Replace dialog and opens the Search report panel, which lists all the changes made.

7 Right-click the Search report tab and select Close Tab Group from the context menu.

Another method for targeting text and code is to select it *before* activating the command. This method can be used in either Design or Code view.

8 In Design view, locate and select the first occurrence of the text *Burkeline Mountains Resort* in the Location column of the Events table. Choose Edit > Find and Replace.

The Find and Replace dialog appears. The selected text is automatically entered into the Find field by Dreamweaver. This technique is even more powerful when used in Code view.

9 Close the Find and Replace dialog. Switch to Code view.

10 With the cursor still inserted in the *Burkeline Mountains Resort* text, click the `<tr>` tag selector at the bottom of the document window.

11 Choose Edit > Find and Replace. The Find and Replace dialog appears.

Observe the Find field. The selected code is automatically entered into the Find field in its entirety by Dreamweaver, including the line breaks and other whitespace. The reason this is so amazing is that there's no way to enter this type of markup in the dialog manually.

12 Select the code in the Find field. Press Delete to remove it. Type `<tr>` and press Enter/Return to insert a line break. Observe what happens.

Pressing Enter/Return did not insert a line break; instead, it activated the Find command, which finds the first occurrence of the `<tr>` element. In fact, you can't manually insert any type of line break within the dialog.

You probably don't think this is much of a problem, since you've already seen that Dreamweaver inserts text or code when it's selected first. Unfortunately, the method used in steps 8 and 10 don't work with large amounts of text or code.

13 Close the Find and Replace dialog box. Click the `<table>` tag selector.

The entire markup for the table is selected.

14 Choose Edit > Find and Replace. Observe the Find field.

This time, Dreamweaver didn't transfer the selected code into the Find field. To get larger amounts of text or code into the Find field, and to enter large amounts of replacement text and code, you need to use copy and paste.

15 Close the Find and Replace dialog. Select the table again, if necessary. Right-click the selected code and choose Copy from the context menu.

16 Press Ctrl+F/Cmd+F to activate the Find and Replace command. Right-click the Find field, and choose Paste from the context menu.

The entire `<table>` selection is pasted into the Find field.

17 Insert the cursor into the Replace field, and press Ctrl+V/Cmd+V.

The entire selection is pasted into the Replace field. Obviously, the two fields contain identical markup, but it illustrates how easy it would be to change or replace large amounts of code.

18 Close the Find and Replace dialog. Save all files.

In this lesson, you created four new pages and learned how to import text from multiple sources. You formatted text as headings and lists and then styled it using CSS. You inserted and formatted two tables, added captions to each one, and styled them to make them responsive. And you reviewed and corrected text using Dreamweaver's spellcheck and Find and Replace tools.

Superpowerfindelicious!

Note the options in the Find In and Search menus. The power and flexibility of Dreamweaver shines brightest here. The Find and Replace command can search in selected text, in the current document, in all open documents, in a specific folder, in selected files of the site, or the entire current local site. But as if those options weren't enough, Dreamweaver also allows you to target the search to the source code, text, advanced text, or even a specific tag.

Optional self-paced exercise

At the end of the lesson, the four pages created are only partially completed. Before proceeding to the next lesson, go ahead and finish each page using the resources in the files **quotes09.txt** and **sidebar2_09.txt**, located in the resources folder. If you have any questions about how the content should be created or formatted, check out the finished files with the same names within the finished_files folder for lesson09. Be sure to save all your changes when you are finished.

Review questions

1 How do you format text to be an HTML heading?

2 Explain how to turn paragraph text into an ordered list and then an unordered list.

3 Describe two methods for inserting HTML tables into a webpage.

4 What element controls the width of a table column?

5 What items will not be found by Dreamweaver's spellcheck command?

6 Describe three ways to insert content in the Find field.

Review answers

1   Use the Format field menu in the Property inspector to apply HTML heading formatting, or press Ctrl+1/Cmd+1, Ctrl+2/Cmd+2, Ctrl+3/Cmd+3, and so on.

2   Highlight the text with the cursor and click the Ordered List button in the Property inspector. Then click the Unordered List button to change the numbered list to bullets.

3   You can copy and paste a table from another HTML file or a compatible program. Or you can insert a table by importing the data from a delimited file.

4   The width of a table column is controlled by the widest <th> or <td> element that creates the individual table cell within the specific column.

5   The spellcheck command finds only words *spelled* incorrectly, not the ones *used* incorrectly.

6   You can type text into the Find field; you can select text before you open the dialog and then allow Dreamweaver to insert the selected text; or you can copy the text or code and then paste it into the field.

10

WORKING WITH IMAGES

Lesson overview

In this lesson, you'll learn how to work with images to include them
in your webpages in the following ways:

- Inserting an image

- Using Photoshop Smart Objects

- Copying and pasting an image from Photoshop and Fireworks

 This lesson will take about 1 hour and 30 minutes to complete. If you have
not already done so, download the project files for this lesson from the
Lesson & Update Files tab on your Account page at www.peachpit.com,
store them on your computer in a convenient location, and define a site
based on the lesson10 folder as described in the "Getting Started" section
of this book. Your Account page is also where you'll find any updates
to the lessons or to the lesson files. Look on the Lesson & Update Files
tab to access the most current content.

Dreamweaver provides many ways to insert and adjust graphics, both within the program and in tandem with other Creative Suite tools, such as Adobe Fireworks and Adobe Photoshop.

Web image basics

The web is not so much a place as it is an experience. And essential to that experience are the images and graphics—both still and animated—that populate most websites. In the computer world, graphics fall into two main categories: vector and raster.

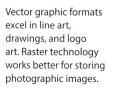

Vector graphic formats excel in line art, drawings, and logo art. Raster technology works better for storing photographic images.

Vector   Raster

Vector graphics

Vector graphics are created by math. They act like discrete objects, which you can reposition and resize as many times as you want without affecting or diminishing their output quality. The best application of vector art is wherever geometric shapes and text are used to create artistic effects. For example, most company logos are built from vector shapes.

Vector graphics are typically stored in the AI, EPS, PICT, or WMF file formats. Unfortunately, most web browsers don't support these formats. The vector format that is supported is SVG (scalable vector graphic). The simplest way to get started with SVG is to create a graphic in your favorite vector-drawing program—such as Adobe Illustrator or CorelDRAW—and then export it to this format. If you are a good programmer, you may want to try creating SVG graphics using XML (Extensible Markup Language). To find out more about creating SVG graphics, check out www.w3schools.com/svg.

Raster graphics

Although SVG has definite advantages, web designers primarily use raster-based images in their web designs. Raster images are built from *pixels,* which stands for *picture elements*. Pixels have three basic characteristics:

- They are perfectly square in shape.
- They are all the same size.
- They display only one color at a time.

Raster-based images are composed of thousands, even millions, of pixels arranged in rows and columns, in patterns that create the illusion of an actual photo, painting, or drawing. It's an illusion, because there is no real photo on the screen, just a bunch of pixels that fool your eyes into seeing an image. And, as the quality of the image increases, the more realistic the illusion becomes. Raster image quality is based on three factors: resolution, size, and color.

The inset image shows an enlargement of the flowers, revealing the pixels that compose the image itself.

Resolution

Resolution is the most well known of the factors affecting raster image quality. It is the expression of image quality, measured in the number of pixels that fit in one inch (ppi). The more pixels you can fit in one inch, the more detail you can depict in the image. But better quality comes at a price. An unfortunate byproduct of higher resolution is larger file size. That's because each pixel must be stored as bytes of information within the image file—information that has real overhead in computer terms. More pixels means more information, which means larger files.

Note: Printers and printing presses use round "dots" to create photographic images. Quality on a printer is measured in dots per inch, or dpi. The process of converting the square pixels used in your computer into the round dots used on the printer is called screening.

72 ppi   300 ppi

Resolution has a dramatic effect on image output. The web image on the left looks fine in the browser but doesn't have enough quality for printing.

Luckily, web images have to appear and look their best only on computer screens, which are based mostly on a resolution of 72 ppi. This is low compared to other applications or output—like printing—where 300 dpi is considered the lowest acceptable quality. The lower resolution of the computer screen is an important factor in keeping most web image files down to a reasonable size for downloading from the Internet.

Size

Size refers to the vertical and horizontal dimensions of the image. As image size increases, more pixels are required to create it, and therefore the file becomes larger. Since graphics take more time to download than HTML code, many designers in recent years have replaced graphical components with CSS formatting to speed up the web experience for their visitors. But if you need or want to use images, one method to ensure snappy downloads is to keep image size small. Even today, with the proliferation of high-speed Internet service, you won't find too many websites that depend on full-page graphics.

Although these two images share the identical resolution and color depth, you can see how image dimensions can affect file size

500KB

1.6MB

Color

Color refers to the color space, or *palette*, that describes each image. Most computer screens display only a fraction of the colors that the human eye can see. And different computers and applications display varying levels of color, expressed by the term *bit depth*. Monochrome, or 1-bit color, is the smallest color space, displaying only black and white, with no shades of gray. Monochrome is used mostly for line-art illustrations, for blueprints, and to reproduce handwriting.

The 4-bit color space describes up to 16 colors. Additional colors can be simulated by a process known as *dithering*, where the available colors are interspersed and juxtaposed to create an illusion of more colors. This color space was created for the first color computer systems and game consoles. Because of its limitations, this palette is seldom used today.

The 8-bit palette offers up to 256 colors or 256 shades of gray. This is the basic color system of all computers, mobile phones, game systems, and handheld devices. This color space also includes what is known as the *web-safe* color palette. Web-safe refers to a subset of 8-bit colors that are supported on both Mac and Windows computers. Most computers, game consoles, handheld devices, and even phones now support higher color palettes, so 8-bit is not as important any more. Unless you need to support non-computer devices, you can probably disregard the web-safe palette altogether.

Today, a few older cellphones and handheld games support the 16-bit color space. This palette is named *high color* and sports a grand total of 65,000 colors. Although this sounds like a lot, 16-bit color is not considered good enough for most graphic design purposes or professional printing.

The highest color space is 24-bit color, which is named *true color*. This system generates up to 16.7 million colors. It is the gold standard for graphic design and professional printing. Several years ago, a new color space was added to the mix: 32-bit color. It doesn't offer any additional colors, but it provides an additional 8 bits of data for an attribute called *alpha transparency*.

Alpha transparency enables you to designate parts of an image or graphic as fully or even partially transparent. This trick allows you to create graphics that seem to have rounded corners or curves, and can even eliminate the white bounding box typical of raster graphics.

24-bit color   8-bit color   4-bit color

Here you can see a dramatic comparison of three color spaces and what the total number of available colors means to image quality.

As with size and resolution, color depth can dramatically affect image file size. With all other aspects being equal, an 8-bit image is over seven times larger than a monochrome image. And the 24-bit version is over three times larger than the 8-bit image. The key to effective use of images on a website is finding the balance of resolution, size, and color to achieve the desired optimal quality.

Raster image file formats

Raster images can be stored in a multitude of file formats, but web designers have to be concerned with only three: GIF, JPEG, and PNG. These three formats are optimized for use on the Internet and compatible with most browsers. However, they are not equal in capability.

GIF

GIF (graphic interchange format) was one of the first raster image file formats designed specifically for the web. It has changed only a little in the last 20 years. GIF supports a maximum of 256 colors (8-bit palette) and 72 ppi, so it's used mainly for web interfaces—buttons and graphical borders and such. But it does have two interesting features that keep it pertinent for today's web designers: index transparency and support for simple animation.

JPEG

JPEG, also written JPG, is named for the Joint Photographic Experts Group that created the image standard back in 1992 as a direct reaction to the limitations of the GIF file format. JPEG is a powerful format that supports unlimited resolution, image dimensions, and color depth. Because of this, most digital cameras use JPEG as their default file type for image storage. It's also the reason most designers use JPEG on their websites for images that must be displayed in high quality.

This may sound odd to you, since "high quality" (as described earlier) usually means large file size. Large files take longer to download to your browser. So why is this format so popular on the web? The JPEG format's claim to fame comes from its patented user-selectable image compression algorithm, which can reduce file size as much as 95 percent. JPEG images are compressed each time they are saved and then decompressed as they are opened and displayed.

Unfortunately, all this compression has a downside. Too much compression damages image quality. This type of compression is called *lossy*, because it loses quality. In fact, the loss in quality is great enough that it can potentially render the image totally useless. Each time designers save a JPEG image, they face a trade-off between image quality and file size.

Here you see the effects of different amounts of compression on the file size and quality of an image.

Low Quality
High compression 130K

Medium Quality
Medium compression 150K

High Quality
Low compression 260K

PNG

PNG (portable network graphics) was developed in 1995 because of a looming patent dispute involving the GIF format. At the time, it looked as if designers and developers would have to pay a royalty for using the .gif file extension. Although that issue blew over, PNG has found many adherents and a home on the Internet because of its capabilities.

PNG combines many of the features of GIF and JPEG and adds a few of its own. For example, it offers support for unlimited resolution, 32-bit color, and full alpha and index transparency. It also provides lossless compression, which means you can save an image in PNG format and not worry about losing any quality when you save the file.

The only downside to PNG is that its most important feature—alpha transparency—is not fully supported in older browsers. As these browsers are retired year after year, this issue is not much of a concern to most web designers.

But as with everything on the web, your own needs may vary from the general trend. Before using any specific technology, it's always a good idea to check your site analytics and confirm which browsers your visitors are actually using.

Previewing the completed file

To get a sense of the files you will work on in this lesson, let's preview the completed pages in the browser.

1 Launch Adobe Dreamweaver CC (2015.1 release) or later.

2 If necessary, select lesson10 from Site drop-down menu in the Files panel.

3 Open **contactus_finished.html** from the lesson10/finished folder. Preview the page in your favorite browser.

   The page includes several images, as well as a Photoshop Smart Object.

4 Drag the right edge of the browser to resize the window. Observe how the layout and images adapt to the changing screen size.

The images align alternately to the left and the right down the page and are small enough to fit any size screen, but they move within the text as the screen narrows. When the browser window gets to the size of a smartphone, the images move to a separate line and center above the text.

> ● **Note:** If you have not already downloaded the project files for this lesson to your computer from your Account page, make sure to do so now. See "Getting Started" at the beginning of the book.

5 Open **news_finished.html** from the lesson10/finished folder. Preview the page in your favorite browser.

6 Drag the right edge of the browser to resize the window. Observe how the layout and images adapt.

The first image stretches across the main content area. As the screen gets smaller, the image scales along with it to match the width of the area. As the screen gets wider, the picture fills the space again.

7 Close your browser and return to Dreamweaver.

The sample files display images of varying sizes and composition. Some images are small enough to fit any size screen; others scale responsively as the size of the page changes. In the following exercises, you will insert these images into these pages using a variety of techniques and format them to work on any screen.

Inserting an image

● **Note:** When working with images in Dreamweaver, you should be sure that your site's default images folder is set up according to the directions in the "Getting Started" section at the beginning of the book.

Images are key components of any webpage, both for developing visual interest and for telling stories. Dreamweaver provides numerous ways to populate your pages with images, using built-in commands and even using copy and paste from other Adobe apps. Let's start with some of the tools built into Dreamweaver itself, such as the Assets panel.

1 In the Files panel, open **contact_us.html** in Live view.

2 Click the first paragraph under the heading *Association Management.*

The HUD appears focused on the p element.

3 Choose Window > Assets to display the Assets panel, if necessary. Click the Images category icon ▣ to display a list of all images stored within the site.

4 Locate and select **elaine.jpg** in the list.

A preview of **elaine.jpg** appears in the Assets panel. The panel lists the image's name, dimensions in pixels, size in kilo- or megabytes, and file type, as well as its full directory path.

5 Note the dimensions of the image: 150 pixels by 150 pixels.

6 At the bottom of the panel, click the Insert button.

Note: The Images window shows all images stored anywhere in the defined site—even ones outside the site's default images folder—so you may see listings for images stored in the lesson subfolders too.

Type	▲	Name	Dimensions	Size	Format	Full Path
📄		biking.jpg	180x145	61KB	jpg	/images/bik...
📄		city.jpg	200x335	80KB	jpg	/images/city...
📄		elaine.jpg	150x150	51KB	jpg	/images/elai...
📄		eric.png	150x150	51KB	png	/images/eric...
📄		farmersmarket.png	450x400	383KB	png	/images/far...
📄		farmersmarket_finished.png	350x365	291KB	png	/images/far...

The position assist dialog appears.

7 Click Nest.

The image appears at the beginning of the paragraph. The HUD now focuses on the `img` element. You can use the HUD to add alt text to the image.

8 Click the Edit HTML Attribute icon 📋.

The HTML Attribute dialog appears.

9 In the Alt text field in the Element HUD, enter **Elaine, Meridien GreenStart President and CEO** as the alternate text.

10 Choose File > Save.

You inserted Elaine's picture in the text, but it doesn't look very nice at its current position. In the next exercise, you will adjust the image position using a CSS class.

Adjusting image positions with CSS classes

The `<img>` element is an inline element by default. That's why you can insert images into paragraphs and other elements. When the image is taller than the font size, the image will increase the vertical space for the line in which it appears. In the past, you could adjust its position using either HTML attributes or CSS, but many of the HTML-based attributes have been deprecated from the language as well as from Dreamweaver. Now you must rely completely on CSS-based techniques.

If you want all the images to align in a certain fashion, you can create a custom rule for the `<img>` tag to apply specific styling. In this instance, the employee photos will alternate from right to left going down the page and have the text wrap around the image to use the space more effectively. To do this, you'll create a custom class to provide options for left and right alignment. You can use the HUD to create and apply the new class all at once.

1 If necessary, open **contact_us.html** in Live view.

2 Click the image for Elaine in the first paragraph of the *Association Management* section. The HUD appears focused on the img element.

3 Click the Add Class/ID icon ⊞.

4 Type `.flt_rgt` in the text field.

The new class name is short for "float right," hinting at what CSS command you're going to use to style the images.

5 Press Enter/Return.

The CSS Source HUD appears.

6 If necessary, select **green_styles.css** from the source drop-down menu. Leave the media query drop-down menu empty.

7 Press Enter/Return to complete the class.
In the CSS Designer, select **green_styles.css** > GLOBAL > `.flt_rgt`.

The new rule appears at the bottom of the list of selectors. No properties are defined yet.

8 Create the following properties:

```
float: right
margin-left: 10px
```

As you learned in Lesson 3, applying a float to the image removes it from the normal flow of the HTML elements, although it still maintains its width and height. The image moves to the right side of the `section` element; the text wraps around on the left. The margin setting keeps the text from touching the edge of the image itself. You will create a similar rule to align images to the left in the next exercise.

Working with the Insert panel

The Insert panel duplicates key menu commands and makes inserting images and other code elements both quick and easy.

1   In Live view, click the first paragraph under the heading *Education and Events.*

2   Choose Window > Insert to display the Insert panel, if necessary.

3   In the Insert panel, choose the HTML category.

4   Click Image.

The position assist HUD appears.

5   Click Nest.

The Select Image Source dialog appears.

6   Select **sarah.jpg** from the site images folder. Click OK/Open.

7 In the Property inspector, enter **Sarah, GreenStart Events Coordinator** in the Alt text field.

8 Click the Add Class/ID icon ⊞.

Type `.flt_lft` and press Enter/Return.

The name is short for "float left."

9 Use the CSS Source HUD to add the class to **green_styles.css**. No media query should be selected.

10 In the CSS Designer, create the following properties in the new rule:

```
float: left
margin-right: 10px
```

The image drops down into the paragraph on the left side, with the text wrapping to its right.

11 Save the file.

Another way to insert images in your webpage is by using the Insert menu.

Using the Insert menu

The Insert menu duplicates all the commands you'll find in the Insert panel. Some users find the menu faster and easier to use. Others prefer the ready nature of the panel, which allows you to focus on one element and quickly insert multiple copies of it at once. Feel free to alternate between the two methods as desired or even create your own custom keyboard shortcuts. In this exercise, you will use the Insert menu to add images.

1 Click the first paragraph under the heading *Transportation Analysis*.

2 Choose Insert > Image, or press Ctrl+Alt+I/Cmd+Option+I.

  The position assist dialog appears.

3 Click Nest.

  The Select Image Source dialog appears.

4 Navigate to the images folder in lesson10.
  Select the file **eric.png** and click Open.

  The **eric.png** image appears in the Dreamweaver layout. Once the classes have
  been created and defined, you simply have to add the appropriate class using
  the HUD.

5 Click the Add Class/ID icon and type: `.flt_rgt`

  As you type, the class will appear in the hinting menu. You can click the name
  or use the arrow keys to highlight it, and you can press Enter/Return to select
  it. As soon as the class is selected, the image floats to the right side of the
  paragraph.

6 In the Property inspector, type **Eric, Transportation Research Coordinator**
  in the Alt text field.

7 Save all files.

So far, you have inserted web-compatible image formats. But Dreamweaver is not
limited to the file types GIF, JPEG, and PNG; it can work with other file types too.
In the next exercise, you will learn how to insert a Photoshop document (PSD) into
a webpage.

Inserting non-web file types

Although most browsers will display only the web-compliant image formats described earlier, Dreamweaver also allows you to use other formats; the program will then automatically convert the file to a compatible format on the fly.

1 Click the first paragraph under the heading *Research and Development*.

2 Choose Insert > Image.
   Nest the image in the first paragraph.
   Navigate to the lesson10/resources folder.
   Select **lin.psd**.

3 Click OK/Open to insert the image.

   The image appears in the layout, and the Image Optimization dialog opens; it acts as an intermediary that allows you to specify how and to what format the image will be converted.

4 Observe the options in the Preset and Format menus.

   The presets allow you to select predetermined options that have a proven track record for web-based images. The Format menu allows you to specify your own custom settings from among five options: GIF, JPEG, PNG 8, PNG 24, and PNG 32.

5 Choose JPEG High For Maximum Compatibility from the Presets menu. Note the Quality setting.

Note: The Image Optimization dialog displays the final file size of the image, indicating how much compression is being applied.

This Quality setting produces a high-quality image with a moderate amount of compression. If you lower the Quality setting, you automatically increase the compression level and reduce the file size; increase the Quality setting for the opposite effect. The secret to effective design is to select a good balance between quality and compression. The default setting for the JPEG High preset is 80, which is sufficient for your purposes.

6 Click OK to convert the image.

Note: When an image has to be converted this way, Dreamweaver usually saves the converted image into the site's default images folder. This is not the case when the images inserted are web-compatible. So before you insert an image, you should be aware of its current location in the site and move it to the proper folder first, if necessary.

The Save Web Image dialog appears with the name lin entered in the Save As field. Dreamweaver will add the .jpg extension to the file automatically. Be sure to save the file to the default site images folder. If Dreamweaver does not automatically point to this folder, navigate to it before saving the file.

7 Click Save.

The Save Web Image dialog closes. The image in the layout is now linked to the JPEG file saved in the default images folder.

8 Enter **Lin, Research and Development Coordinator** in the Alt text field.

▶**Tip:** The image HUD and the Property inspector can be used interchangeably to enter alt text.

The image appears in Dreamweaver at the cursor position. The image has been resampled to 72 ppi but still appears at its original dimensions, so it's larger than the other images in the layout. You can resize the image in the Property inspector.

9 If necessary, click the Toggle Size Constrain icon 🔒 to display the closed lock. Change the Width value to **150px** and press Enter/Return.

● **Note:** Whenever you change HTML or CSS properties, you may need to press Enter/Return to complete the modification.

When the lock icon appears closed, the relationship between width and height is constrained, and the two change proportionally to each other: Change one and they both change. The change to the image size is only temporary at the moment, as indicated by the Reset ⊘ and Commit ✔ icons. In other words, the HTML attributes specify the size of the image as 150 pixels by 150 pixels, but the JPEG file holds an image that's still 300 pixels by 300 pixels—four times as many pixels as it needs to have.

10 Click the Commit icon ✔.

The image is now resized to 150 by 150 pixels permanently.

11 Apply the `flt_lft` class to this image using the HUD. Save all files.

In Live view, the image now appears like the others in the layout; however, this image has a difference. But you can't see it in Live view.

12 Switch to Design view.

In Design view you can now see an icon in the upper-left corner of the image that identifies this image as a Photoshop Smart Object.

Right size, wrong size

Until the latest mobile devices appeared on the scene, deciding what size and resolution to use for web images was pretty simple. You picked a specific width and height, and saved the image at 72 pixels per inch. That's all you needed to do.

But today, web designers want their sites to work well for all visitors, no matter what type or size device they want to use. So the days of picking one size and one resolution may be gone forever. But what's the answer? At the moment, there isn't one perfect solution.

One trend simply inserts an image that is larger or higher resolution, and resizes it using CSS. This allows the image to display more clearly on high-resolution screens, like Apple's Retina display. The downside is that lower-resolution devices are stuck downloading an image that's larger than they need. This not only slows the loading of the page for no reason, but it can incur higher data charges for smartphone users.

Another idea is to provide multiple images optimized for different devices and resolutions and to use JavaScript to load the proper image as needed. But many users object to using scripts for such basic resources as images. Others want a standardized solution.

So W3C is working on a technique that uses a new element named `<picture>`, which will not require JavaScript at all. Using this new element you would select several images and declare how they should be used and then the browser would load the appropriate image. Unfortunately, this element is so new that Dreamweaver doesn't support it yet, and few browsers even know what it is.

Implementing a responsive workflow for images is outside the scope of this course. For the purposes of these lessons, you will simply learn how to adapt standard web images to the current responsive template using CSS and media queries.

Working with Photoshop Smart Objects (optional)

● **Note:** Dreamweaver and Photoshop can work only with the existing quality of an image. If your initial image quality is unacceptable you may not be able to fix it in Photoshop. You will have to re-create the image or pick another.

Unlike other images, Smart Objects maintain a connection to their original Photoshop (PSD) file. If the PSD file is altered in any manner and then saved, Dreamweaver identifies those changes and provides the means to update the web image used in the layout. The following exercise can be completed only if you have Photoshop installed on your computer along with Dreamweaver.

1 If necessary, open **contact_us.html** in Design view.
   Scroll down to the **lin.jpg** image in the *Research and Development* section. Observe the icon in the upper-left corner of the image.

The icon indicates that the image is a Smart Object. The icon appears only within Dreamweaver itself; visitors see the normal image in the browser as you saw originally in Live view. If you want to edit or optimize the image, you can simply right-click the image and choose the appropriate option from the context menu.

To make substantive changes to the image, you will have to open it in Photoshop. (If you don't have Photoshop installed, copy lesson10/resources/smartobject/**lin.psd** into the lesson10/resources folder to replace the original image, and then skip to step 6.) In this exercise, you will edit the image background using Photoshop.

2   Right-click the **lin.jpg** image.

● **Note:** The exact name of the apps appearing in the menu may differ depending on what version of Photoshop you have installed and your operating system. If Photoshop is not installed at all, you may see no program listed.

Choose Edit Original With > Adobe Photoshop CC 2015 from the context menu.

Photoshop CC 2015 launches—if it is installed on your computer—and loads the file.

3   In Photoshop, choose Window > Layers to display the Layers panel, if necessary. Observe the names and states of any existing layers.

The image has two layers: Lin and New Background. New Background is turned off.

4 Click the eye icon 👁 for the New Background layer to display its contents.

The background of the image changes to show a scene from a park.

5 Save the Photoshop file.

6 Switch back to Dreamweaver.
Position the cursor over the Smart Object icon.

A tool tip appears indicating that the original image has been changed. You don't have to update the image at this time, and you can leave the out-of-date image in the layout for as long as you want. Dreamweaver will continue to monitor its status as long as it's in the layout. But for this exercise, let's update the image.

7 Right-click the image and choose Update From Original from the context menu.

This Smart Object, and any other instances of it, changes to reflect the new background. You can check the status of the Smart Object by positioning the pointer over the image. A tool tip will appear showing that the image is synced. You can also insert the same original PSD image multiple times in the site using different dimensions and image settings under different filenames. All the Smart Objects will stay connected to the PSD and will allow you to update them as the PSD changes.

8 Save the file.

As you can see, Smart Objects have several advantages over a typical image work-flow. For frequently changed or updated images, using a Smart Object can simplify updates to the website in the future.

Copying and pasting images from Photoshop (optional)

As you build your website, you will need to edit and optimize many images before you use them in your site. Adobe Photoshop is an excellent program for performing these tasks. A common workflow is to make the needed changes to the images and then manually export the optimized GIF, JPEG, or PNG files to the default images folder in your website. But sometimes simply copying images and pasting them directly into your layout is faster and easier.

1 Launch Adobe Photoshop, if necessary.
Open **matthew.tif** from the lesson10/resources folder.
Observe the Layers panel.

The image has only one layer. In Photoshop, by default you can copy only one layer at a time to paste into Dreamweaver. To copy multiple layers, you have to merge or flatten the image first, or you have to use the command Edit > Copy Merged to copy images with multiple active layers.

2 Choose Select > All, or press Ctrl+A/Cmd+A, to select the entire image.

3 Select Edit > Copy, or press Ctrl+C/Cmd+C, to copy the image.

4 Switch to Dreamweaver. Scroll down to the Information Systems section in **contact_us.html**. Insert the cursor at the beginning of the first paragraph in this section and before the name *Matthew*.

5 Press Ctrl+V/Cmd+V to paste the image from the clipboard.

The image appears in the layout, and the Image Optimization dialog opens.

6 Choose the preset PNG24 for Photos (Sharp Details), and choose PNG 24 from the Format menu. Click OK.

The Save Image dialog appears.

7 Name the image **matthew.png** and select the default site images folder, if necessary. Click Save.

8 If necessary, select the image for Matthew and enter **Matthew, Information Systems Manager** in the Alt text field in the Property inspector.

The **matthew.png** image appears in the layout. As in the earlier exercise, the PNG image is larger than the other images.

9 In the Property inspector, change the image dimensions to **150px** by **150px**. Click the Commit icon ✔ to apply the change. Click OK in the dialog that appears acknowledging that the change is permanent.

10 Apply the `flt_rgt` class to **matthew.png** using the Class menu in the Properties inspector.

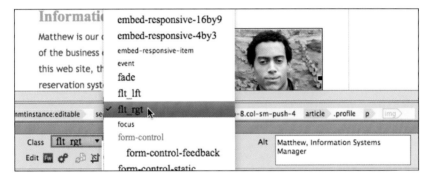

● **Note:** Raster images can be scaled down in size without losing quality, but the opposite is not true. Unless a graphic has a resolution higher than 72 ppi, scaling it larger without noticeable degradation may not be possible.

The image appears in the layout at the same size as the other images and aligned to the right. Although this image came from Photoshop, it's not "smart" like a Photoshop Smart Object and can't be updated automatically. It does, however, give you an easy way to load the image into Photoshop or another image editor to perform any modifications.

▶ **Tip:** If no image-editor program is displayed, you may need to browse for a compatible editor. The executable program file is usually stored in the Program Files folder in Windows and in the Applications folder on a Mac.

11 In the layout, right-click **matthew.png**.
Choose Edit With > Photoshop CC 2015 from the context menu.

The program launches and displays the PNG file from the site images folder. If you make changes to this image, you merely have to save the file to update the image in Dreamweaver.

● **Note:** The exact name displayed in the menu may differ depending on the program version or operating system installed.

12 In Photoshop, press Ctrl+L/Cmd+L to open the Levels dialog.
Adjust the brightness and contrast.
Save and close the image.

● **Note:** This exercise is geared specifically to Photoshop, but the changes can be made in most image editors.

● **Note:** Although Dreamweaver automatically reloads any modified file, most browsers won't. You will have to refresh the browser display before you see any changes.

13 Switch back to Dreamweaver. Scroll down to view the **matthew.png** image in the Information Systems section.

The image should be updated in the layout automatically. Since you saved the changes under the original filename, no other action is necessary. This method saves you several steps and avoids any potential typing errors.

14 Save all the files.

Today, the modern web designer has to contend with a multitude of visitors using different browsers and devices. Depending on the size of the images and how they are inserted, you may need to use several different strategies to get them to work effectively in your page design.

For example, the images used on the *Contact Us* page are small enough that they should be usable all the way down to the size needed on a smartphone, but they'll need some work to make them adapt better to smaller screens.

Adapting images to smaller screens

To get the current images to make the most of the available space as the pages respond to the size of the screen, you can create a few specific rules in the appropriate media queries. The first step is to observe how images adapt to the current design, and then you'll create an effective strategy for reformatting them.

1 Open **contact_us.html**.
Preview the page in the default browser.

2 Resize the width of the browser window as necessary to engage each of the existing media queries. Observe how the images adapt to the different designs.

The images are small enough that they adapt well to desktop and tablet screen sizes. On the smallest screens, the text is starting to get crowded, wrapping around the edges of the images. One fix would be to remove the float and center the images.

3 In Dreamweaver, switch to Live view if necessary and click your custom media query (max-width: 426px).

4 In CSS Designer, choose **green_styles.css** > (max-width:426px).
Create a new rule: .flt_lft, .flt_rgt

5 Add the following properties to the new rule:

```
max-width: 95%
display: block
margin: 0px auto
float: none
```

▶ **Tip:** For this new rule to work, it must appear within the media query markup and after the rules it is designed to reset. If your layout does not look like the screen shot, check the structure and order of your CSS rules.

These new settings put the images on their own line and center them. The `max-width` property makes sure that larger images automatically scale down with the screen. In the next exercise, you will insert a much larger image that will have to use a different responsive strategy.

Inserting images by drag and drop

Most of the programs in the Creative Suite offer drag-and-drop capabilities. Dreamweaver is no exception.

1 Open **news.html** from the site root folder in Live view.

2 Choose Window > Assets to display the Assets panel, if necessary.

The Assets panel is no longer opened by default in the Dreamweaver workspace. You can leave it as a floating dialog or dock it to keep it out of the way.

3 Drag the Assets panel to dock it beside the Files tab, if necessary.

4 In the Assets panel, click the Images icon ⊡.

5 Drag **skyline.png** from the panel, and position the cursor between the first paragraph and the heading *Green Buildings earn more Green*.

▶ **Tip:** If you don't see specific image files listed in the Assets panel, click the Refresh icon ↻ to reload site images.

If you position the cursor correctly, you will see a green line between the heading and the paragraph, indicating where the image will be inserted.

Unlike the images used in the previous exercises, **skyline.png** was inserted between the <h2> and the <p> elements. The image is also too large for the column. Part of it is obscured behind Sidebar 2. Luckily, Dreamweaver has a new built-in way to deal with just this situation.

6   Click the Edit HTML Attributes icon ⊟ on the new image.

The HTML Attributes HUD appears.

7   Select the Make Image Responsive checkbox.

The image now conforms to the width of the column. But what happens when the screen gets smaller? You can check the behavior in Live view, or you can preview the page in a browser window.

8   Enter **Green buildings are top earners** in the Property inspector's Alt text field.

9   Save all files.

10   Drag the Scrubber to the left, and observe how the image adapts to the changes to the layout.

The image scales automatically as the document window changes sizes. The option in the HTML Attributes HUD applies the Bootstrap .img-responsive class to the image. This class forces the image to fit within the existing element and scale as needed.

Optimizing images with the Property inspector

Optimized web images try to balance image dimensions and quality against file size. Sometimes you may need to optimize graphics that have already been placed on the page. Dreamweaver has built-in features that can help you achieve the smallest possible file size while preserving image quality. In this exercise, you'll use tools in Dreamweaver to scale, optimize, and crop an image for the web.

1 If necessary, open **news.html** in Design view or switch to it.

2 Insert the cursor at the beginning of the *Shopping green saves energy* heading. Choose Insert > Image.
Insert **farmersmarket.png** from the site images folder.

3 Enter **Buy local to save energy** in the Alt text field.

4 Apply the flt_rgt class to the image.

The image is too large. There is barely any room for the image in the column. It could really use some cropping. To save time, you can use tools in Dreamweaver to fix the image composition.

5 If necessary, choose Window > Properties to display the Property inspector.

Whenever an image is selected, image-editing options appear to the right of the image source field in the Property inspector. The buttons here allow you to edit the image in Photoshop or Fireworks or to adjust various settings in place. See the sidebar "Dreamweaver's graphic tools" at the end of the lesson for an explanation of each button.

There are two ways to reduce the dimensions of an image in Dreamweaver. The first method changes the size of the image temporarily by imposing user-defined dimensions.

6   Select **farmersmarket.png**. If necessary, click the Toggle Size Constrain icon 🔒 in the Property inspector to lock the image proportions.
Change the image width to **350 pixels** and press the Tab key.

▶ **Tip:** Dimensions may also be entered manually if you know the final proportions.

When the size constraint is locked, the height automatically conforms to the new width. Note that Dreamweaver indicates that the new size is not permanent by displaying the current specifications in bold and also by displaying the Reset ⊘ and Commit ✔ icons.

7   Click the Commit icon ✔.

A dialog appears that indicates the change will be permanent.

8   Click OK.

Dreamweaver can also crop images.

9   With the image still selected, click the Crop icon ⊠ in the Property inspector.

A dialog appears indicating that the action will permanently change the image.

10 Click OK.

Crop handles appear slightly inset from the edges of the image. We want to crop the width but not the height.

11 Drag the crop handles to set the image to a width of 300 pixels and a height of 312 pixels.

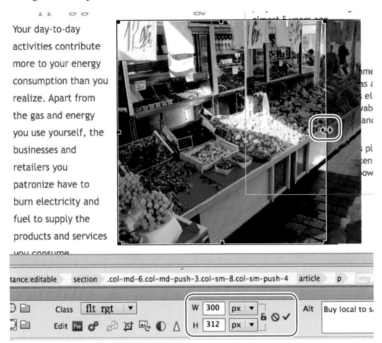

Your day-to-day activities contribute more to your energy consumption than you realize. Apart from the gas and energy you use yourself, the businesses and retailers you patronize have to burn electricity and fuel to supply the products and services you consume.

12 Press Enter/Return to apply the change.

13 Save all files.

Most designers will edit and resize images prior to bringing them into Dreamweaver, but it's nice to know that these tools are available for any last-minute changes or fast turnarounds.

In this lesson, you learned how to insert images and Smart Objects into a Dreamweaver page, copy and paste from Photoshop, and use the Property inspector to edit images.

There are numerous ways to create and edit images for the web. The methods examined in this lesson show but a few of them and are not meant to recommend or endorse one method over another. Feel free to use whatever methods and workflow you desire based on your own situation and expertise.

Dreamweaver's graphic tools

All Dreamweaver's graphic tools appear in the Property inspector when an image is selected in Design view. Here are the seven tools:

Edit—Opens the selected image in the defined external graphics editor if you have one installed. You can assign a graphics-editing program to any given file type in the File Types/Editors category of the Preferences dialog. The button's image changes according to the program chosen. For example, if Fireworks is the designated editor for the image type, a Fireworks icon **Fw** is shown; if Photoshop is the editor, you'll see a Photoshop icon **Ps**. If neither app is installed you will see a generic edit icon.

Edit Image Settings—Opens the Image Optimization dialog, allowing you to apply user-defined optimization specifications to the selected image.

Update from Original—Updates any placed Smart Object to match any changes to the original source file.

Crop—Permanently removes unwanted portions of an image. When the Crop tool is active, a bounding box with a series of control handles appears within the selected image. You can adjust the bounding box size by dragging the handles or by entering the final dimensions. When the box outlines the desired portion of the image, double-click the graphic to apply the cropping.

Resample—Permanently resizes an image. The Resample tool is active only when an image has been resized.

Brightness and Contrast—Offers user-selectable adjustments to an image's brightness and contrast; a dialog presents, for each value, sliders that can be adjusted independently. A live preview is available so that you can evaluate adjustments before committing to them.

Sharpen—Affects the enhancement of image details by raising or lowering the contrast of pixels on a scale from 0 to 10. As with the Brightness and Contrast tool, Sharpen offers a real-time preview.

You can undo most graphics operations by choosing Edit > Undo until the containing document is closed or you quit Dreamweaver.

Review questions

1 What are the three factors that determine raster image quality?

2 What file formats are specifically designed for use on the web?

3 Describe at least two methods for inserting an image into a webpage using Dreamweaver.

4 True or false: All graphics have to be optimized outside of Dreamweaver.

5 What is the advantage of using a Photoshop Smart Object over copying and pasting an image from Photoshop?

Review answers

1 Raster image quality is determined by resolution, image dimensions, and color depth.

2 The compatible image formats for the web are GIF, JPEG, PNG, and SVG.

3 One method to insert an image into a webpage using Dreamweaver is to use the Insert panel. Another method is to drag the graphic file into the layout from the Assets panel. Images can also be copied and pasted from Photoshop and Fireworks.

4 False. Images can be optimized even after they are inserted into Dreamweaver by using the Property inspector. Optimization can include rescaling, changing format, or fine-tuning format settings.

5 A Smart Object can be used multiple times in different places on a site, and each instance of the Smart Object can be assigned individual settings. All copies remain connected to the original image. If the original is updated, all the connected images are immediately updated as well. When you copy and paste all or part of a Photoshop file, however, you get a single image that can have only one set of values applied to it.

11

WORKING WITH NAVIGATION

Lesson overview

In this lesson, you'll apply several kinds of links to page elements by doing the following:

- Creating a text link to a page within the same site

- Creating a link to a page on another website

- Creating an email link

- Creating an image-based link

- Creating a link to a location within a page

This lesson will take about 1 hour and 45 minutes to complete. If you have not already done so, download the project files for this lesson from the Lesson & Update Files tab on your Account page at www.peachpit.com, and store them on your computer in a convenient location, as described in the "Getting Started" section of this book. Your Account page is also where you'll find any updates to the lessons or to the lesson files. Look on the Lesson & Update Files tab to access the most current content. Before you begin this lesson, define a new site based on the lesson11 folder using the method described in the "Getting Started" section at the beginning of the book.

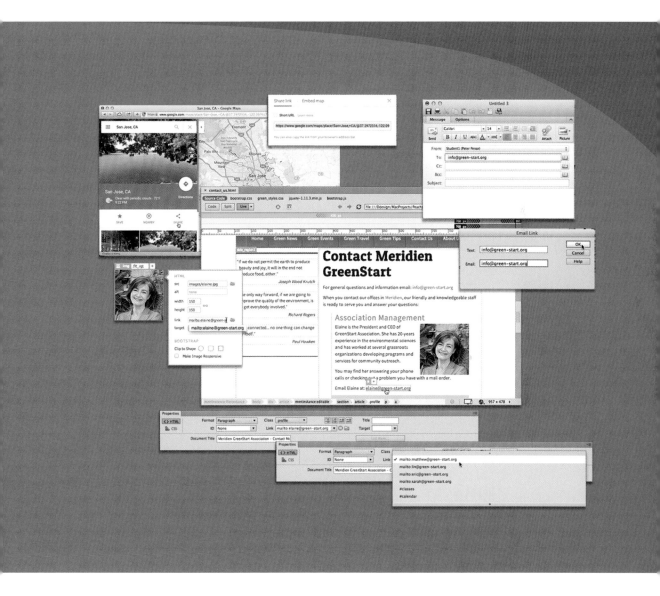

Dreamweaver can create and edit many types
of links—from text-based links to image-based
links—and does so with ease and flexibility.

Hyperlink basics

The World Wide Web, and the Internet in general, would be a far different place without the hyperlink. Without hyperlinks, HTML would simply be ML (markup language). The *hypertext* in the name refers to the functionality of the hyperlink. So what is a hyperlink?

A hyperlink, or *link*, is an HTML-based reference to a resource available on the Internet or within the computer hosting a web document. The resource can be anything that can be stored on and displayed by a computer, such as a webpage, an image, a movie, a sound file, a PDF—in fact, almost any type of computer file. A hyperlink creates an interactive behavior specified by HTML and CSS, or by the programming language you're using, and is enabled by a browser or other application.

An HTML hyperlink consists of the anchor \<a\> element and one or more attributes.

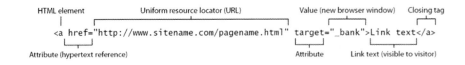

Internal and external hyperlinks

The simplest hyperlink—an internal hyperlink—takes the user to another part of the same document or to another document stored in the same folder or hard drive on the web server that hosts the site. An external hyperlink is designed to take the user to a document or resource outside your hard drive, website, or web host.

Internal and external hyperlinks may work differently, but they have one thing in common: They are enabled in HTML by the \<a\> *anchor* element. This element designates the address of the destination, or *target*, of the hyperlink, and can then specify how it functions using several attributes. You'll learn how to create and modify the \<a\> element in the exercises that follow.

Relative vs. absolute hyperlinks

A hyperlink address can be written in two ways. When you refer to a target by where it is stored in relation to the current document, it is known as a *relative* link. This is like telling someone that you live next door to the blue house. If she were driving down your street and saw the blue house, she would know where you live. But those directions don't really tell her how to get to your house or even to your neighborhood. A relative link frequently will consist of the resource name and perhaps the folder it is stored within, such as `logo.jpg` or `images/logo.jpg`.

Sometimes, you need to spell out precisely where a resource is located. In those instances, you need an *absolute* hyperlink. This is like telling someone you live at 123 Main Street in Meridien. This is typically how you refer to resources outside your website. An absolute link includes the entire uniform resource locator, or URL, of the target, and may even include a filename—such as http://forums.adobe.com/index.html—or just a folder within the site.

Both types of links have advantages and disadvantages. Relative hyperlinks are faster and easier to write, but they may not work if the document containing them is saved in a different folder or location in the website. Absolute links always work no matter where the containing document is saved, but they can fail if the targets are moved or renamed. A simple rule that most web designers follow is to use relative links for resources within a site and absolute links for resources outside the site. Of course, whether you follow this rule or not, it's important to test all links before deploying the page or site.

Previewing the completed file

To see the final version of the file you will work on in this lesson, let's preview the completed page in the browser.

1 Launch Adobe Dreamweaver CC (2015.1 release) or later.

2 If necessary, press F8 to open the Files panel. Select lesson11 from the site list.

3 In the Files panel, expand the lesson11 folder.

4 In the Files panel, right-click **aboutus_finished.html** in the lesson11/finished folder.
Choose Preview in Browser from the context menu.

Note: Before beginning this exercise, download the project files and define a new site based on the lesson11 folder using the instructions in the "Getting Started" section at the beginning of the book.

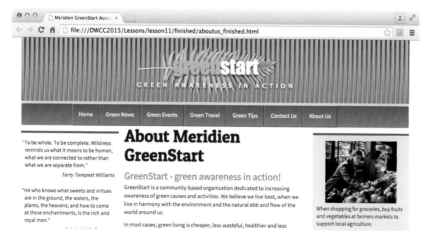

The **aboutus_finished.html** file appears in your default browser. This page features only internal links in the horizontal menu.

5 Position the cursor over the horizontal navigation menu. Hover over each button, and examine the behavior of the menu.

The menu is the same one created and formatted in Lesson 5, "Creating a Page Layout."

6 Click the *Green News* link.

The browser loads the finished *Green News* page.

7 Position the cursor over the *About Us* link. Observe the browser to see whether it's displaying the link's destination anywhere on the screen.

▶ **Tip:** Most browsers will display the destination of a hyperlink in the status bar at the bottom of the browser window. In some browsers, this status bar may be turned off by default.

Typically, the browser shows the link destination in the status bar.

8 Click the *Contact Us* link.

The browser loads the finished *Contact Us* page, replacing the *Green News* page. The new page includes internal, external, and email links.

9 Position the cursor over the *Meridien* link in the second paragraph of the main content area.
Observe the status bar.

The status bar displays the http://google.com/maps link.

10 Click the *Meridien* link.

A new browser window appears and loads Google Maps. The link is intended to show the visitor where the Meridien GreenStart Association offices are located.

If desired, you can even include address details or the company name in this link so that Google can load the exact map and directions.

Note that the browser opens a separate window or document tab when you click the link. This is a good behavior to use when directing visitors to resources outside your site. Since the link opens in a separate window, your own site is still open and ready to use. This practice is especially helpful if your visitors are unfamiliar with your site and may not know how to get back to it once they click away.

11 Close the Google Maps window.

The *Contact Us* page is still open in the browser. Note that each employee has a link applied to their email address.

12 Click an email link for one of the employees.

Note: Many web visitors don't use email programs installed on their computers. They use web-based services like AOL, Gmail, Hotmail, and so on. For these visitors, email links like the one you tested won't work. The best option is to create a web-hosted form on your site that sends the email to you via your own server.

The default mail application launches on your computer. If you have not set up this application to send and receive mail, the program will usually start a wizard to help you set up this functionality. If the email program is set up, a new message window, similar to the one pictured in the screen shot, appears with the email address of the employee automatically entered in the To field.

13 Close the new message window, and exit the email program.

14 Scroll down to the *Education and Events* section.
Click the *events* link.

The browser loads the *Green Events and Classes* page. The browser focuses on the table containing the list of upcoming events at the top of the page.

15 In the horizontal menu, click the *Contact Us* link.

The *Contact Us* page loads again.

16 Scroll down to the *Education and Events* section.
Click the *classes* link.

The browser loads the *Green Events and Classes* page again, but this time the browser focuses on the table containing the list of upcoming classes at the bottom of the page.

17 Click the *Return to top* link that appears above the class schedule. You may need to scroll up or down the page to see it.

The browser jumps back to the top of the page.

18 Close the browser and switch to Dreamweaver, if necessary.

You have tested a variety of different types of hyperlinks: internal, external, relative, and absolute. In the following exercises, you will learn how to build each type.

Creating internal hyperlinks

Creating hyperlinks of all types is easy with Dreamweaver. In this exercise, you'll create relative text-based links to pages in the same site, using a variety of methods. You can create links in Design view, Live view, and Code view.

Creating relative links

Dreamweaver provides several methods for creating and editing links. Links can be created in all three program views.

1 Open **about_us.html** from the site root folder in Live view.

2 In the horizontal menu, position the cursor over any of the horizontal menu items. Observe the type of cursor that appears.

The pointer indicates that the menu item is structured as a hyperlink. The styling changes as you position the cursor over each link and then move it away. The links in the horizontal menu are not editable in the normal way. But this is something you can actually see only in Design view.

3 Switch to Design view.
Position the cursor over any item of the horizontal menu again.

The "slash" icon ⃠ appears indicating that this section of the page is uneditable. The horizontal menu was not part of one of the editable regions you created in Lesson 8, "Working with Templates." That means it's considered part of the template and is locked with Dreamweaver. To add hyperlinks to this menu, you'll have to first open the template.

4   Choose Window > Assets. In the Assets panel Template category, right-click **mygreen_temp**, and choose Edit from the context menu.

5   Switch to Design view, if necessary.
    In the horizontal menu, insert the cursor into the *Green News* link.

    The horizontal menu is editable in the template.

▶ **Tip:** When editing or removing an existing hyperlink, you don't need to select the entire link; you can just insert the cursor anywhere in the link text. Dreamweaver assumes you want to change the entire link by default.

6   If necessary, choose Window > Properties to open the Property inspector. Examine the contents of the Link field in the Property inspector.

To create links, the HTML tab must be selected in the Property inspector. The Link field shows a hyperlink placeholder (#). The home page doesn't exist yet, but the link can be created by typing the name of the file or resource into this field.

7   In the Link field, click the Browse for File icon 🗀 .

● **Note:** The link won't have the typical hyperlink appearance— a blue underscore— because of the special formatting you applied to this menu in Lesson 5.

The Select File dialog appears.

8 Navigate to the site root folder, if necessary.
Select **news.html** from the site root folder. Click Open.

The link `../news.html` appears in the Link field in the Property inspector.

You've created your first text-based hyperlink. Since the template is saved in a subfolder, Dreamweaver adds the path element notation (../) to the filename so that the link properly resolves once the template pages are updated. This notation tells the browser or operating system to look in the parent directory of the current folder. Dreamweaver then rewrites the link simply to `"news.html"` when the template is applied to a page that is modified automatically based on where the pages are saved. If necessary, you can type links in the field manually too.

9 Insert the cursor in the *Home* link.

The home page does not exist yet. But that doesn't stop you from entering the link text by hand.

10 In the Link field, select the hash (#) symbol, type `../index.html` to replace the placeholder and press Enter/Return.

At any time, you may insert a link by typing it manually just this way. But, entering links by hand can introduce a variety of errors that can break the very link you are trying to create. If you want to link to a file that already exists, Dreamweaver offers other interactive ways to create links.

11 Insert the cursor in the *Green Events* link.

12 Click the Files tab to bring the panel to the top, or choose Window > Files.

You need to make sure you can see the Property inspector and the target file in the Files panel.

13 In the Property inspector, drag the Point to File icon ⊕ —next to the Link field—to **events.html** in the site root folder displayed in the Files panel.

▶ **Tip:** If a folder in the Files panel contains a page you want to link to but the folder is not open, drag the Point to File icon over the folder, and hold it in place to expand that folder so that you can point to the desired file.

Dreamweaver enters the filename and any necessary path information into the Link field.

14 Modify the rest of the menu as shown using any of the methods you've learned:

Green Travel: **../travel.html**

Green Tips: **../tips.html**

Contact Us: **../contact_us.html**

About Us: **../about_us.html**

● **Note:** The **index. html** and **travel.html** pages will be created later.

For files that have not been created, you will always have to enter the link manually. Remember that all the links added to the template pointing to files in the site root folder must include the **../** notation so that the link resolves properly. Remember also that Dreamweaver will modify the link as needed once the template is applied to the child page.

Creating a home link

Most websites display a logo or company name, and this site is no different. The GreenStart logo appears in the header element—a product of two background graphics, a gradient, and some text. Frequently, such logos are used to create a link back to the site home page. In fact, this practice has become a virtual standard on the web. Since the template is still open, it's easy to add such a link to the GreenStart logo.

1 Select the *GreenStart* text in the `<header>` element.

The text component of the logo is highlighted. Dreamweaver keeps track of links you create in each editing session until you close the program. You can access these previously created links from the Property inspector.

Note: You can select any range of text to create a link—from one character to an entire paragraph or more; Dreamweaver will add the necessary markup to the selection.

2 In the Property inspector Link field, choose `../index.html` from the drop-down menu.

This selection will create a link to the home page you will create later. The `<a>` tag now appears in the tag selector interface, and the logo has changed color to match the default styling of hyperlinks. Although you may want normal hyperlinks to be styled this way, the logo is not supposed to be blue. It's a simple fix with CSS.

3 In the CSS Designer, choose **green_styles.css** > GLOBAL.
Create the following selector:

```
header h2 a:link, header h2 a:visited
```

This selector will target the "default" and "visited" states of the link within the logo.

4 Add the following properties to the rule:

```
color: inherit
text-decoration: none
```

Note: Design view will not render all the styling properly, but it will appear correctly in Live view and in a browser.

5 Switch to Live view.

These properties will cancel the hyperlink styling and return the text to its original appearance. By using `inherit` for the color value, the color applied by the `header h2` rule will be passed automatically to the text. That way, any time the color in the `header h2` rule changes, the hyperlink will be styled in turn without any additional work or redundant code.

So far, all the links you've created and the changes you've made are only on the template. The whole purpose of using the template is to make updating pages in your site easy.

Updating links in child pages

To apply the links you've created to all the existing pages based on this template, all you have to do is save it.

1 Choose File > Save.

The Update Template Files dialog appears. You can choose to update pages now or wait until later. You can even update the template files manually, if desired.

2 Click Update.

● **Note:** When you close templates or web pages, Dreamweaver may ask you to save changes to **green_styles.css.** Whenever you see these warnings, always save the changes; otherwise you could lose all your newly created rules and properties.

Dreamweaver updates all pages created by this template. The Update Pages dialog appears, and displays a report listing the updated pages. If you don't see the list of updated pages, click the Show Log option in the dialog.

3 Close the Update Pages dialog.
Close **mygreen_temp.dwt.**

Dreamweaver prompts you to save **green_styles.css**.

4 Click Save.

The file **about_us.html** is still open. Note the asterisk in the document tab; this indicates that the page has been changed but not saved.

5 Save **about_us.html** and preview it in a browser.
Position the cursor over the *Home* and *Green News* links.

If you display the status bar in your browser, you can see the links applied to each item. When the template was saved, it updated the locked regions of the page, adding the hyperlinks to the horizontal menu. Child pages that are closed at the time of updating are automatically saved. Open pages must be saved manually or you will lose changes applied by the template.

Tip: Thoroughly test every link you create on every page.

6 Click the *Contact Us* link.

The *Contact Us* page loads to replace the *About Us* page in the browser.

7 Click the *About Us* link.

The *About Us* page loads to replace the *Contact Us* page. The links were added even to pages that weren't open at the time.

8 Close the browser.

You learned three methods for creating hyperlinks with the Property inspector: typing the link manually, using the Browse for File function, and using the Point to File tool.

Creating an external link

The pages you linked to in the previous exercise were stored within the current site. You can also link to any page—or other resource—stored on the web if you know the URL.

Creating an absolute link in Live view

In the previous exercise, you used Design view to build all your links. As you build pages and format content, you'll use Live view frequently to preview the styling and appearance of your elements. Although some aspects of content creation and editing are limited in Live view, you can still create and edit hyperlinks. In this exercise, you'll apply an external link to some text using Live view.

1 Open **contact_us.html** from the site root folder in Live view.

2 In the second <p> element in the MainContent region, note the word *Meridien*.

You'll link this text to the Google Maps site.

Tip: For this exercise, you can use any search engine or web-based mapping application.

Note: In some browsers, you can type the search phrase directly in the URL field.

Note: We're using Adobe's headquarters in place of the fictional city of Meridien. Feel free to use another search term.

3 Launch your favorite browser. In the URL field, type **maps.google.com** and press Enter/Return.

Google Maps appears in the browser window.

4 Type **San Jose, CA** into the search field and press Enter/Return.

Note: The technique for sharing map links is implemented differently in various browsers and search engines and may change over time.

San Jose appears on a map in the browser. In Google Maps, somewhere on the screen you should see a settings or share icon.

5 Open the settings interface as appropriate for your chosen mapping application.

Search engines and browsers may display their link-sharing and embedding interface slightly differently than the one pictured. Google Maps, MapQuest, and Bing usually offer at least two separate code snippets: one for use within a hyperlink and the other to generate an actual map that you can embed in your site.

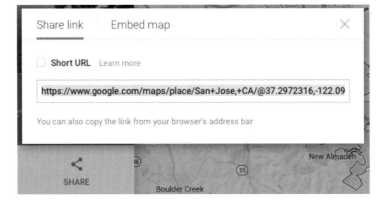

Note how the link contains the entire URL of the map, making it an *absolute* link. The advantage of using absolute links is that you can copy and paste them anywhere in the site without worrying whether the link will resolve properly.

6 Select and copy the link.

7 Switch to Live view in Dreamweaver.
   Select the word *Meridien*.

▶ **Tip:** Double-click to select text in Live view.

In Live view, you can select an entire element or insert the cursor within the element to edit or add text or apply hyperlinks, as desired. When an element or section of text is selected, a HUD will appear. The Text HUD allows you to apply `<strong>` or `<em>` tags to the selection, or (as in this case) to apply hyperlinks.

8 Click the Hyperlink icon ✗ in the Text HUD.

Press Ctrl+V/Cmd+V to paste the link in the Link field.
Press Enter/Return to complete the link.

The selected text displays the default formatting for a hyperlink.

9 Save the file and preview it in the default browser. Test the link.

When you click the link, the browser takes you to the opening page of Google Maps, assuming you have a connection to the Internet. But there is a problem: Clicking the link replaced the *Contact Us* page in the browser; it didn't open a new window as when you previewed the page at the beginning of the lesson. To make the browser open a new window, you need to add a simple HTML attribute to the link.

10 Switch to Dreamweaver.
    Click the *Meridien* link in Live view.

The Element HUD appears. The Property inspector displays the value of the existing link.

Tip: You can access the Target attribute in the Property inspector in Live, Design, and Code views whenever a link is selected.

11 Choose _blank from the Target field menu in the Property inspector.

For general questions and information email: info@green-start.org

When you contact our offices in Meridien, our friendly and knowledgeable staff is ready to serve you and answer your questions:

mmtinstance:editable   section   .col-md-6.col-md-push-3.col-sm-8.col-sm-push-

Class   col-md-...

Link   https://www.google.com/m...

Title

Target

Default
_blank
new
_parent
_self
_top

12 Save the file, and preview the page in the default browser again. Test the link.

This time when you click the link, the browser opens a new window or document tab.

13 Close the browser windows, and switch back to Dreamweaver.

As you can see, Dreamweaver makes it easy to create links to internal or external resources.

Setting up email links

Tip: The Email Link menu cannot be accessed in Live view. But you can use the menu in Design view or Code view or just create the links by hand in any view.

Another type of link doesn't take the visitor to another page; rather, it opens the visitor's email program. Email links can create automatic, pre-addressed email messages from your visitors for customer feedback, product orders, or other important communications. The code for an email link is slightly different from the normal hyperlink, and—as you probably guessed already—Dreamweaver can create the proper code for you automatically.

1 If necessary, open **contact_us.html** in Design view.

2 Select the email address (info@green-start.org) in the first paragraph underneath the heading and press Ctrl+C/Cmd+C to copy the text.

3 Choose Insert > HTML > Email Link.

The Email Link dialog appears. The text selected in the document window is automatically entered into the Text field.

4 Insert the cursor in the Email field and press Ctrl+V/Cmd+V to paste the email address, if necessary.

▶ **Tip:** If you select the text before you access the dialog, Dreamweaver enters the text in the field for you automatically.

5 Click OK. Examine the Link field in the Property inspector.

Dreamweaver inserts the email address into the Link field and also enters the `mailto:` notation, which tells the browser to automatically launch the visitor's default email program.

6 Save the file and preview it in the default browser. Test the email link.

If your computer has a default email program installed, it will launch and create a new email message using the email address provided in the link. If there is no default email program, your computer's operating system may ask you to identify one.

7 Close any open email program, related dialogs, or wizards. Switch to Dreamweaver.

You can also create email links by hand.

8 Select and copy the email address for Elaine.

9 Type `mailto:` in the Property inspector link field.

Paste Elaine's email address directly after the colon.

Press Enter/Return to complete the link.

10 Save the file.

The text `mailto:elaine@green-start.org` appears in the Text HUD link field in Live view. You can use the HUD to add links to images too.

Creating an image-based link

Image-based links work like any other hyperlink and can direct users to internal or external resources. You can use the Insert menu in Design or Code views or apply links and other attributes using the HUD interface in Live view.

Creating image-based links using the Element HUD

In this exercise, you will create and format an image-based link using the email addresses of each GreenStart employee via the Element HUD.

1 If necessary, open **contact_us.html** in Live view from the site root folder.

2 Select the image of Elaine in the *Association Management* section.

To access the hyperlink option, you must open the Edit HTML Attributes menu.

3 In the Element HUD, click the Edit HTML Attributes icon ▤ .

The menu opens and displays options for the image attributes `src`, `alt`, `link`, `target`, `width`, and `height`.

● **Note:** Normally, an image formatted with a hyperlink displays a blue border, similar to the blue underscore that text links get. But the predefined Bootstrap CSS turns this styling off. In non-Bootstrap sites, you may want to create a similar rule.

▶ **Tip:** Make sure there is no space after the colon or the link will not work properly.

4 If the email address is still in memory from the previous exercise, simply enter `mailto:` and paste the address in the Link field.

Otherwise, enter `mailto:elaine@green-start.org` in the link field after the colon.

Press the ESC key to close the HUD.

The hyperlink that is applied to the image will launch the default email program in the same fashion as it did with the text-based link earlier.

5 Select and copy the email address for Sarah.

Repeat steps 2–4 to create an email link for Sarah's image.

6 Create image links for the remaining employees using the appropriate email address for each.

All the image-based links on the page are complete. You can also create text-based links using the Text HUD.

Creating text links using the Text HUD

In this exercise, you will create text-based email links as needed for the remaining employees.

1 If necessary, open **contact_us.html** in Live view.

2 Select and copy the email address for Sarah.

The Text HUD appears around the selected text.

3 Click the Link icon ⚓.

A link field appears. A folder icon displays on the right side of the link field. If you were linking to a file on the website, you could click the folder to target the file. In this case, we're creating an email link.

4 Insert the cursor in the link field, if necessary.

Enter `mailto:` and paste Sarah's email address and press Enter/Return.

5 Using the Text HUD, create email links for the remaining email addresses displayed on the page.

6 Save all files.

Attack of the killer robots

Although on the surface it sounds like a good idea to add email links to make it easier for your customers and visitors to communicate with you and your staff, email links are a double-edged sword. The Internet is awash in bad actors and unethical companies that use intelligent programs, or robots, to constantly search for live email addresses that they can flood with unsolicited email and spam. Putting a plain email address on your site as shown in these exercises is like putting a sign on your back that says "kick me."

In place of active email links, many sites use a variety of methods for limiting the amount of spam they receive. One technique uses images to display the email addresses, since robots can't read data stored in pixels (yet). Another leaves off the hyperlink attribute and types the address with extra spaces, like this:

```
elaine @ green-start .org
```

However, both of these techniques have drawbacks; if visitors try to use copy and paste it forces them to go out of their way to remove the extra spaces or try to type your email address from memory. Either way, the chances of you receiving any communication decreases with each step the user has to accomplish without additional help.

At this time, there is no foolproof way to prevent someone from using an email address for nefarious purposes. Coupled with the fact that fewer users actually have a mail program installed on their computers anymore, the best method for enabling communication for your visitors is to provide a means built into the site itself. Many sites create web-hosted forms that collect the visitor's information and message and then pass it along using server-based email functionality.

Targeting page elements

As you add more content, the pages get longer and navigating to that content gets more difficult. Typically, when you click a link to a page, the browser window loads the page and displays it starting at the very top. But it can be very helpful when you provide convenient methods for users to link to a specific point on a page.

HTML 4.01 provided two methods to target specific content or page structures: a *named anchor* and an *id* attribute. In HTML5, the named anchor method has been deprecated in favor of ids. If you have used named anchors in the past, don't worry, they won't suddenly cease to function. But from this point on, you should start using ids exclusively.

Creating internal targeted links

In this exercise, you'll work with id attributes to create the target of an internal link. You can add ids in Live, Design, or Code view.

1 Open **events.html** in Live view.

2 Scroll down to the table containing the class schedule.

When users move down this far on the page, the navigation menus are out of sight and unusable. The farther down the page they read, the farther they are from the primary navigation. Before users can navigate to another page, they have to use the browser scroll bars or the mouse scroll wheel to get back to the top of the page. Adding a link to take users back to the top can vastly improve their experience on your site. Let's call this type of link an *internal targeted* link.

Internal targeted links have two parts: the link itself and the target. Which one you create first doesn't matter.

3 Click the Class table.
Click the `article` tag selector.

The HUD appears focused on the `article` element.

4 Open the Insert panel.
Select the HTML category.
Click the Paragraph item.

The position assist interface opens.

5 Click Before.

A new paragraph element appears in the layout, with the placeholder text *This is the content for Layout P Tag.*

6 Select the placeholder text.
   Type **Return to top** to replace it.

The text is inserted between the two tables, formatted as a <p> element. The text would look better centered.

7 In the CSS Designer, choose **green_styles.css** > GLOBAL.
   Create a new selector: `.ctr`

8 Create the following property for `.ctr`:
   `text-align: center`

9 Click the Add Class/ID icon ⊞ for the selected <p> element.

10 Type `.ctr` in the text field, or choose `.ctr` from the hinting menu and press Enter/Return.

The *Return to top* text is aligned to the center. The tag selector now displays `p.ctr`.

11 Select the text *Return to top*.

Click the Link icon and type #top in the Link field.

Press Enter/Return to complete the link.

By using #top, you have created a link to a target within the current page. When users click the *Return to top* link, the browser window jumps to the position of the target. This target doesn't exist yet. For this link to work properly, you need to insert the destination as high on the page as possible.

12 Save all files. Switch to Design view.

13 Scroll to the top of **events.html**.

Position the cursor over the header element.

The mouse icon indicates that this part of the page (and its related code) is uneditable, because the header and horizontal navigation menu are based on the site template. Putting the target at the very top is important, or a portion of the page may be obscured when the browser jumps to it. Since the top of the page is part of an uneditable region, the best solution is to add the target directly to the template.

Creating a link destination using an id

By adding a unique id to the template, you will be able to access it automatically throughout the site wherever you want to add a link back to the top of a page.

1 Open the template **mygreen_temp.dwt** from the Templates folder in Design view.

Tip: When applying classes or ids, you can insert the cursor in the element or select the tag selector. The attribute will automatically be applied to the first containing element.

2 Click in the text *greenstart* in the `<header>`.
Select the h2 tag selector.
In the Property inspector, type **top** in the id field and press Enter/Return.

Note: An id can be created and applied to any HTML element. They don't have to be referenced in the style sheet at all.

The tag selector changes to h2#top; otherwise, the page shows no visible difference. The big difference is in how the page reacts to the internal hyperlink.

3 Save the file and update all template child pages. Close the template.

4 Switch to or open **events.html**, if necessary.
Save the file, and preview it in a browser.

5 Scroll down to the Class table.
Click the *Return to top* link.

The browser jumps back to the top of the page.

Now that the id has been inserted in every page of the site by the template, you can copy the *Return to top* link and paste it anywhere in the site you want to add this functionality.

6 In Dreamweaver, switch to Live view.
Select and copy the `<p>` element containing the text *Return to top* and its link.

7 Insert the cursor in the Class table.
Using the tag selector, select the `<article>` element.
Press Ctrl+V/Cmd+V to paste.

A new `p.ctr` element and link appear at the bottom of the page.

8 Save the file and preview it in the browser. Test both *Return to top* links.

Both links can be used to jump back to the top of the document. In the next exercise, you'll learn how to create link targets using element attributes.

Creating a destination link in the Element HUD

There's no need to add any extra elements to create hyperlink destinations when you can simply add an id attribute to a handy element nearby. In this exercise, you will use the Element HUD to add an id.

1   Open **events.html** in Live view.
    Insert the cursor in the Events table.
    Click the `table` tag selector.

    The Element HUD and the Property inspector display the attributes currently applied to the Events table. You can add an id using either tool.

2   Click the Add Class/ID icon ⊞ .
    Type a hash mark (#).

    If any ids were defined in the style sheet but unused on the page, a list would appear. Since nothing appears, it means that there are no unused ids. Creating a new one is easy.

3   Type `calendar` and press Enter/Return.

The CSS Source HUD appears. We do not need the id in any style sheet.

4   Press ESC to close the HUD.

    The tag selector now displays `table#calendar`. Since ids are unique identifiers, they are perfect for targeting specific content on a page. We also need to create an id for the Class table.

Note: When creating ids, remember that they need to have names that are used only once per page. They are case sensitive, so look out for typos.

Note: If you add the id to the wrong element, simply delete it and try again.

5 Repeat steps 1–4 to add the id `#classes` to the Class table.

The tag selector now displays `table#classes`.

6 Save all files.

You'll learn how to link to these ids in the next exercise.

Targeting id-based link destinations

By adding unique ids to both tables, you have provided an ideal target for internal hyperlinks to navigate to a specific section of your webpage. In this exercise, you will create a link to each table.

1 If necessary, open **contact_us.html** in Live view.
Scroll down to the *Education and Events* section.

▶ **Tip:** You can select single words by double-clicking them.

2 Select the word *events* in the first paragraph of the section.

3 Using the Text HUD, create a link to the file **events.html**.

every minute.

She can also create custom events for people with special needs such as handicap access or special die **B** *I* **8** Enter Link accommodations for existing events and classes. So, let Sarah know if you have any personal requirements.

Browse for file...

Email Sarah at: sarah@green-start.org

This link will open the file, but you're not finished. You now have to direct the browser to navigate down to the Events table.

4 Type #calendar at the end of the filename to complete the link and press Enter/Return.

● **Note:** Hyperlinks cannot contain spaces; make sure the id reference follows the filename immediately.

The word *events* is now a link targeting the Events table in the **events.html** file.

5 Select the word *classes*.

Create a link to the **events.html** file.

Type #classes to complete the link and press Enter/Return.

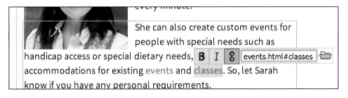

6 Save the file and preview the page in a browser.

Test the links to the *Events* and *Class* tables.

The links open the *Events* page and navigate to the appropriate tables.

Checking your page

Dreamweaver can check your page automatically for valid HTML, accessibility, and broken links. In this exercise, you'll check your links and learn what you can do in case of a browser compatibility problem.

1 If necessary, open **contact_us.html** in Design view.

2 Choose Site > Check Links Sitewide.

Note: The Link Checker may find some suspicious links in a Bootstrap JavaScript file. Ignore any of these errors.

A Link Checker panel opens. The Link Checker panel reports broken links to the files **index.html** and **travel.html** you created for nonexistent pages. You'll make these pages later, so you don't need to worry about fixing these broken links now. The Link Checker will find broken links to external sites, should you have any.

3 Right-click the Link Checker tab, and choose Close Tab Group from the context menu.

You've made big changes to the pages in this lesson by creating the main navigation menu, links to specific positions on a page, to email, and to an external site. You also applied links to images. Finally, you checked your page for broken links.

Adding destination links to the same page (optional)

Using the skills you have just learned, open **events.html** and create destination links for the words *Events* and *Classes* that appear in the first paragraph.

Remember that the words will link to the tables on the same page. Can you figure out how to construct these links properly? If you have any trouble, check out the **events_finished.html** file for the answer.

Review questions

1   Describe two ways to insert a link into a page.

2   What information is required to create a link to an external webpage?

3   What's the difference between standard page links and email links?

4   What attribute is used to create destination links?

5   What limits the usefulness of email links?

6   Can links be applied to images?

7   How can you check to see whether your links will work properly?

Review answers

1   Select text or a graphic and then, in the Property inspector, click the Browse for File icon next to the Link field and navigate to the desired page. A second method is to drag the Point to File icon to a file within the Files panel.

2   Link to an external page by typing or copying and pasting the full web address (a fully formed URL) in the Link field of the Property inspector or the Text HUD.

3   A standard page link opens a new page or moves the view to a position somewhere on the page. An email link opens a blank email message window if the visitor has an email application installed.

4   You can apply unique id attributes to any element to create a link destination.

5   Email links may not be very useful because many users do not use built-in email programs, and the links will not automatically connect with Internet-based email services.

6   Yes, links can be applied to images and used in exactly the same way text-based links are.

7   Run the Link Checker report to test links on each page individually or sitewide. You should also test them in a browser.

12 ADDING INTERACTIVITY

Lesson overview

In this lesson, you'll add Web 2.0 functionality to your webpages by doing the following:

- Use Dreamweaver behaviors to create an image rollover effect

- Insert a Bootstrap Accordion widget

This lesson will take about 2 hours to complete. If you have not already done so, download the project files for this lesson from the Lesson & Update Files tab on your Account page at www.peachpit.com, store them on your computer in a convenient location, and define a new site based on the lesson12 folder as described in the "Getting Started" section of this book. Your Account page is also where you'll find any updates to the lessons or to the lesson files. Look on the Lesson & Update Files tab to access the most current content.

Dreamweaver can create sophisticated interactive
effects with behaviors and accordion panels using
Adobe's Bootstrap and jQuery frameworks.

Learning about Dreamweaver behaviors

● **Note:** If you have not already downloaded the project files for this lesson to your computer from your Account page, make sure to do so now. See "Getting Started" at the beginning of the book.

● **Note:** To access Dreamweaver Behaviors, you must have a file open.

The term *Web 2.0* was coined to describe a major change in the user experience on the Internet—from mostly static pages, featuring text, graphics, and simple links, to a new paradigm of dynamic webpages filled with video, animation, and interactive content. Dreamweaver has always led the industry in providing a variety of tools to drive this movement, from its tried-and-true collection of JavaScript behaviors, jQuery, and Bootstrap widgets to the latest support for jQuery Mobile. This lesson explores two of these capabilities: Dreamweaver behaviors and Bootstrap widgets.

A Dreamweaver *behavior* is predefined JavaScript code that performs an action—such as opening a browser window or showing or hiding a page element—when it is triggered by an event, such as a mouse click. Applying a behavior is a three-step process:

1 Create or select the page element that you want to trigger the behavior.

2 Choose the behavior to apply.

3 Specify the settings or parameters of the behavior.

The triggering element often involves a hyperlink applied to a range of text or to an image. In some cases, the behavior is not intended to load a new page, so it employs a dummy link enabled by the hash sign (#), similar to ones that you used in Lesson 11, "Working with Navigation." The Swap Image behavior you will use in this lesson does not require a link to function, but keep this in mind when you work with other behaviors.

Dreamweaver offers more than 16 built-in behaviors, all accessed from the Behaviors panel (Window > Behaviors). Hundreds of other useful behaviors can be downloaded from the Internet for free or a small fee. Some are available from the online Adobe Add-ons website, which can be added to the program by clicking the Add Behavior icon ⊞ in the Behaviors panel and choosing Get More Behaviors from the pop-up menu or by choosing Window > Browse Add-ons.

When the Adobe Add-ons page loads in the browser, click the link to download the plug-in, extension, or other add-on. Often you can simply double-click the add-on to install it.

The following are some examples of the functionality available to you using the built-in Dreamweaver behaviors:

• Opening a browser window

• Swapping one image for another to create what is known as a *rollover effect*

• Fading images or page areas in and out

• Growing or shrinking graphics

• Displaying pop-up messages

- Changing the text or other HTML content within a given area

- Showing or hiding sections of the page

- Calling a custom-defined JavaScript function

Not all behaviors are available all the time. Certain behaviors become available only in the presence and selection of certain page elements, such as images or hyperlinks. For example, the Swap Image behavior must be applied to an image.

Each behavior invokes a unique dialog that provides relevant options and specifications. For instance, the dialog for the Open Browser Window behavior enables you to open a new browser window; set its width, height, and other attributes; and set the URL of the displayed resource. After the behavior is defined, it is listed in the Behaviors panel with its chosen triggering action. As with other behaviors, these specifications can be modified at any time.

Behaviors are extremely flexible, and multiple behaviors can be applied to the same trigger. For example, you could swap one image for another and change the text of the accompanying image caption—and do it all with one click. Although some effects may appear to happen simultaneously, behaviors are actually triggered in sequence. When multiple behaviors are applied, you can choose the order in which the behaviors are processed.

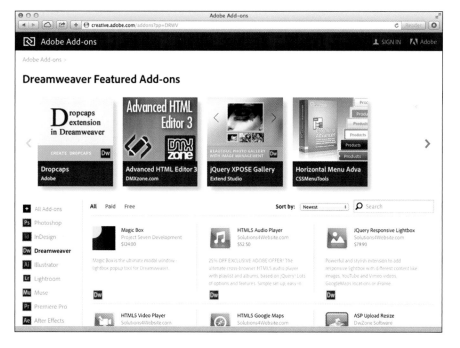

Adobe add-ons offer tons of resources for many of the applications in Creative Cloud, including both free and paid add-ons.

To learn more about Adobe Add Ons, check out creative.adobe.com/addons.

Previewing the completed file

In the first part of this lesson, you'll create a new page for GreenStart's travel services. Let's preview the completed page in a browser.

1 Launch Adobe Dreamweaver CC (2015.1 release) or later.
  If necessary, define a site based on the lesson12 folder.
  Name the site **lesson12**.

2 Open **travel_finished.html** and preview the page in the default browser.

  The page includes Dreamweaver behaviors.

3 If Microsoft Internet Explorer is your default browser, a message may appear in the browser window indicating that it has prevented scripts and ActiveX controls from running. If so, click Allow Blocked Content.

  This message appears only when the file is previewed from your hard drive. It doesn't appear when the file is actually hosted on the Internet.

4 Position the cursor over the *Tour Eiffel* heading.
  Observe the image to the right of the text.

  The existing image swaps for one of the Eiffel Tower.

5 Move the pointer to the *Paris Underground* heading.

  Observe the image to the right of the text.

  As the pointer moves off the *Tour Eiffel* heading, the image reverts to the Eco-Tour ad. Then, as the pointer moves over the heading *Paris Underground*, the ad image swaps for one of underground Paris.

6 Pass the pointer over each <h3> heading, and observe the image behavior.

  The image alternates between the Eco-Tour ad and images of each of the tours. This effect is the Swap Image behavior.

7 When you're finished, close the browser window and return to Dreamweaver.

8 Close **travel-finished.html**.

In the next exercise, you'll learn how to work with Dreamweaver behaviors.

Working with Dreamweaver behaviors

Adding Dreamweaver behaviors to your layout is a simple point-and-click operation. But before you can add the behaviors, you have to create the travel page.

1 Create a new page from **mygreen_temp**.

2 Save the file as **travel.html** in the site root folder.
Switch to Design view, if necessary.

3 Open **sidebars12.html** in Design view from the lesson12/resources folder.
Insert the cursor into the first paragraph.
Examine the tag selectors.

The paragraph is a child of a `<blockquote>` within an `aside` element. The classes and structure in the new file are identical to Sidebar 1 in the site template.

4 Select the `aside` tag selector.

5 Copy the `aside` element from **sidebars12.html**.

6 Switch to **travel.html**.
Insert the cursor into the first quotation.
Select the `aside` tag selector.

7 Paste the new content.

The new content replaces the placeholder.

8 Close **sidebars12.html**.

9 Open **travel-text.html** in Design view from the lesson12/resources folder.

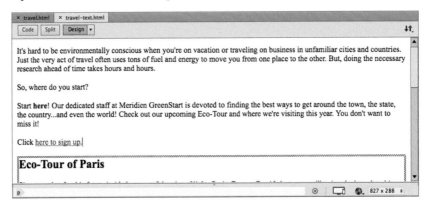

The **travel-text.html** file contains content in some paragraphs and a table for the travel page. Note that the text and table are unformatted.

10 Press Ctrl+A/Cmd+A to select all the text, and press Ctrl+C/Cmd+C to copy the contents of **travel-text.html**.
Close the file.

11 In **travel.html**, select the placeholder *Add main heading here.*
Type **Green Travel** to replace the text.

12 Select the heading placeholder *Add subheading here.*
Type **Eco-Touring** to replace it.

13 Select the p tag selector for the *Add content here* text.
Press Ctrl+V/Cmd+V to paste.

The content from **travel-text.html** appears, replacing the placeholder text. It assumes the default formatting for text and tables applied by the style sheet you created in Lesson 9, "Working with Text, Lists, and Tables."

Next, let's insert the Eco-Tour ad, which will be the base image for the Swap Image behavior.

14 In the table, double-click the *SideAd* placeholder.

Select **ecotour.png** from the images folder.

Click OK/Open.

The placeholder is replaced by the Eco-Tour ad. But before you can apply the Swap Image behavior, you have to identify the image you want to swap. You do this by giving the image an id.

15 Select **ecotour.png** in the layout.

In the Property inspector, select the existing id SideAd.

Type ecotour and press Enter/Return.

Enter Eco-Tour of Paris in the Alt field.

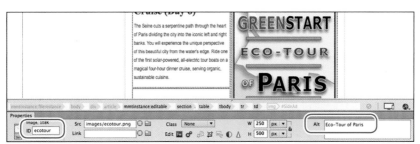

> ▶ **Tip:** Although it takes more time, giving all your images unique ids is a good practice.

16 Save the file.

Next, you'll create a Swap Image behavior for **ecotour.png**.

Applying a behavior

As described earlier, many behaviors are context sensitive, based on the elements or structure present. A Swap Image behavior can be triggered by any document element, but it affects only images displayed within the page.

1 Choose Window > Behaviors to open the Behaviors panel.

2 Insert the cursor in the *Tour Eiffel* text, and select the <h3> tag selector.

3 Click the Add Behavior icon ➕.

Choose Swap Image from the behavior menu.

> ◉ **Note:** Feel free to dock the Behaviors panel with the other panels in the interface.

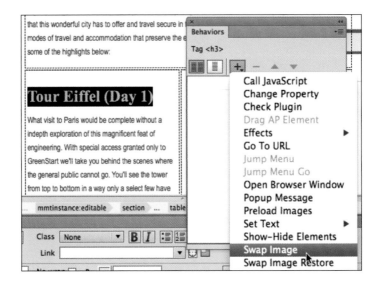

Note: Items listed as unnamed <img> are images without id attributes. If you wish to swap them too, you'll have to first give them ids.

The Swap Image dialog lists any images on the page that are available for this behavior. This behavior can replace one or more of these images at a time.

4   Select the image "ecotour" item and click Browse.

5   In the Select Image Source dialog, select **tower.jpg** from the site images folder. Click OK/Open.

Note: The Preload Images option forces the browser to download all images necessary for the behavior when the page loads. That way, when the user clicks the trigger, the image swap occurs without any lags or glitches.

6   In the Swap Image dialog, select the Preload Images option, if necessary, and click OK.

A Swap Image behavior is added to the Behaviors panel with an attribute of onMouseOver. Attributes can be changed, if desired, using the Behaviors panel.

7 Click the onMouseOver attribute to open the pop-up menu, and examine the other available options.

The menu provides a list of trigger events, most of which are self-explanatory. For now, however, leave the attribute as onMouseOver.

8 Save the file.
Switch to Live view to test the behavior.
Position the cursor over the *Tour Eiffel* text.

When the cursor passes over the text, the Eco-Tour ad is replaced by the image of the Eiffel Tower. But there is a small problem. When the cursor moves away from the text, the original image doesn't return. The reason is simple: You didn't tell it to. To bring back the original image, you have to add another command—Swap Image Restore—to the same element.

Applying a Swap Image Restore behavior

In some instances, a specific action requires more than one behavior. To bring back the Eco-Tour ad once the mouse moves off the trigger, you have to add a restore function.

1 Switch to Design view.
Insert the cursor in the *Tour Eiffel* heading and examine the Behaviors panel.

The inspector displays the currently assigned behavior. You don't need to select the element completely; Dreamweaver assumes you want to modify the entire trigger.

2 Click the Add Behavior icon ![+]

Choose Swap Image Restore from the drop-down menu.

Click OK in the Swap Image Restore dialog to complete the command.

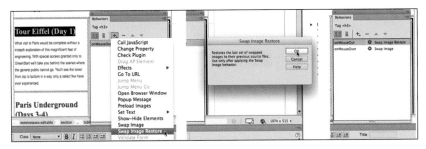

The Swap Image Restore behavior appears in the Behaviors panel with an attribute of onMouseOut.

3 Switch to Code view and examine the markup for the *Tour Eiffel* text.

```
95    <td scope="col">
96    <h3 onMouseOver="MM_swapImage('SideAd','','images/ecotour.png',1)"
97    onMouseOut="MM_swapImgRestore()">Tour Eiffel (Day 1)</h3>
98    <p>What visit to Paris would be complete without a indepth exploration
```

The trigger events—onMouseOver and onMouseOut—were added as attributes to the <h3> element. The rest of the JavaScript code was inserted in the document's <head> section.

4 Save the file and switch to Live view to test the behavior.

Test the text trigger *Tour Eiffel*.

When the pointer passes over the text, the Eco-Tour image is replaced by the one of the Eiffel Tower, and then reappears when the pointer is withdrawn. The behavior functions as desired, but nothing is visibly "different" about the text. There is nothing here to prompt a user to roll their pointer over the heading. The result will be that many users will miss the swap image effect altogether.

Users sometimes need to be encouraged or directed to these types of effects. Many designers use hyperlinks for this purpose, since users are already familiar with how they function. Let's replace the current effect with one based on a hyperlink.

Removing applied behaviors

Before you can apply a behavior to a hyperlink, you need to remove the current Swap Image and Swap Image Restore behaviors.

1 Switch to Design view.

Open the Behaviors panel, if necessary.

Insert the cursor in the *Tour Eiffel* text.

The Behaviors panel displays the two applied events. Which one you delete first doesn't matter.

2 Select the Swap Image event in the Behaviors panel.
Click the Remove Event icon [−].

3 Select the Swap Image Restore event.
In the Behaviors panel, click the Remove Event icon.

Both events are now removed. Dreamweaver also removes any unneeded JavaScript code.

4 Save the file and check the text in Live view again.

The text no longer triggers the Swap Image behavior. To reapply the behavior, you need to add a link or link placeholder to the heading.

Adding behaviors to hyperlinks

Behaviors can be added to hyperlinks even if the link doesn't load a new document. For this exercise, you'll add a link placeholder (#) to the heading to support the desired behavior.

1 Select only the text *Tour Eiffel* in the <h3> element.
Type # in the Property inspector Link field.
Press Enter/Return to create the link placeholder.

The text displays with the default hyperlink styling. The tag selector for the a tag appears.

2 Insert the cursor in the *Tour Eiffel* link.
Click the Add Behavior icon [+].
Choose Swap Image from the pop-up menu.

As long as the cursor is still inserted anywhere in the link, the behavior will be applied to the entire link markup.

3 In the Swap Image dialog, select the item `image "ecotour"`.
Browse and select **tower.jpg** from the images folder.
Click OK/Open.

4 In the Swap Image dialog, select the **Preload Images** option and the **Restore Images onMouseOut** option, if necessary, and click OK.

The Swap Image event appears in the Behaviors panel along with a Swap Image Restore event. Since the behavior was applied all at once, Dreamweaver provides the restore functionality as a productivity enhancement.

5 Apply a link placeholder (#) to the text *Paris Underground*.
Apply the Swap Image behavior to the link.
Use **underground.jpg** from the images folder.

6 Repeat step 5 for the *Seine Dinner Cruise* text.
Select the image **cruise.jpg**.

7 Repeat step 5 for the *Champs Élysées* text.
Select the image **champs.jpg**.

The Swap Image behaviors are now complete, but the text and link appearances don't match the site's color scheme. Let's create custom CSS rules to format them accordingly. You will create two rules: one for the heading element and another for the link itself.

8 In the CSS Designer, select **green_styles.css** > GLOBAL.
Create the new selector: `article table h3`

9 Create the following properties in the new rule:

```
margin-top: 0px
margin-bottom: 5px
font-size: 130%
font-family: "Arial Narrow", Verdana, "Trebuchet MS", sans-serif
```

10 Select **green_styles.css** > GLOBAL.

Create a new selector:

```
table h3 a:link, table h3 a:visited
```

11 Create the following properties in the new rule:

```
color: #090
font-weight: bold
```

The headings are now more prominent and styled to match the site theme.

12 Save all files.

Test the behaviors in Live view.

Note how the links are underlined when the mouse moves over them. The Swap Image behavior should work successfully on all links. If one or more of the links do not function, check to make sure the behavior was assigned to the link successfully.

Making it responsive

Once you're satisfied that all the rollover effects are functioning properly, you should check to make sure that the new components adapt properly to the responsive page design too. You can check the functionality in Dreamweaver or in any modern browser installed on your computer.

1 If necessary, open **travel.html**.
Switch to Live view.

2 Drag the Scrubber to the left to test how the new table responds to the existing set of media queries.

The table adapts to the changing screen in a fashion similar to the tables created and styled in Lesson 9. Everything seems to display fine, although the Eco-Tour ad does not scale or resize in any way.

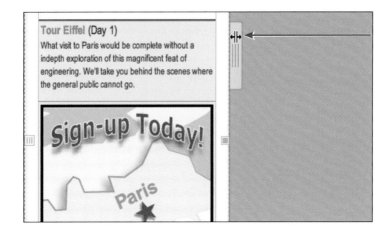

At a width of 426 pixels, the two columns merge and the cells begin to stack one atop the other, including the cell containing the ad. The image does not appear beside the text describing the tours. At this point, the purpose of the rollover effect will be lost completely, as does the need for the ad itself. The simplest plan would be just to hide the ad on smaller screens and allow the text to speak for itself.

At this moment, there's a custom id applied to the ad image but nothing applied to the cell containing it. CSS can hide the image, but it will leave the blank cell behind. Instead, let's create a custom class to hide the cell and its contents.

3 Drag the Scrubber all the way to the right to restore the table layout to two columns.

4 Select the Eco-Tour image.

5 Select the `td` tag selector.

The HUD appears focused on the `td` element.

6 Click the Add Class/ID icon $\boxed{+}$.

7 Enter `.hide_ad` in the HUD text field. If the CSS Source HUD appears press the ESC key to close it.

8 If necessary, open the CSS Designer.
Select **green_styles.css** > (max-width: 426px).
Create a new selector: `table .hide_ad`

This rule limits the styling to elements within a table when the screen drops down to the smallest media query.

9 Create the following property:
`display: none.`
The table cell and ad will hide whenever the screen is 426 pixels or narrower.

10 Drag the Scrubber to the left until it is narrower than 426 pixels.
Observe the changes to the table and its content.

The Eco-Tour ad hides once the screen is narrower than 426 pixels. It reappears as soon as the screen gets wider than 426 pixels.

11 Save all files.

12 Close **travel.html**.

In addition to eye-catching effects such as the dynamic behaviors you've just been learning about, Dreamweaver also provides structural components—such as jQuery and Bootstrap widgets—that conserve space and add more interactive flair to your website.

Working with Bootstrap Accordion widgets

The Bootstrap Accordion widget allows you to organize a lot of content into a compact space. In the Accordion widget, the tabs are stacked, and when opened, they expand vertically rather than side by side. Let's preview the completed layout.

1 In the Files panel, select **tips_finished.html** from the lesson12 folder and preview it in your primary browser.

The page content is divided among three panels using the Bootstrap Accordion widget.

2 Click each panel in turn to open and close each.

When you click a tab, the panel slides open with a smooth action. The panels are set to a specific height; if the content is taller than the default panel size, the panel adjusts its height automatically. When the panels open and close, the bulleted lists of green tips are revealed. The accordion allows you to display more content in a smaller, more efficient footprint.

3 Close your browser and return to Dreamweaver.
Close **tips_finished.html**.

Inserting a Bootstrap Accordion widget

In this exercise, you'll incorporate a Bootstrap Accordion widget into one of your existing layouts.

1 Open **tips.html** in Live view.

The page consists of three bulleted lists separated by <h2> headings. These lists take up a lot of vertical space on the page, requiring the user to scroll down two or more screens to read them. Keeping content on one screen as much as possible will make it easier to access and read.

One technique to maximize screen real estate is using tabbed or accordion panels. Dreamweaver offers both types of components in jQuery and Bootstrap frameworks. Since we're using a Bootstrap layout, let's use a Bootstrap Accordion.

2 Insert the cursor in the *At Home* heading, and select the <h2> tag selector.

3 Open the Insert panel.
Select the Bootstrap category.
Click the Accordion item.

The position assist HUD appears.

4 Click Before.

Dreamweaver inserts the Bootstrap Accordion widget element above the heading, but inside the `<article>` element. The default element is a three-panel Accordion widget that appears with the top panel (*Collapsible Group 1*) open. The HUD appears above the new object, focused on a `div` element with a class of `.panel-group` and an id of `#accordion1`.

The next step is to move the existing lists into the panel. Since two of the panels are hidden by default, the easiest way to work with the content will be in Code view.

5 Switch to Code view.

6 Scroll down, and insert the cursor in the first bullet:
`<li>Wash clothes in cold water.</li>` (approximately line 87).

7 Select the `ul` tag selector.
Press Ctrl+X/Cmd+X to cut the whole list.

> ▶ **Tip:** As you work in Code view, you may need to click the Refresh button from time to time in the Property inspector to see the tag selectors.

```
86   <h2>At Home</h2>
87   <ul>
88   <li>Wash clothes in cold water</li>
89   <li>Hang clothes to dry</li>
```

mmtinstance:fileinstance body div article mmtinstance:editable section .col-md-6.col-md-push-3.col-sm-8.col-sm-push-4 article

Properties

<> HTML Format None Class col-md-... B I Title <ul>

8 Delete the code **<h2>At Home</h2>**.

9 Scroll up and select the heading *Collapsible Group 1* (approximately line 63). Edit the heading to say: At Home

```
62   <div class="panel-heading" role="tab">
63   <h4 class="panel-title"><a data-toggle="collapse" data-parent="#accordion1" href=
     "#collapseOne1">At Home</a></h4>
64   </div>
65   <div id="collapseOne1" class="panel-collapse collapse in">
66   <div class="panel-body">Content for Accordion Panel 1</div>
67   </div>
```

The new heading structure is based on an <h4> element.

10 Select and delete the text placeholder *Content for Accordion Panel 1* (approximately line 66).

```
62   <div class="panel-heading" role="tab">
63   <h4 class="panel-title"><a data-toggle="collapse" data-parent="#accordion1" href=
     "#collapseOne1">Collapsible Group 1</a></h4>
64   </div>
65   <div id="collapseOne1" class="panel-collapse collapse in">
66   <div class="panel-body">Content for Accordion Panel 1</div>
67   </div>
```

The text appears in the <div> without any other structure. Make sure you do not delete the <div>.

11 Press Ctrl+V/Cmd+V to paste the list.

```
63   <h4 class="panel-title"><a data-toggle="collapse" data-parent="#accordion1" href=
     "#collapseOne1">Collapsible Group 1</a></h4>
64   </div>
65   <div id="collapseOne1" class="panel-collapse collapse in">
66   <div class="panel-body"><ul>
67   <li>Wash clothes in cold water</li>
68   <li>Hang clothes to dry</li>
69   <li>Turn off lights in empty rooms</li>
70   <li>Use motion sensors to turn lights on</li>
71   <li>Plan driving errands to combine trips</li>
72   <li>Walk more, drive less</li>
73   <li>Install Compact Fluorescent lighting (CFL)</li>
```

The list markup appears in <div class="panel-body">. The first Accordion panel group is complete. You have to repeat this process for the other two lists.

12 Scroll down and select the "At Work" tip list (approximately line 112).

13 Using the ul tag selector as in step 7, press Ctrl+X/Cmd+X to cut the list.

14 Click the <article> tag selector. Press Delete.

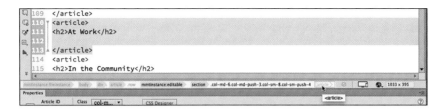

```
109  </article>
110  <article>
111  <h2>At Work</h2>
112
113  </article>
114  <article>
115  <h2>In the Community</h2>
```

The `<article>` and the heading *At Work* are deleted.

15 Select the heading *Collapsible Group 2* and type **At Work** to replace it (approximately line 93).

```
91  <div class="panel panel-default">
92  <div class="panel-heading">
93  <h4 class="panel-title"><a data-toggle="collapse" data-parent="#accordion1" href=
    "#collapseTwo1">At Work</a></h4>
94  </div>
95  <div id="collapseTwo1" class="panel-collapse collapse">
96  <div class="panel-body">Content for Accordion Panel 2</div>
97  </div>
```

16 Delete the placeholder text *Content for Accordion Panel 2* and paste the list you cut from step 13 (approximately line 96).

```
92  <div class="panel-heading">
93  <h4 class="panel-title"><a data-toggle="collapse" data-parent="#accordion1" href=
    "#collapseTwo1">At Work</a></h4>
94  </div>
95  <div id="collapseTwo1" class="panel-collapse collapse">
96  <div class="panel-body"><ul>
97  <li>Use recycled paper.</li>
98  <li>Print on both sides of the paper</li>
99  <li>Turn your computer screen off when you leave your desk</li>
```

17 Repeat steps 12–16 to create the content section for *In the Community*.

When you're finished, all three lists are now contained within Accordion 1, and all the empty `<article>` elements have been deleted.

18 Switch to Live view.

You inserted a Bootstrap Accordion and added content to it.

19 Test the panels by clicking each heading.

When clicked, the panel should open, revealing the list contained within. When you click a different heading, the new panel opens, closing the old one.

20 Save all files.

In the next exercise, you'll learn how to apply the site color scheme to the Accordion widget.

Styling a Bootstrap Accordion

As with the basic layout and the other Bootstrap components created by Dreamweaver, the accordion is formatted by the Bootstrap CSS and JavaScript files. You should avoid editing these files directly unless you know what you are doing. Instead, you'll apply the site design theme to Accordion 1 using your own custom style sheet as before. Let's start with the tabs.

1 Click the *At Home* tab.
   Examine the tag selectors.

The tab is composed of three main elements: <div.panel-heading>, <h4.panel-title>, and <a>. But that's only on the surface. Behind the scenes, the Bootstrap JavaScript and CSS functions are manipulating the HTML and CSS to produce the various behaviors controlling the accordion. As you move your mouse over the tabs and click them, class attributes are being changed on the fly to produce the hover effects and animated panels.

As you learned earlier, hyperlinks exhibit four basic behaviors: link, visited, hover, and active. The Bootstrap framework is taking advantage of these default states to apply the various effects you see when interacting with Accordion 1 for the *At Home* list.

Your job will be to create several new rules that will override the default styling and apply the GreenStart theme instead. The first step is to format the default state of the tabs. Since only one tab can be open at a time, the closed state is considered the default state.

2 Click the *At Home* tab heading to close the tab content.

The tabs are currently styled a light gray. You need to identify any rules that format the background color of the Accordion tab. Be aware that there may be more than one rule affecting these properties.

One trick that can help you identify rules that are styling a specific element is to notice how the selected element is displayed in the document window. For example, when you clicked the heading initially, only the <a> element was selected, as shown below.

You can see how the HUD outlines the heading text.

3 Click the h4 tag selector for the closed tab.

When you click the h4 tag selector, the HUD outlines the <h4> element but does not extend to the entire tab.

The outline is a literal indication of how far the styling of the heading extends. That means you can ignore rules styling the a and h4 elements if you want to set the background of the entire tab.

4 Click the next element in the tag selector interface.

The element <div.panel-heading> is selected. Note how the HUD outlines the entire tab.

5 Click the Current button in the CSS Designer.
Examine the rules and properties applied to this element.

The very first rule displayed in the Selectors window, .panel-default > .panel-heading, applies a background color. To apply the site color theme, you need to override this rule.

6 Click the All button.

Choose **green_styles.css** > GLOBAL.

Create a new selector:

```
article .panel-default > .panel-heading
```

Since some elements already feature the site theme, it's a simple matter to grab this styling using the CSS Designer. Let's format the tabs the same way the footer is styled.

7 Select the `footer` rule in **green_styles.css** in the Selectors window.

8 Right-click the `footer` rule.

Select Copy Styles > Copy Background Styles from the context menu.

9 Right-click the rule `article .panel-default > .panel-heading` and select Paste Styles from the context menu.

The background color and gradient properties are added to the new rule.

10 Add the following property:

```
color: #FFC
```

This styling will apply to the default state of the Accordion tabs. We'll add some interactive styling later, but first let's flesh out the styling of the accordion.

11 Choose **green_styles.css** > GLOBAL.
Create a new selector:
```
article #accordion1
```

12 Create the following properties:

```
border: solid 1px #060
border-radius: 5px
```

This new rule defines a border around the entire accordion.

13 Create a new selector: `article .panel-body`
Create the following property: `background-color: #CFC`

This rule adds a background color to the content panels.

Finally, let's give the accordion a little flair by adding a rollover behavior to the tabs. Although it's mainly used for links, the `:hover` pseudo-class can be used anytime you want to create interactive effects.

14 Right-click the rule
`article .panel-default > .panel-heading`.
Select Duplicate from the context menu.

A duplicate of the rule appears in the Selectors window, complete with the same styling.

15 Edit the new selector by adding the highlighted markup:

```
article .panel-default > .panel-heading:hover
```

The new rule will format the tabs whenever you position the cursor over the tab. But at the moment, the styling is identical to the original.

16 Edit the background gradient property.

Change the angle to **180**

17 Change the `color` property to **#FFF**

18 Save all files.

19 Position the cursor over each tab to test the new behavior.

The gradient background inverts as the cursor moves over and away from each tab. There is only one distraction in the overall effect. The default hyperlink styling adds an underline to the heading when the cursor passes over it.

Although this may be an acceptable behavior in a normal text-based link, it's rather distracting in the Accordion tab. To turn this effect off, you first have to find the rule that's responsible for creating it.

20 Select the Current button in the CSS Designer.

21 Click the heading *At Home* in the first tab. Examine the rules listed in the Selectors window. Try to identify any rules adding the underline effect.

The third rule, `a:hover, a:focus`, applies the underline effect. We don't want to turn this styling off for all hyperlinks, just for links in the Accordion tabs.

22 Create a new selector in **green_styles.css** > GLOBAL.

The name `.panel-heading .panel-title a` appears in the window.

23 Press the up arrow key to make the selector less specific.

24 Add the highlighted markup to the name:

```
.panel-title a:hover,
.panel-title a:focus
```

This rule will style the hover state of the tab heading.

25 Create the following property:

```
text-decoration: none
```

26 Test the rollover effect.

The underline no longer appears in the Accordion tabs.

27 Save all files.

The accordion is just one of over 100 Bootstrap and jQuery widgets and components offered by Dreamweaver. They allow you to incorporate advanced functionality into your website, while requiring little or no programming skill. All of these components can be accessed via either the Insert menu or panel.

Adding interactivity to your webpages opens new possibilities of interest and excitement for your visitors, engaging them in new ways. It can easily be overdone, but a wise use of interactivity can help bring in new visitors and keep your frequent visitors coming back for more.

Review questions

1   What is a benefit of using Dreamweaver behaviors?

2   What three steps must be used to create a Dreamweaver behavior?

3   What's the purpose of assigning an id to an image before applying a behavior?

4   What does a Bootstrap Accordion widget do?

5   What Dreamweaver tools are helpful in troubleshooting CSS styling on dynamic elements?

Review answers

1   Dreamweaver behaviors add interactive functionality to a webpage quickly and easily.

2   To create a Dreamweaver behavior, you need to create or select a trigger element, select a desired behavior, and specify the parameters.

3   The id is essential for selecting the specific image during the process of applying a behavior.

4   A Bootstrap Accordion widget includes multiple collapsible panels that hide and reveal content in a compact area of the page.

5   The Current mode of the CSS Designer helps identify any existing CSS styling and create new specifications.

13 WORKING WITH WEB ANIMATION AND VIDEO

Lesson overview

In this lesson, you'll learn how to incorporate web-compatible animation and video components into your webpage and do the following:

- Insert web-compatible animation
- Insert web-compatible video

This lesson will take about 40 minutes to complete. Download the project files for this lesson from the Lesson & Update Files tab on your Account page at www.peachpit.com, store them on your computer in a convenient location, and define a new site based on the lesson13 folder, as described in the "Getting Started" section of this book. Your Account page is also where you'll find any updates to the lessons or to the lesson files. Look on the Lesson & Update Files tab to access the most current content.

Dreamweaver allows you to integrate HTML5-compatible animation and video.

Understanding web animation and video

The web can provide a variety of experiences to the average user. One second, you are downloading and reading a best-selling novel. Next, you're listening to your favorite radio station or performing artist. Then, you're watching live television coverage or a feature-length movie. Before Adobe Flash, animation and video were hard to incorporate onto websites. That's because HTML was invented at a time when even static images were difficult to use on the Internet; video was a dream far off in the future.

Video and animation content was eventually provided in a variety of formats using a hodgepodge of applications, plug-ins, and coder-decoders (codecs) that could transfer data across the Internet to your computer and browser. Often this was accomplished with enormous difficulties and incompatibilities. Frequently, a format that worked in one browser was incompatible with another. Applications that worked in Windows didn't work on the Mac. Most formats required their own proprietary players or plug-ins.

For a time, Adobe Flash brought order to this chaos. It provided a single platform for creating both animation and video. Flash started as an animation program and changed the web for everyone. A few years ago, it revolutionized the industry again by making it a simple task to add video to a site. By inserting a video into Flash and saving the file as a SWF or FLV file, web designers and developers were able to take advantage of the almost universal distribution of the Flash Player (installed on over 90 percent of all desktop computers). No more worries over formats and codecs—Flash Player took care of all that.

With the invention and rise in popularity of smartphones and tablet devices over the last decade, Flash has fallen on hard times. For most manufacturers, the power and capability of Flash were too difficult to support on these devices, and it was abandoned. Flash is not dead. It's still unmatched for its multimedia power and functionality. But today, all bets are off when it comes to animation and video. The techniques for creating web-based media are being reinvented. As you may have guessed, this trend away from Flash is ringing in a new era of chaos on the web media front. Half a dozen or more codecs are competing to become the "be-all, end-all" format for video distribution and playback for the web.

The only ray of sunshine in this morass is that HTML5 was developed with built-in support for both animation and video. Great strides have already been made to replace much of the capability of Flash-based animation using native HTML5 and CSS3 functionality. The status of video is not as clear. So far, a single standard has not yet emerged, which means that to support all the popular desktop and mobile browsers, you'll have to produce several different video files. In this lesson, you'll learn how to incorporate different types of web animation and video into your site.

Previewing the completed file

To see what you'll work on in this lesson, preview the completed page in a browser. The finished page is based on the travel page you created in Lesson 12, "Adding Interactivity."

1 Launch Adobe Dreamweaver CC (2015.1 release) or later.

2 If necessary, define a site based on the lesson13 folder. Press F8 to open the Files panel, and choose lesson13 from the site list drop-down menu.

3 Open **travel_finished.html** from the finished folder. Preview the page in your default browser.

The page includes two media elements: the banner animation at the top of the `main_content` region and the video inserted below. Depending on the browser used to view the page, the video may be generated from one of four different formats: MP4, WebM, Ogg, or Flash Video.

4 Note that the banner ad plays when the page loads and loops after it calls you to sign up for the Eco-Tour.

5 To view the video, click the Play button. If you do not see a Play button, your browser may be showing a Flash fallback version of the video. Move the cursor over the video to display the control skin, and click the Play button.

● **Note:** Internet Explorer may block dynamic content from playing when it's on your local hard drive. You will probably have to click a button to allow this content to play.

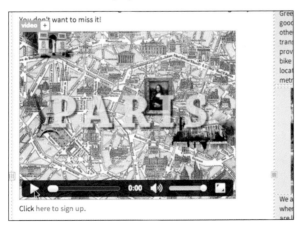

Different browsers support different types of video. Depending on the video format your browser supports, you may notice that the controls fade if you move the cursor away from the video, but that they return once you position the cursor over the video again.

6   When you're finished previewing the media, close your browser. Return to Dreamweaver and close **travel_finished.html**.

Video and animation provide powerful venues for rich web content, and Dreamweaver makes it a simple matter to insert this type of content.

Adobe Edge Animate

The animation used in this lesson was built in Edge Animate—a program developed by Adobe not to replace Flash but to create web animation and interactive content natively using HTML5, CSS3, and JavaScript. Edge Animate is available to all Creative Cloud subscribers.

Check out www.adobe.com/products/edge-animate.html for more information about Edge Animate.

Adding web animation to a page

Dreamweaver has a built-in and simplified workflow for inserting Edge Animate compositions, making the process a point-and-click operation. Dreamweaver takes advantage of a feature in Edge Animate designed to assist in deploying compositions to other programs and workflows, such as Adobe InDesign, Adobe Dreamweaver, and Apple's iBooks Author. The File > Publish Settings command (shown in the figure) enables you to export your Edge Animate compositions into a single file or folder.

By defining your Publish settings appropriately, you can create a complete set of files that are compatible with these applications. For the purposes of this exercise, we published an OAM file for you, which is an archive file format that contains all the constituent elements needed to support the animation in Dreamweaver.

1   Open **travel.html** from the lesson13 site root folder in Live view.

The banner will be inserted above the main heading. But we have to take an interim step to get it into this page. At the time of this writing, Dreamweaver can't insert OAM files into child pages still connected to a template. So you will have to insert the animation into an empty page and then manually transfer the code to the travel page.

2   Select File > New.

The New Document dialog appears.

3   Choose HTML in the Document Type section of the dialog.

4   Choose None in the Framework section.

5 Click Create.

A new blank document appears. Before you can insert the banner, you have to save the file.

6 Save the file as **animation_transfer.html**.
If necessary, switch to Live view.

7 Choose Insert > HTML > Animated Composition. You may also use the Animated Composition option in the Insert panel's HTML category.

8 Navigate to the lesson13/resources folder.
Select **ecotour.oam**.

9 Click OK/Open to insert the composition.

The banner should appear and begin to play. It is designed to loop over and over.

10 Save the file and switch to Code view.

11 Examine the HTML code.

The file contains the structure of a basic webpage, including `<head>` and `<body>` sections, as well as the Edge Animate stage and support code.

Tip: When selecting large amounts of code, click or drag the line numbers.

12 In the Code view window, select and copy all the markup contained between the `<!--Adobe Edge Runtime-->` and `<!--Adobe Edge Runtime End-->` comments.

13 Click the **travel.html** document tab and switch to Code view.

14 In the Code view window, scroll to the `<head>` section. Insert the cursor at the end of the notation `<!-- InstanceBeginEditable name="doctitle" -->` and press Enter/Return to create a new line (approximately line 7).

15 Paste the runtime markup copied in step 12.

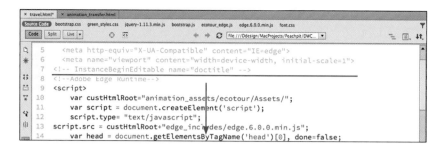

The next step is to transfer the composition stage.

Note: When selecting the stage, don't forget the closing </div> tag.

16 Switch to **animation_transfer.html**.

17 In Code view, select the markup
`<div id="Stage" class="EDGE-204064396"> </div>` and copy it
(approximately line 40).

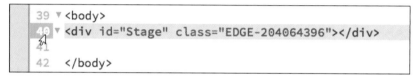

18 Switch to **travel.html**.

19 In the Code view window, scroll to the `<body>` section. Insert the cursor before
the markup `<h1>Green Travel</h1>` (approximately line 114) and paste the
stage.

20 Press Return/Enter to move the heading to a new line, if necessary.

21 Switch to Live view.

The banner animation plays automatically in Live view once the code is processed.

It may seem like a miracle that this amazing banner animation was created by one simple file, but what you cannot see is that Dreamweaver just created in the site root directory a new folder that is populated by more than a dozen files.

22 Open the Files panel and examine the list of folders in the site root.

◆ **Warning:** Dreamweaver will not automatically upload all the support files needed for the Edge Animate composition. Be sure to upload the entire contents of the **animation_assets** folder when publishing the site to the web.

Local Files		Size	Type	Modifi
▼ 📁 Site – lesson13 (Ddesign:MacProjects:Peachpit:DW…			Folder	10/
📄 about_us.html		7KB	HTML File	10/
▼ 📁 animation_assets			Folder	10/
▼ 📁 ecotour			Folder	10/
▼ 📁 Assets			Folder	10/
📄 ecotour.html		2KB	HTML File	10/
📄 ecotour_edge.js		8KB	JS File	10/
📄 ecotour_oam.xml		3KB	XML File	10/
▼ 📁 edge_includes			Folder	10/
📄 edge.6.0.0.min.js		102KB	JS File	10/
▼ 📁 images			Folder	10/
🖼 Arc.png		28KB	PNG File	10/
🖼 catacombs.png		15KB	PNG File	10/
🖼 champs.png		13KB	PNG File	10/
🖼 cruise.png		25KB	PNG File	10/
🖼 ecotour-base.png		1.77MB	PNG File	10/

The folder named **animation_assets** now appears in the root directory. The folder was generated automatically and contains all the files needed to support the composition. The entire folder must be uploaded to the web host when **travel.html** is posted.

23 Save all files.

Congratulations! You've successfully incorporated an HTML5- and CSS3-based animation in your page.

Poster child

The widespread popularity and support of HTML5 should mean that your animation will run in most browsers and mobile devices. But there's a very small possibility that the animation may be incompatible with older computers and software. Edge Animate can include either a down-level stage or a static poster image that will be viewed in these circumstances.

To add or create a down-level stage or poster within Edge Animate, select the project stage and then add the appropriate content using the Properties panel.

Adding web video to a page

Implementing HTML5-compatible video in your site is a bit more involved than it was when you had to insert only a single Flash-based file. Unfortunately, no single video format is supported by all browsers in use today. To make sure your video content plays everywhere, you'll have to supply several different formats. Dreamweaver CC now provides a built-in technique to add multiple video files so you won't have to do all the coding yourself. In this exercise, you will learn how to insert HTML5-compatible video on a page in your site.

1   If necessary, open **travel.html** in Live view.

   You will insert the video in the main_content section of the page.

2   Click the paragraph *Click here to sign up*.

   The HUD appears focused on the p tag.

● **Note:** Open the Property inspector and dock it to the bottom of the document window, if necessary.

3   Choose Insert > HTML > HTML5 Video.

   The Position Assist HUD appears.

4 Click Before.

An HTML5-compatible video placeholder appears on the page, and the Property inspector displays new options for targeting the video source files. Note that this interface enables you to specify up to three video source files and one Flash fallback file. The first step is to select your primary video source.

5 In the Property inspector, click the Browse icon ▥ in the Source field. Navigate to the **movies** folder and select the **paris.mp4** file. Click OK/Open.

The MP4 video replaces the video placeholder. Note that Alt Source 1 is automatically populated with a WebM version of the movie.

The MP4 file format will be the primary video format loaded. MP4, also known as MPEG-4, is a video format based on Apple's QuickTime standard. It is supported natively by iOS-compatible devices, such as the iPhone and iPad, as well as by Apple's Safari browser. Many experts advise loading MP4 files first; otherwise, iOS devices may ignore the video element altogether.

WebM is an open-source, royalty-free video format sponsored by Google. It is compatible with Firefox 4, Chrome 6, Opera 10.6, and Internet Explorer 9 and later.

To round out our HTML5 video selections, the next format you'll load is a lossy, open-source multimedia format: Ogg. It is designed for the distribution of multimedia content that is free of copyright and other media restrictions.

● **Note:** Ogg is a container format. When the container contains a video, it uses the extension .ogv.

6 Click the Browse icon 🗂 for the Alt Source 2 field. Select the file **paris.theora. ogv** from the **movies** folder and click OK/Open.

These three formats support all the modern desktop and mobile browsers. But to support older software and devices, using a stalwart old friend—Flash video—may be necessary. By adding it last, you ensure that only browsers that don't support the other three formats will load the Flash content. Although many are abandoning Flash, Dreamweaver still provides support for inserting both FLV and SWF files.

7 Click Browse in the Flash Fallback field.

Select the **paris.flv** file from the **movies** folder and click OK/Open.

8 Save the file.

9 If necessary, switch to Live view.

In some browsers, the `<video>` element won't generate a preview of the video content. You can add an image placeholder by using the Poster field in the Property inspector.

10 If necessary, select the `<video>` tag selector.

In the Property inspector, click Browse in the Poster field.

11 In the **movies** folder, select **paris-poster.png** and click OK/Open.

A preview image has been applied to the `<video>` element. It won't be visible in Dreamweaver, but you may see the poster in the browser. The advantage of using a poster is that something will always appear on the page, even in the rare browsers that do not support HTML5 or Flash video formats.

12 Save all files.

Video controls appear below the poster depending on what video format is displayed. In the next exercise, you will learn how to configure these controls and how the video will respond to the user.

Buggy video

At this point, you would normally be finished and ready to test your video configuration in multiple browsers. Unfortunately, the Flash fallback using an FLV source file is missing some essential support files and will not play the FLV correctly as is. Dreamweaver has a bug affecting the proper support of both FLV and SWF video using the new HTML5 video workflow described in this section.

The Dreamweaver engineers promised to fix this issue in a subsequent cloud update, but until then you can correct the issue yourself by simply replacing the new code element using the legacy Flash video workflow, like this:

1 Select the `<video>` tag selector.

2 Switch to Code view. If necessary, select Source Code in the Related Files interface.

3 Select the entire `<embed>` element containing the reference to **paris.flv** and delete it.

4 Choose Insert > HTML > Flash Video.

5 In the Insert FLV dialog, click the Browse icon. Select **paris.flv** from the **movies** folder and click OK/Open.

The filename **paris.flv** appears in the URL field of the dialog. Flash video supplies its own controls via a SWF skin interface. You can choose your own skin design in this dialog.

6 Choose **Corona Skin 2** from the Skin pop-up menu.

Before you can insert the file, you have to specify the dimensions of the video.

7 In the Width field, enter: **400**
In the Height field, enter: **300**

You can use the options below these fields to specify whether you want the video to autoplay and autorewind.

8 Click OK to insert the FLV video.

The `<embed>` element is now replaced by an `<object>` tag, along with all the code necessary to run the Flash video and even detect the presence and version of the needed Flash Player. This is the simplest method to insert FLV-compatible video so that it will play properly in all browsers that don't support HTML5 video.

Choosing HTML5 video options

The final step for configuring the video is to decide what other HTML5-supported options to specify. The options are displayed within the Property inspector whenever the `<video>` element is chosen. The options are selectable in all views.

1   If necessary, open **travel.html** in Live view.
    Select the `<video>` tag selector.
    Observe the left side of the Property inspector.

    - **Controls** displays visible video controls.

    - **AutoPlay** starts the video automatically after the webpage loads.

    - **Loop** causes the video to replay from the beginning automatically once it finishes.

    - **Muted** silences the audio.

    - **Preload** specifies the method in which the video loads.

2   If necessary, select the Controls option and deselect the AutoPlay, Loop, and Muted options. Set Preload to **none**.

    Video is very memory- and bandwidth-intensive. This is especially true for phones and tablets. Setting Preload to none prevents any video resources from downloading until the user actually clicks the video. It may take the video a few more seconds to download when launched, but your visitors will appreciate that you are respectful of their minutes and data plan.

    The `<video>` element is now complete, but it's not responsive. Adding a simple rule can take care of that issue.

3   Select the `video` tag selector, if necessary.

4   In the CSS Designer, select **green_styles.css** > GLOBAL.
    Create a new selector: `video`

5   Create the following properties:
    `max-width: 100%`
    `height: auto`

6 Preview the page in Live view or in a browser. If the video controls are not visible, move your cursor over the still image to display them. Click the Play button to view the movie.

Chrome   Firefox   Safari

Depending on where you preview the page, you will see one of the four video formats. For example, in Live view you will see the MP4-based video. The controls will appear differently depending on what format is displayed. This movie has no sound, but the controls will often include a speaker button to adjust the volume or mute the audio.

7 Drag the Scrubber to the left to check the display of the video at various screen widths.

The video resizes as needed to fit the available space.

You've embedded three HTML5-compatible videos and an FLV fallback, which gives you support for most browsers and devices that can access the Internet. But you've learned only one possible technique for supporting this evolving standard. To learn more about HTML5 video and how to implement it, check out the following links:

- http://tinyurl.com/video-HTML5-1
- http://tinyurl.com/video-HTML5-2
- http://tinyurl.com/video-HTML5-3

To learn more about implementing video for mobile devices, check out these links:

- http://tinyurl.com/fluid-video
- http://tinyurl.com/fluid-video-1

Review questions

1   What advantage does HTML5 have over HTML 4 regarding web-based media?

2   What programming language(s) created the HTML5-compatible animation used in this lesson?

3   True or false: To support all web browsers, you can select a single video format.

4   In browsers or devices that do not support video, what can you do to provide some form of content to these users?

5   What video format is recommended to support older browsers?

Review answers

1   HTML5 has built-in support for web animation, video, and audio.

2   The animation used in this lesson was created by Adobe Edge Animate natively using HTML5, CSS3, and JavaScript.

3   False. A single format supported by every browser has not emerged. Developers recommend incorporating four video formats to support the majority of browsers: MP4, WebM, Ogg, and FLV.

4   You can add a static poster image (GIF, JPG, or PNG) via an option in the Property inspector to provide a preview of the video content in incompatible browsers and devices.

5   FLV (Flash video) is recommended as the fallback format for older browsers because of the widespread installation of the Flash Player.

14 PUBLISHING TO THE WEB

Lesson overview

In this lesson, you'll publish your website to the Internet and do the following:

- Define a remote site
- Define a testing server
- Put files on the web
- Cloak files and folders
- Update out-of-date links sitewide

 This lesson will take about one hour to complete. If you have not already done so, download the project files for this lesson from the Lesson & Update Files tab on your Account page at www.peachpit.com, store them on your computer in a convenient location, and define a new site based on the lesson14 folder, as described in the "Getting Started" section of this book. Your Account page is also where you'll find any updates to the lessons or to the lesson files. Look on the Lesson & Update Files tab to access the most current content.

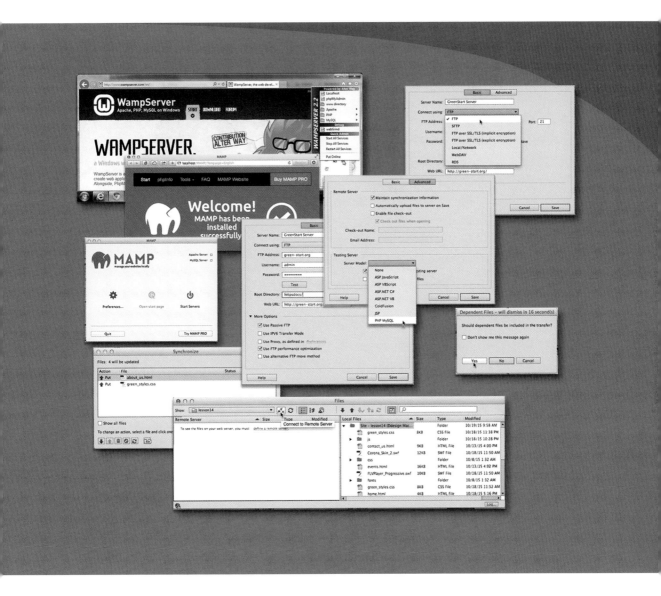

The goal of all the preceding lessons is to design, develop, and build pages for a remote website. But Dreamweaver doesn't abandon you there. It also provides powerful tools to upload and maintain any size website over time.

Defining a remote site

● **Note:** If you have not already downloaded the project files for this lesson to your computer from your Account page and defined a site based on this folder, make sure to do so now. See "Getting Started" at the beginning of the book.

Dreamweaver's workflow is based on a two-site system. One site is in a folder on your computer's hard drive and is known as the *local site*. All work in the previous lessons has been performed on your local site. The second site, known as the *remote site*, is established in a folder on a web server, typically running on another computer, and is connected to the Internet and publicly available. In large companies, the remote site is often available only to employees via a network-based intranet. Such sites provide information and applications to support corporate programs and products.

Dreamweaver supports several methods for connecting to a remote site:

- **FTP** (File Transfer Protocol)—The standard method for connecting to hosted websites.

- **SFTP** (Secure File Transfer Protocol)—A protocol that provides a method to connect to hosted websites in a more secure manner to preclude unauthorized access or interception of online content.

- **FTP over SSL/TLS** (implicit encryption)—A secure FTP (FTPS) method that requires all clients of the FTPS server be aware that SSL is to be used on the session. It is incompatible with non-FTPS-aware clients.

- **FTP over SSL/TLS** (explicit encryption)—A legacy-compatible, secure FTP method where FTPS-aware clients can invoke security with an FTPS-aware server without breaking overall FTP functionality with non-FTPS-aware clients.

- **Local/network**—A local or network connection is most frequently used with an intermediate web server, known as a *staging server*. Staging servers are typically used to test sites before they go live. Files from the staging server are eventually published to an Internet-connected web server.

- **WebDav** (Web Distributed Authoring and Versioning)—A web-based system also known to Windows users as Web Folders and to Mac users as iDisk.

- **RDS** (Remote Development Services)—Developed by Adobe for ColdFusion and primarily used when working with ColdFusion-based sites.

Dreamweaver now can upload larger files faster and more efficiently and as a background activity, allowing you to return to work more quickly. In the following exercises, you'll set up a remote site using the two most common methods: FTP and Local/Network.

Setting up a remote FTP site

The vast majority of web developers rely on FTP to publish and maintain their sites. FTP is a well-established protocol, and many variations of the protocol are used on the web—most of which are supported by Dreamweaver.

1   Launch Adobe Dreamweaver CC (2015.1 release) or later.

2   Choose Site > Manage Sites or choose Manage Sites from the site list drop-down menu in the Files panel.

◆ **Warning:** To complete the following exercise, you must have a remote server already established. Remote servers can be hosted by your own company or contracted from a third-party web-hosting service.

3   In the Manage Sites dialog is a list of all the sites you may have defined.

Make sure that the current site, lesson14, is selected.

Click the Edit icon ✐.

4 In the Site Setup dialog for lesson14, click the Servers category.

The Site Setup dialog allows you to set up multiple servers, so you can test several types of installations, if desired.

5 Click the Add New Server icon ✚.
Enter **GreenStart Server** in the Server Name field.

6 From the Connect Using pop-up menu, choose FTP.

7 In the FTP Address field, type the URL or IP (Internet protocol) address of your FTP server.

▶ **Tip:** If you are in the process of moving an existing site to a new Internet Service Provider (ISP), you may not be able to use the domain name to upload files to the new server. In that case, the IP address can be used to upload files initially.

If you contract a third-party service as a web host, you will be assigned an FTP address. This address may come in the form of an IP address, such as 192.168.1.100. Enter this number into the field exactly as it was sent to you. Frequently, the FTP address will be the domain name of your site, such as **ftp.green-start.org**. But don't enter the characters *ftp* into the field.

8 In the Username field, enter your FTP user name.
In the Password field, enter your FTP password.

Usernames may be case sensitive, but password fields almost always are; be sure you enter them correctly. Often, the easiest way to enter them is to copy them from the confirmation email from your hosting company and paste them into the appropriate fields.

▶ **Tip:** Check with your web-hosting service or IS/IT manager to obtain the root directory name, if any.

9 In the Root Directory field, type the name of the folder that contains documents publicly accessible to the web, if any.

Some web hosts provide FTP access to a root-level folder that might contain nonpublic folders—such as cgi-bin, which is used to store common gateway interface (CGI) or binary scripts—as well as a public folder. In these cases, type the public folder name—such as public, public_html, www, or wwwroot—in the Root Directory field. In many web host configurations, the FTP address is the same as the public folder, and the Root Directory field should be left blank.

10 Select the Save option if you don't want to re-enter your username and password every time Dreamweaver connects to your site.

11 Click Test to verify that your FTP connection works properly.

▶ **Tip:** If Dreamweaver does not connect to your host, first check the username and password, as well as the FTP address and root directory for any errors.

Dreamweaver displays an alert to notify you that the connection was successful or unsuccessful.

12 Click OK to dismiss the alert.

If Dreamweaver connects properly to the webhost, skip to step 14. If you received an error message, your web server may require additional configuration options.

13 Click the More Options triangle to reveal additional server options.

Consult the instructions from your hosting company to select the appropriate options for your specific FTP server:

- **Use Passive FTP**—Allows your computer to connect to the host computer and bypass a firewall restraint. Many web hosts require this setting.

- **Use IPV6 Transfer Mode**—Enables connection to IPV6-based servers, which use the most recent version of the Internet transfer protocol.

- **Use Proxy**—Identifies a secondary proxy host connection as defined in your Dreamweaver preferences.

- **Use FTP Performance Optimization**—Optimizes the FTP connection. Deselect this option if Dreamweaver can't connect to your server.

- **Use Alternative FTP Move Method**—Provides an additional method to resolve FTP conflicts, especially when rollbacks are enabled or when moving files.

Troubleshooting your FTP connection

Connecting to your remote site can be frustrating the first time you attempt it. You can experience numerous pitfalls, many of which are out of your control. Here are a few steps to take if you have issues connecting:

- If you can't connect to your FTP server, double-check your username and password and re-enter them carefully. Remember that usernames may be case sensitive on some servers, while passwords frequently are. (This is the most common error.)

- Select Use Passive FTP and test the connection again.

- If you still can't connect to your FTP server, deselect the Use FTP Performance Optimization option and click Test again.

- If none of these steps enable you to connect to your remote site, check with your IS/IT manager or your remote site administrator or web-hosting service.

Once you establish a working connection, you may need to configure some advanced options.

14 Click the Advanced tab. Select among the following options for working with your remote site:

- **Maintain Synchronization Information**—Automatically notes the files that have been changed on the local and remote sites so that they can be easily synchronized. This feature helps you keep track of your changes and can be helpful if you change multiple pages before you upload. You may want to use cloaking with this feature. You'll learn about cloaking in an upcoming exercise. This feature is usually selected by default.

- **Automatically Upload Files To Server On Save**—Transfers files from the local to the remote site when they are saved. This option can become annoying if you save often and aren't yet ready for a page to go public.

- **Enable File Check-Out**—Starts the check-in/check-out system for collaborative website building in a workgroup environment. If you choose this option, you'll need to enter a check-out name and, optionally, an email address. If you're working by yourself, you do not need to select this option.

It is acceptable to leave any or all these options unselected, but for the purposes of this lesson, select the Maintain Synchronization Information option, if necessary.

15 Click Save to finalize the settings in the open dialogs.

The server setup dialog closes, revealing the Servers category in the Site Setup dialog. Your newly defined server is displayed in the window.

16 Click the Remote radio button to the right of the server name if necessary.

Site Setup for lesson14					
Site	Here you'll select the server that will host your pages on the web. The settings for this dialog box come from your Internet Service Provider (ISP) or your web administrator.				
Servers					
Version Control					
▶ Advanced Settings					
	Name	Address	Connection	Remote	Testing
	GreenStart Server	green-start.org	FTP	◉	○

17 Click Save to finish setting up your new server.

A dialog appears, informing you that the cache will be re-created because you changed the site settings.

18 Click OK to build the cache. When Dreamweaver finishes updating the cache, click Done to close the Manage Sites dialog.

You have established a connection to your remote server. If you don't currently have a remote server, you can substitute a local testing server instead as your remote server.

Installing a testing server

When you produce sites with dynamic content, you need to test functionality before the pages go live on the Internet. A testing server can fit that need nicely. Depending on the applications you need to test, the testing server can simply be a subfolder on your actual web server, or you can use a local web server such as Apache or Internet Information Services (IIS) from Microsoft.

For detailed information about installing and configuring a local web server, check out the following links:

- Apache/ColdFusion—http://tinyurl.com/setup-coldfusion
- Apache/PHP—http://tinyurl.com/setup-apachephp
- IIS/ASP—http://tinyurl.com/setup-asp

Once you set up the local web server, you can use it to upload the completed files and test your remote site. In most cases, your local web server will not be accessible from the Internet or be able to host the actual website for the public.

Establishing a remote site on a local or network web server (Optional)

If your company or organization uses a staging server as a "middleman" between web designers and the live website, it's likely you'll need to connect to your remote site through a local or network web server. Local/network servers are often used as testing servers to check dynamic functions before pages are uploaded to the Internet.

1 Launch Adobe Dreamweaver CC (2015.1 release) or later.

2 Choose Site > Manage Sites.

3 In the Manage Sites dialog, make sure that lesson14 is selected. Click the Edit icon ✏.

4 In the Site Setup for lesson14 dialog, select the Servers category.

5 Click the Add New Server icon ✚ if you have already installed a local testing server.
In the Server Name field, enter **GreenStart Local**.

6 From the Connect Using pop-up menu, choose Local/Network.

7 In the Server Folder field, click the Browse icon 📁.

Select the local web server's HTML folder, such as C:\wamp\www\lesson14.

8 In the Web URL field, enter the appropriate URL for your local web server. If you are using WAMP or MAMP local servers, your web URL will be something like http://localhost:8888/lesson14 or http://localhost/lesson14.

You must enter the correct URL, or Dreamweaver's FTP and testing features may not function properly.

● **Note:** The paths you enter here are contingent on how you installed your local web server and may not be the same as the ones displayed.

9 Click the Advanced tab, and as with the actual web server, select the appropriate options for working with your remote site: Maintain Synchronization Information, Automatically Upload Files To Server On Save, and/or Enable File Check-Out.

Although leaving these three options unselected is acceptable, for the purposes of this lesson, select the Maintain Synchronization Information option if necessary.

10 If you'd like to use the local web server as the testing server too, select the server model in the Advanced section of the dialog. If you are creating a dynamic site using a specific programming language, like ASP, ColdFusion, or PHP, select the matching Server Model from the drop-down menu so you'll be able to test the pages of your site properly.

11 Click Save to complete the remote server setup.

12 In the Site Setup dialog for lesson14, select Remote. If you want to use the local server as a testing server too, select Testing. Click Save.

13 In the Manage Sites dialog, click Done. If necessary, click OK to rebuild the cache.

Only one remote and one testing server can be active at one time, but you may have multiple servers defined. One server can be used for both roles, if desired. Before you upload files for the remote site, you may need to cloak certain folders and files in the local site.

Cloaking folders and files

Not all the files in your site root folder may need to be transferred to the remote server. For example, there's no point in filling the remote site with files that won't be accessed or that will remain inaccessible to website users. Minimizing files stored on the remote server may also pay financial dividends, since many hosting services base part of their fee on how much disk space your site occupies. If you selected Maintain Synchronization Information for a remote site using FTP or a network server, you may want to cloak some of your local materials to prevent them from being uploaded. *Cloaking* is a Dreamweaver feature that allows you to designate certain folders and files that will not be uploaded to or synchronized with the remote site.

▶ **Tip:** You might consider uploading the template files to the server as means of creating a backup.

Folders you don't want to upload include the Templates and resource folders. Some other non-web-compatible file types used to create your site, like Photoshop (.psd), Flash (.fla), or Microsoft Word (.doc) files, also don't need to be on the remote server. Although cloaked files will not upload or synchronize automatically, you may still upload them manually, if desired. Some people like to upload these items to keep a backup copy of them off-site.

The cloaking process begins in the Site Setup dialog.

1 Choose Site > Manage Sites.

2 Select lesson14 in the site list, and click the Edit icon ✏ .

3 Expand the Advanced Settings category and select the Cloaking category. Select the Enable Cloaking and Cloak Files Ending With checkboxes, if necessary.

The field below the checkboxes displays the extensions .fla and .psd.

4 Insert the cursor after *.psd,* and insert a space, if necessary.
Type **.doc .txt .rtf**

Be sure to insert a space between each extension. By specifying the extensions of file types that don't contain desired web content, you prevent Dreamweaver from uploading and synchronizing these file types automatically no matter where they appear in the site.

5 Click Save. If Dreamweaver prompts you to update the cache, click OK. Then, click Done to close the Manage Sites dialog.

Although you have cloaked several file types automatically, you can also cloak specific files or folders manually from the File panel.

6 Open the Files panel.
The Files panel appears.

7 Right-click the resources folder.
From the context menu, choose Cloaking > Cloak.

The Templates folder is not needed on the remote site because your webpages do not reference these assets in any way. But if you work in a team environment, it may be handy to upload and synchronize these folders so that each team member has up-to-date versions of each on their own computers. For this exercise, let's assume you work alone.

8 Apply cloaking to the Templates folder.

9 In the warning dialog that appears, click OK.

Using the Site Setup dialog and the Cloaking context menu, you cloaked file types, folders, and files. The synchronization process will ignore cloaked items and will not upload or download them automatically.

Wrapping things up

Over the last 13 lessons, you have built an entire website, beginning with a starter layout and then adding text, images, movies, and interactive content, but a few loose strings remain for you to tie up. Before you publish your site, you'll need to create one important webpage and make some crucial updates to your site navigation.

The file you need to create is one that is essential to every site: a home page. The home page is usually the first page most users see on your site. It is the page that loads automatically when a user enters your site's domain name into the browser window. Since the page loads automatically, there are a few restrictions on the name and extension you can use.

Basically, the name and extension depend on the hosting server and the type of applications running on the home page, if any. Today, the majority of home pages will simply be named *index*. But *default*, *start*, and *iisstart* are also used.

Extensions identify the specific types of programming languages used within a page. A normal HTML home page will use an extension of .htm or .html. Extensions like .asp, .cfm, and .php, among others, are required if the home page contains any dynamic applications specific to that server model. You may still use one of these extensions—if they are compatible with your server model—even if the page contains no dynamic applications or content. But be careful—in some instances, using the wrong extension may prevent the page from loading altogether. Whenever you're in doubt, use .html, because it's supported in all environments.

The specific home page name or names honored by the server are normally configured by the server administrator and can be changed, if desired. Most servers are configured to honor several names and a variety of extensions. Check with your IS/IT manager or web server support team to ascertain the recommended name and extension for your home page.

1 Create a new page from the site template.
   Save the file as **index.html**, or use a filename and extension compatible with your server model.

2 Open **home.html** from the lesson14 site root folder in Design view.

   The file contains content for the new home page.

3 Insert the cursor in the heading *Welcome to Meridien GreenStart*.
   Select the `section` tag selector, and copy the content.

4   In **index.html**, select Design view.
    Click the heading *Add main heading here.*
    Select the `section` tag selector and paste.

● **Note:** Pasting to replace an element works only in Design and Code views.

5   Replace the quotation placeholder with the first `<aside>` element in **home.html**.

6   Replace Sidebar 2 with the second `<aside>` element in **home.html**.

    Note the hyperlink placeholders in the `main_content` region.

7   Insert the cursor in the *News* link and click the `a` tag selector.
    In the Property inspector, browse and connect the link to **news.html**.

8   Repeat step 2 with each link.
    Connect the links to the appropriate pages in your site root folder.

9   Save and close all files.

The home page is complete. Let's assume you want to upload the site at its current state of completion even though some pages have yet to be created. This happens in the course of any site development. Pages are added and deleted over time; missing pages will be completed and uploaded at a later date. Before you can upload the site to a live server, you should always update any out-of-date links and remove dead ones.

Putting your site online (optional)

◆ **Warning:** Dreamweaver does a good job trying to identify all the dependent files in a particular workflow. But in some cases, it may miss files crucial to a dynamic or extended process. It is imperative that you do your homework to identify these files and make sure they are uploaded.

For the most part, the local site and the remote site are mirror images, containing the same HTML files, images, and assets in identical folder structures. When you transfer a webpage from your local site to your remote site, you are publishing, or *putting,* that page. If you *put* a file stored in a folder on your local site, Dreamweaver transfers the file to the equivalent folder on the remote site. It will even automatically create the remote folder or folders if they do not already exist. The same is true when you download files.

Using Dreamweaver, you can publish anything—from one file to a complete site—in a single operation. When you publish a webpage, by default Dreamweaver asks if you would also like to put the dependent files too. Dependent files are the images, CSS, HTML5 movies, JavaScript files, server-side includes (SSI), and all other files necessary to complete the page.

You can upload one file at a time or the entire site at once. In this exercise, you will upload one webpage and its dependent files.

● **Note:** This exercise is optional since it requires that you set up a remote server beforehand.

1 Open the Files panel and click the Expand icon 🗗, if necessary.

2 Click the Connect To Remote Server icon ✖ to connect to the remote site.

If your remote site is properly configured, the Files panel will connect to the site and display its contents on the left half of the panel. When you first upload files, the remote site may be empty or mostly empty. If you are connecting to your Internet host, specific files and folders created by the hosting company may appear. Do not delete these items unless you check to see whether they are essential to the operation of the server or your own applications.

3 In the local file list, select **index.html**.
In the Document toolbar, click the Put icon ⬆.

By default, Dreamweaver will prompt you to upload dependent files. If a dependent file already exists on the server and your changes did not affect it, you can click No. Otherwise, for new files or files that have had any changes, click Yes.

4 Click Yes.

Dreamweaver uploads **index.html** and all images, CSS, JavaScript, server-side includes, and other dependent files needed to properly render the selected HTML file.

The Files panel enables you to upload multiple files as well as the entire site at once.

5 Select the site root folder for the local site, and then click the Put icon ⬆ in the Files panel.

Note: Dependent files include but are not limited to images, style sheets, and JavaScript used within a specific page and are essential to the proper display and function of the page.

Dialogs appear, asking you to confirm that you want to upload dependent files and the entire site.

6   Click Yes and OK as appropriate.

Dreamweaver begins to upload the site. It will re-create your local site structure on the remote server. Dreamweaver uploads pages in the background so that you can continue to work in the meantime. If you want to see the progress of the upload, click the Log button in the lower-right corner of the Files panel.

7   Click the Log button.

Tip: If you are using a third-party web-hosting service, be aware that they often create placeholder pages on your domain. If your home page does not automatically appear when you access your site, check to make sure that there is no conflict with the web-host's placeholder pages.

If you click the Log button before all the files have been uploaded, you will see a list featuring the filenames and the status of the selected operation. When the upload is finished, the dialog provides a report.

```
File activity incomplete. 2 file(s) or folder(s) were not completed.
Files updated: 58
Files skipped: 12

File Transfer failed due to following reasons:
- Internal data error. Failed to send network data.
- Access denied.  The file may not exist, or there could be a permission prol

Files with errors: 2
movies:paris.theora.ogv
movies:paris.mp4

Finished: 10/18/15 7:54 PM
```

Save Log...   Hide   Close

Note that none of the cloaked lesson folders were uploaded. Dreamweaver will automatically ignore all cloaked items when putting a folder or an entire site. If desired, you can manually select and upload individually cloaked items.

8 Right-click the Templates folder and choose Put from the context menu.

Note: A file that is uploaded or downloaded will automatically overwrite any version of the file at the destination.

Dreamweaver prompts you to upload dependent files for the Templates folder.

9 Click Yes to upload dependent files.

The Templates folder is uploaded to the remote server. The log report shows that Dreamweaver checked for dependent files but did not upload the files that had not changed.

Note that the remote Templates folder displays a red slash, indicating that it, too, is cloaked. At times, you will want to cloak local and remote files and folders to prevent these items from being replaced or accidentally overwritten. A cloaked file will not be uploaded or downloaded automatically. But you can manually select any specific files and perform the same action.

The opposite of the Put command is Get, which downloads any selected file or folder to the local site. You can get any file from the remote site by selecting it in the Remote or Local pane and clicking the Get icon ⬇. Alternatively, you can drag the file from the Remote pane to the Local pane.

10 If you were able to successfully upload your site, use a browser to connect to the remote site on your network server or the Internet. Type the appropriate address in the URL field—depending on whether you are connecting to the local web server or to the actual Internet site—such as http://localhost/*domain_name* or http://www.*domain_name*.com.

Note: When accessing Put and Get, it doesn't matter whether you use the Local or Remote pane of the Files panel. Put always uploads to Remote; Get always downloads to Local.

The GreenStart site appears in the browser.

11 Click to test the hyperlinks to view each of the completed pages for the site.

Once the site is uploaded, keeping it up-to-date is an easy task. As files change, you can upload them one at a time or synchronize the whole site with the remote server.

Synchronization is especially important in workgroup environments where files are changed and uploaded by several individuals. You can easily download or upload files that are older, overwriting files that are newer in the process. Synchronization can ensure that you are working with only the latest versions of each file.

Synchronizing local and remote sites

Synchronization in Dreamweaver keeps the files on your server and your local computer up to date. It's an essential tool when you work from multiple locations or with one or more coworkers. Used properly, it can prevent you from accidentally uploading or working on out-of-date files.

At the moment, your local and remote sites are identical. To better illustrate the capabilities of synchronization, let's make a change to one of the site pages.

1 Open **about_us.html** in Design view.

2 Collapse the Files panel.

Clicking the collapse button re-docks the panel on the right side of the program.

3 In the CSS Designer, select **green_styles.css** > GLOBAL.
   Create a new selector: `.green`

4 Add the following property to the new rule:
   `color: #090`

5 In the main heading, select the characters *Green* in the heading *About Meridien GreenStart*.

6 Apply the green class to this text.

7 Apply the green class to each occurrence of the word *"green"* anywhere on the page where the text is not already green in color.

8 Save all files and close the page.

9 Open and expand the Files panel. In the Document toolbar, click the Synchronize icon ⟳.

The Synchronize Files dialog appears.

⬤ **Note:** The Synchronize icon looks similar to the Refresh icon but is located on the right side of the Files panel.

10 From the Synchronize pop-up menu, choose the option Entire 'lesson14' Site. From the Direction menu, choose the Get And Put Newer Files option.

Choose specific options in this dialog that meet your needs and workflow.

11 Click Preview.

⬤ **Note:** Synchronize does not compare cloaked files or folders.

The Synchronize dialog appears, reporting what files have changed and whether you need to get or put them. Since you just uploaded the entire site, only the files you modified—**about_us.html** and **green_styles.css**—appear in the list, which indicates that Dreamweaver wants to put them to the remote site.

Synchronization options

During synchronization, you can choose to accept the suggested action or override it by selecting one of the other options in the dialog. Options can be applied to one or more files at a time.

⬇ **Get**—Downloads the selected file(s) from the remote site

⬆ **Put**—Uploads the selected file(s) to the remote site

🗑 **Delete**—Marks the selected file(s) for deletion

🚫 **Ignore**—Ignores the selected file(s) during synchronization

🔄 **Synchronized**—Identifies the selected file(s) as already synchronized

▦ **Compare**—Uses a third-party utility to compare the local and remote versions of a selected file

12 Click OK to put the two files.

If other people access and update files on your site, remember to run synchronization *before* you work on any files to be certain you are working on the most current versions of each file in your site. Another technique is to set up the Check-out/ Check-in functionality in the advanced options of the server's setup dialog.

In this lesson, you set up your site to connect to a remote server and uploaded files to that remote site. You also cloaked files and folders and then synchronized the local and remote sites.

Congratulations! You've designed, developed, and built an entire website and uploaded it to your remote server. By finishing all the exercises in this book, you have gained experience in all aspects of the design and development of a standard website compatible with desktop computers and mobile devices. Now you are ready to build and publish a site of your own. Good luck!

Review questions

1 What is a remote site?

2 Name two types of file transfer protocols supported in Dreamweaver.

3 How can you configure Dreamweaver so that it does not synchronize certain files in your local site with the remote site?

4 True or false: You have to manually publish every file and associated image, JavaScript file, and server-side include that are linked to pages in your site.

5 What service does synchronization perform?

Review answers

1 A remote site is typically the live version of the local site stored on a web server connected to the Internet.

2 FTP (file transfer protocol) and local/network are the two most commonly used file transfer methods. Other file transfer methods supported in Dreamweaver include Secure FTP, WebDav, and RDS.

3 Cloaking the files or folders prevents them from synchronizing.

4 False. Dreamweaver can automatically transfer dependent files, if desired, including embedded or referenced images, CSS style sheets, and other linked content, although some files may be missed.

5 Synchronization automatically scans local and remote sites, comparing files on both to identify the most current version of each. It creates a report window to suggest which files to get or put to bring both sites up to date, and then it will perform the update.

APPENDIX
Tiny URLs

PAGE	TINYURL	FULL URL
LESSON 7		
	http://tinyurl.com/adobe-media-queries	http://www.adobe.com/devnet/archive/dreamweaver/articles/introducing-media-queries.html
	http://tinyurl.com/w3c-media-queries	http://www.w3.org/TR/css3-mediaqueries/
	http://tinyurl.com/media-queries-smashing	http://www.smashingmagazine.com/2010/07/how-to-use-css3-media-queries-to-create-a-mobile-version-of-your-website/
LESSON 13		
	http://tinyurl.com/video-HTML5-1	http://www.w3schools.com/html/html5_video.asp
	http://tinyurl.com/video-HTML5-2	http://www.808.dk/?code-html-5-video
	http://tinyurl.com/video-HTML5-3	http://www.htmlgoodies.com/html5/client/how-to-embed-video-using-html5.html#fbid=Dp-CQRBOvYc
	http://tinyurl.com/fluid-video	https://ulrich.pogson.ch/complete-responsive-videos-breakdown
	http://tinyurl.com/fluid-video-1	https://css-tricks.com/NetMag/FluidWidthVideo/Article-FluidWidthVideo.php
LESSON 14		
	http://tinyurl.com/setup-coldfusion	http://www.adobe.com/devnet/archive/dreamweaver/articles/setup_cf.html?PID=4166869
	http://tinyurl.com/setup-apachephp	http://www.adobe.com/devnet/archive/dreamweaver/articles/setup_php.html?PID=4166869
	http://tinyurl.com/setup-asp	http://www.adobe.com/devnet/archive/dreamweaver/articles/setup_asp.html?PID=4166869

INDEX

A

\<a\> element, 60, 175, 344
absolute hyperlinks, 345, 355–358
Accordion widgets. *See* Bootstrap
    Accordion widgets
Add Behavior icon, 374, 379, 382, 383
Add Class/ID icon, 158, 187, 320, 364
Add New Server icon, 422, 427
Add Selector icon, 159, 225, 248, 276
Adobe Add-ons, 15, 374, 375
Adobe Authorized Training Centers, 15
Adobe Creative Cloud, 4
Adobe Dreamweaver. *See* Dreamweaver
Adobe Edge Animate, 404, 405
Adobe Flash, 402
Adobe forums, 15
Adobe Generator. *See* Generator
Adobe Muse, 59
Adobe Photoshop. *See* Photoshop
All mode, CSS Designer, 48, 94, 149
alpha transparency, 315, 317
animation. *See* web animation
\<article\> element, 62, 78, 215, 263, 389
\<aside\> element, 62, 182, 184, 211, 212
Assets panel, 250, 261, 318–319, 335
\<audio\> tag, 62

B

background color, 163, 176, 396
background images
    adding to headers, 160–163
    gradients as, 164, 177, 179, 397
banner animation, 405–409
Beginner workspace, 33
behaviors, 377–387
    adding to hyperlinks, 383–385
    applying, 379–382
    overview of, 374–375
    removing applied, 382–383
    responsive design and, 385–387
    review questions/answers on, 399
    Swap Image behavior, 379–381
    Swap Image Restore behavior, 381–382

Berners-Lee, Tim, 58
bit depth, 314
\<blockquote\> element, 60, 183, 185, 273
\<body\> element, 60, 84–85
Bootstrap, 131–141
    adding HTML5 elements to, 139–141
    code inconsistency cleanup, 174
    column width manipulation, 217–221
    component width management,
      189–191
    creating layouts using, 133–139
    hiding unwanted content using,
      210–214
    mobile device design and, 208–221
    read-only style sheet, 189
Bootstrap Accordion widgets, 387–398
    inserting into layouts, 388–392
    styling, 392–398
borders
    indented text, 276–277
    navigation menu, 177–178
    table row, 287
box model, 74–75
\<br\> tag, 60, 262
Brightness and Contrast tool, 340
Browse icon, 11, 349, 411, 412
browsers. *See* web browsers

C

\<canvas\> tag, 62
caption elements, 294–296
cascade theory, 79–82
cells, styling table, 287–289
character entities, 61
Check Spelling dialog, 302–303
child pages, 241–253
    adding content to, 243–247
    creating new, 242–243
    formatting content in, 247–250
    hyperlink updates on, 353–355
    updating, 250–253, 353–355
class attributes, 87–88, 97–98

E

Edge Animate program, 404, 405
Edge Web Fonts, 193–198
Edit HTML Attributes icon, 319, 336, 360
Edit Image Settings tool, 340
Edit image tool, 340
editable regions
    formatting content in, 247–250
    inserting into templates, 237–239
Element HUD, 50, 357, 360–361, 367
element references, 3
<em> tag, 60, 357
email links, 347, 358–362
    creating, 358–360
    image-based, 360–361
    text-based, 361–362
    warning about, 362
embedded formatting, 77
Emmet feature, 52–54
exporting Photoshop assets, 114–116
external hyperlinks, 344, 355–358
Extract workspace, 35–36
eye icon, 114, 330

F

<figcaption> tag, 62
<figure> tag, 62
file formats
    for raster images, 316–317
    for vector graphics, 312
    for video files, 412
Find and Replace feature, 304–307
Flash, Adobe, 402
floating panels, 31–32
FLV file format, 412, 414, 417
fonts
    Edge Web, 193–198
    size specifications for, 200–202
    stacks of, 194, 198–200
    typefaces vs., 193
    web-hosted, 198
<footer> tag, 62
<form> tag, 60
forums, Adobe, 15
FTP (File Transfer Protocol), 420
FTP over SSL/TLS connection method, 420
FTP sites
    connection options, 423
    steps for setting up, 421–425
    troubleshooting connections to, 424

G

Generator, 112–118
    creating multiple assets using, 116–118
    exporting assets from Photoshop using,
        114–116
    steps for working with, 113–114
Get icon, 435, 438
Getting Started tab, 21
GIF file format, 316
Google Maps, 355–357
gradient backgrounds, 163–165, 177, 179,
    397
graphic tools, 340
graphics
    raster, 312–317
    vector, 312
    See also images
grouping panels, 32

H

<h1> to <h6> tags, 60
<head> tag, 60, 231, 237
<header> element, 62, 146
headers, 146–167
    background images for, 160–163
    color background for, 163
    creating for text, 264–266
    CSS Designer options for, 148–157
    custom classes for, 158–160
    entering text for, 146–148
    formatting text for, 153–157
    gradient effects for, 163–165
    responsive design for, 298
heads-up displays (HUDs), 50–51
<hgroup> tag, 62
hiding elements, 210–214
high color, 315
hinting menu, 156, 182, 211
home page
    hyperlinks to, 352–353
    setting up, 430–431
<hr> tag, 60
HTML (HyperText Markup Language),
    56–65
    character entities, 61
    code structure, 59
    CSS comparison, 69–70
    current version, 62–64
    defaults, 70–72
    historical origins, 58–59
    review questions/answers on, 65
    table formatting and, 280
    tags, 58–59, 60–61

K

keyboard shortcuts, 40–41

L

layouts
    page, 120–143
    predefined, 124–141
    template creation from, 236–237
    workspace, 33–35
lesson files
    downloading and unzipping, 6–7
    recommended order for using, 8
`<li>` element, 60, 272
`<link>` element, 61, 81
Link Checker panel, 370
linked CSS formatting, 77
links. *See* hyperlinks
Linting support, 52
lists, 269–279
    creating, 270–273
    indented text in, 273–277
    ordered and unordered, 272–273
    responsive, 277–279
Live Source Code mode, 27–28
Live view, 25, 127, 135
    previewing pages in, 259, 286, 355, 416
    table styling in, 286
local site, 9, 420
Locked icon, 243
Log button, 434
lossy compression, 316

M

Manage Sites dialog, 421
map links, 356–357
Marcotte, Ethan, 107
max-width specification, 49, 335
measurement systems, 156
media content. *See* web animation; web
    video
media queries, 207, 221–231
    adding rules to, 224–226
    explanation of, 130
    identifying, 221–224
    resources on, 231
    syntax used in, 208
    VMQ interface and, 129–131
Media Query Definition dialog, 224
media type property, 207
menus. *See* navigation menus
`<meta>` tag, 61, 240, 241

metadata
    image-related, 320
    inserting into templates, 239–241
min-width specification, 49, 224, 335
mobile device design, 204–233
    Bootstrap framework and, 208–221
    column width manipulation and,
        217–221
    copying/pasting CSS properties,
        226–230
    lists and, 277–279
    media queries and, 207–208, 221–231
    media type property and, 207
    mobile-first design and, 206, 214–217
    responsive design and, 206–208
    review questions/answers on, 232–233
    Scrubber tool and, 208–210
    steps for completing, 230–231
    tables and, 296–302
mobile-first design, 206, 214–217
mobile-optimized sites, 213
mockups, 112
monochrome, 314
MP4 file format, 412
Muse, Adobe, 59

N

named anchors, 363
`<nav>` element, 62, 175
navigation, 342–371
    basics of, 344–345
    checking on pages, 369–370
    email links for, 358–362
    external hyperlinks for, 355–358
    image-based links for, 360–361
    internal hyperlinks for, 348–355
    review questions/answers on, 371
    targeting page elements, 363–369
    text-based links for, 361–362
    See also hyperlinks
navigation menus, 167–182
    adding new items to, 170–174
    centering, 180–182
    cleaning up, 174
    hyperlinks in, 178–179
    steps for creating, 167–170
    styling, 175–180
New Document dialog, 125
New Feature guides, 22–23
New Features tab, 20